C000285861

Debra Bourne grew up surrounded by animals and books. She has spent most of her career working to provide people with information on wild animals and how to care for them. She enjoyed running the mile and 1500 metres at school, but only got hooked on long-distance running in her late thirties. Debra ran her first half-marathon in 2009 and her first ultramarathon in January 2012. Meanwhile, in 2011 she found parkrun, discovered the joys of volunteering and became Event Director of Lloyd parkrun in Croydon, south-east England, which has changed her life.

much more than just
a run in the park

DEBRA BOURNE

Chequered Flag
PUBLISHING

First published in the UK by Chequered Flag Publishing
PO Box 4669, Sheffield, S6 9ET
www.chequeredflagpublishing.co.uk

Copyright © Debra Bourne, 2014
The moral right of the author has been asserted

All rights reserved
This book is sold subject to the condition that it may not, by way of
trade or otherwise, be lent, resold, hired out or otherwise circulated
without the publisher's prior consent in any form of binding or
cover other than that in which it is published and without a similar
condition including this condition being imposed on the subsequent
purchaser

A CIP record for this book is available from the British Library

Printed in the EU by Print Group Sp. z o.o.

ISBN 9780956946072

To Paul, for giving us parkrun.

And to parkrunners everywhere, past, present and future.

Contents

Foreword

by Bruce Fordyce
Country Manager, parkrun South Africa

Marathon runners hate having their routine interrupted, so when Paul Sinton-Hewitt suggested that I run Bushy parkrun back in April 2011, I have to admit I was quite irritated. I had big plans for the following day's London Marathon. The plan for the day before had been to rest, put my feet up, and prepare for a hard 26 miler. The last thing I felt like was a five kilometre run through some park where I believed I would be trying not to be impaled by red deer antlers and hoping not to trip over great knobbly oak tree roots.

parkrun: much more than just a run in the park

But Paul was persistent, and so was our friend Peter Fordham, and on that Saturday I found myself listening to a volunteer with a loudhailer addressing an excited, bubbling crowd of runners and walkers. (Some pushed prams, others carried toddlers on their backs. Some strolled arm-in-arm.)

As someone used to the cut and thrust of intense competition, I had never seen anything like this phenomenon. Yes, there were some very fast runners, and my 18:37 was only good enough for nineteenth spot* but it was the slower runners, the joggers and even the walkers who made a lasting impression. They all seemed to be having so much fun. They were the backbone of this amazing parkrun concept. They were the ones who gave me goose bumps and had my pulse racing. I tried to think of an appropriate adjective and, as corny as it sounded, the word 'happy' jumped into my mind. Everyone seemed so happy to be there. Most impressive of all was the sight of the volunteers tirelessly and happily beavering away at their parkrun tasks. Immediately I knew that I had to bring parkrun to South Africa.

Just two and a half years later I find myself even more excited about parkrun than I was on that April day at Bushy. We all know about its astonishing growth and the incredible future projections but those are just facts and figures. It is the human touch that moves me. When Bob Norris (Event Director Nahoon Point) tells me that strangers hug him in the streets of East London, I understand. When Stefan and Jenna van der Merwe (North Beach) talk about their passion for parkrun and its capacity for making a huge difference in the lives of thousands, I understand. Again, when people enthusiastically clap visiting parkrunners, I understand. parkrun is not a simple five kilometre fun run. It is changing the lives of tens of thousands of people for the better. Soon that will be millions. Gill and I still marvel at the idea that we can discuss parkrun with Tim Oberg (Australia), Tom Williams (UK), Lian and Noel de Charmoy (New Zealand), Matt Shields (Ireland), Jakub Fedorowicz (Poland), Rick Brauer (USA) and all the other international parkrun country managers. No wonder parkrun is a topic of conversation at dinner parties, sport governing bodies and even parliaments, and no wonder the Queen has recognised the gravitas of parkrun by honouring Paul appropriately.

As a once-competitive athlete, I always wondered how I would move on from the days of podium finishes and the odd newspaper headline. I was particularly keen to avoid becoming one of those 'has-been' sportsmen who prop up bar counters somewhere and in return for another drink bore people with tales of their long-gone glory.

Iain Morshead (Ebotse parkrun) allayed my fears with these words: 'Your racing career and your wins and records you achieved for yourself, Bruce; parkrun is for others and will be your legacy.'

He was almost correct. But he referred to me and to parkrun in the singular. parkrun is indeed for everyone but it is *our* legacy. We all stand now in a position to make a huge and lasting difference to world health and happiness. That is a legacy of which we can all be truly proud.

* Tom Williams would never forgive me if I neglected to point out that he finished eighteenth, one second ahead of me. I should point out, however that my percentage age-grade score was 83.29%, Tom's 71.97%!

Prologue

It's 8 o'clock on an autumnal Saturday morning in an English park. The sun is just rising and mist hides the belt of trees on the far side of the sports field. Three people approach from different directions and start pulling out folding tables, assembling feather flags and pushing tape-linked plastic posts into the ground to form a long funnel shape. Shortly, they disperse across the park, carrying bags full of marker arrows, greeting the familiar early morning dog walkers: 'Nice morning! I'm glad the rain stopped.' Rays of sunshine creep through the branches of the old oak and make the dewdrops on the grass sparkle.

By 8.30 the mists have burned away. Now there's a small group of people by the tables, chatting, pulling on bright yellow tabards saying 'volunteer' across the back, and picking up small objects.

'Are the numbers all there?'

'Yes, I checked them last night.'

'And the timer? Have you started it up yet?'

'No, not yet – let's do that.'

A variety of short and long beeping noises are heard. Soon, some of the group wearing the volunteer tabards scatter, walking off across the park, while others stay and greet new arrivals.

By 8.40, more people are appearing and exchanging brief greetings with the volunteers before starting their warm-up routines, running knees-up or briefly running off into the park only to reappear a few minutes later.

Slightly tentatively, someone approaches the tables, a sheet of paper in one hand. 'Hi, um, I've not been here before…'

'Welcome! First time parkrunner? You've got your barcode? That's great; no, we don't need it now but keep it safe; you'll need it when you've finished the run. Do you want to see a map of the course? It's quite simple – just follow the arrows, the paths, and the other runners. Collect a finish token at the end and come over here to be registered – and have fun!'

During the next fifteen minutes people converge from all directions. The area between the tables and the finish funnel fills up with runners of all ages, taking off jackets and sweatshirts, double-tying shoelaces, running up and down the edge of the field. A couple of dogs, attached to their respective owners on short leads, are looking eagerly around and whining. The space under and around the tables is filling up as well, with bags, discarded footwear and outer clothing.

8.55. 'Five minutes.' The call goes out and the mass of people congregate at an imaginary line alongside the funnel. Fit-looking runners in shorts, vests and cross-country spikes; runners in long running trousers and sweatshirts; runners wearing headbands or baseball caps or even woolly hats; kids jiggling beside their parents; teenagers with wires dangling from their ears, the inevitable MP3 player or smartphone strapped to an arm or clutched in one hand; dogs straining at their leads near the outside of the group. There is clothing of all colours, with a distinct scattering of white, bright red and a lesser number of stark black running shirts, with numbers emblazoned across the back: 10, 50 and 100 respectively.

'Good morning! Welcome to the parkrun. I'm your Run Director today. Just a few announcements and then you'll be off.'

After welcoming first-timers, thanking the volunteers and providing reminders about safety, finally the moment the impatient runners have been waiting for.

'Timers, are you ready? Three, two, one, go!'

The diverse mass sets off, the bunched crowd soon spreading out to form a small leading edge and a long tail. They disappear round the corner and into the trees, a few already dropping from a jog into their first walking break.

At the same time, this scene, with minor variations, is being repeated in many parks all over England and Wales. In Scotland, Northern Ireland and Ireland, everything starts thirty minutes later to make sure it's light, while in Australia and South Africa the start time is earlier, before it gets too hot.

But regardless of where they are in the world, what they have in common is that they are parkruns: timed, five kilometre runs, for people of all ages and all abilities, fun, friendly – and free.

1

In the beginning...

Has to be the finest contribution to athletics in the region. Exceptional in every respect. The friendliest event anywhere. You make new friends every week.

Chris Phelan, talking about Bushy Park Time Trial in Runner's World, early 2007

It's Saturday 2 October 2004 in Bushy Park in the London Borough of Richmond-upon-Thames, and thirteen runners are about to set off on a five kilometre timed run through the park, organised by Paul Sinton-Hewitt. Paul is feeling nervous. Everyone lines up and he takes a quick picture; he calls 'go' and they set off, soon running out of sight down past the playground. Paul sees them running across at about the one kilometre mark, down towards the cricket pitch, then they disappear from view again. He waits for what seems like a very

4

long time, but it is actually only ten more minutes before Chris Owens and Matthew Morgan come back into view – around the corner, down the final stretch and to the finish neck and neck. They cross the line side by side, smiling, hands clasped and raised in homage to the very first London Marathon finish in 1981, in which Dick Beardsley and Inge Simonsen finished in similar fashion. Both are clocked in at 18:47, although Paul hands Chris the first metal washer/finish token, hand stamped with number 1, and Matt gets the 2. Chris and Matthew go to Paul's car and write their positions by their names on the clipboard in the car's open boot, leaving the number-stamped metal washers there for next week, before standing by the finish line, doing their stretches and chatting to each other while waiting for the rest of the runners to come back. Rachel Rowan is the first woman home, in 21:01. Less than half an hour after the start, the last runners, beginner Tanya Wolken and her husband Simon Lawrence, finish safely: job done. Nobody knows it yet, not even Paul, but this initial Bushy Park Time Trial is the first run of something that's going to be quite amazing.

parkrun is, at heart, a very simple concept: provide runners with a five kilometre (3.1 mile) course against which they can test their progress. That's what Paul was aiming for with the original Bushy Park Time Trial (BPTT) and it's what parkruns worldwide are still providing today – although it has also become much more than that. By repeatedly running the same course, it is easy to see whether you've improved. Running with other people provides an element of competition, encouraging you to run faster, push yourself harder. But because this isn't actually a race, and because it's on every week, the pressure is not the same. If you have a bad run it's no big deal – you can try again next week. Or you can run as a pacer for one of your friends, helping them to run faster, without having to fork out a race fee.

Compared with a race, entering a parkrun is simplicity itself. No need to send in entry forms, arrive hours before the start to make sure you can find the venue, get your number and timing chip, queue for the toilets and so on. You just turn up and run. Simple.

It all started in 2004…

Paul Sinton-Hewitt first mentioned his idea for a Bushy Park Time Trial to Duncan Gaskell during a conversation at their favourite coffee shop in Teddington. Paul was injured and looking for a way to keep in touch with the running community. He had been made redundant from his previous job, so had some time on his hands. While living in South Africa, Paul had benefited from time trials held by several of the running clubs around Johannesburg, used by runners training for marathons or Comrades, the biggest ultramarathon in the world, to judge their progress, and he thought it would be good to start a weekly time trial for members of his running club, Ranelagh Harriers, and other local clubs.

Originally Paul intended to hold the time trial in Richmond Park, with a course from Robin Hood Gate along the Beverley Brook, but Duncan said there was no way he could help every week, not with a forty minute journey to get there. Jim Desmond also talked Paul out of the Richmond Park route, and two weeks later Paul was back at the café proposing a route in Bushy Park, which the others preferred, particularly because it was closer to where they all lived.

Duncan suggested that monthly would be more practical, perhaps the last Saturday in each month, but on this aspect Paul was immovable: it was going to be weekly. Since Paul was obviously going ahead with this mad idea, Duncan and Jim decided to support him.

Robin Drummond remembers when Paul told him about his plan and asked if Ranelagh would support it. 'I told him he would need to ask the committee, so he came to the committee meeting and made his case. Half the committee members said that it would never work – who was going to want to run this time trial every week? And who was going to volunteer? But the others said it might not work but why not try?' Alan Hedger, the club's main race official, and Ken Powley, the club's course measurer, went down to Bushy Park and measured Paul's suggested course. 'It was important for the credibility of the time trial,' Robin said, 'that this was an exact, recognised distance against which runners could test themselves.' Robin also had some number punches, so Paul went round to Robin's house with fifty steel washers and they hand-punched numbers into them.

Like Jim and Duncan, practically everyone at Ranelagh Harriers agreed that trying to hold the time trial weekly would be impossible, but Paul held firm. His reasoning was, 'If it's always in the same place, at the same time, every week, then people don't have to think about when it takes place – they can just turn up. It makes it really easy.' Additionally, Paul felt that if it was weekly, nobody would worry about missing one, since they only had seven days to wait until the next event. The fact that people would get so keen on parkrun – one might say obsessive – that they would run it every single week never occurred to Paul or anyone else involved at this early stage.

Urging from Andrew Lane, pointing out the difficulties of getting people to turn up for an 8 o'clock start on a Saturday during an English winter, did result in a later start time: 9 o'clock.

I started Bushy Park Time Trial because I believed, and still believe, that people shouldn't have to pay for running a 5K. We'd been beneficiaries of the running community for a long time, and we felt that offering this service to the running community was something we ought to do, to give back to that community.
                                        Paul Sinton-Hewitt, parkrun founder

Alan Hedger assisted at that first run, and then every other Saturday for several more weeks until more volunteers stepped forward. He helped initially because, as Ranelagh Harriers' main race official, he thought he ought to go and give Paul a hand with this new venture, 'and it worked quite well.'

The parkrun pioneers were a mixture, from experienced club runners to beginners; their reasons for being at that first run also varied. Chris Owens wanted to support Paul in his efforts to get the Bushy Park Time Trial up and running. He, like many others, thought that every week was too often, because if he was going to run a time trial, he wanted to really push himself, but he went to that first run. John Kipps had heard about the time trial through Ranelagh and noted that, 'It was for free, and didn't sound too competitive and it didn't look like too many people would be there, so I thought I might be able to do quite well,' so he cycled there. Andrew Lane, another experienced runner and a member of Stragglers Running Club, used to run with Paul, who had been helpful when he was running Comrades in 2004. He wanted to support Paul in this venture, and 'I thought that the best way to do that was to turn up for the first run.'

Peter Wright, a keen runner with Ranelagh Harriers for many years, saw the note in the Ranelagh newsletter and 'it just sort of appealed; it was different to the races I was doing.' He thought that the distance was very accessible and the Saturday morning format was good: he could do this and then get on with his weekend. Steve Rowland, like Chris Owens, went on that first day to support Paul, 'to make sure he had a few runners there. I had no idea then what it would lead to even in the short term.'

Rachel Rowan turned up because 10K and 5K were her favourite distances at the time and Bushy Park was right on her doorstep, so this event was very convenient. Rachel Stanhope, an international rower, was encouraged to run by her husband, Steve, who was already a regular runner. They could not both run at the same time because one of them had to watch their children; on this occasion Steve pushed Rachel out the door to go run – after all, it was just around the corner. Tanya Wolken had only just started running, encouraged by her husband Simon Lawrence, an experienced and competitive runner. He thought it would be, 'a good distance for Tanya without overtaking where she had got to in her training programme; that was the main reason we were there.'

Julie Drummond, despite being a veteran runner, was a bit nervous on the morning of the first event, even though it was labelled as not a race. She was pleased it started early so that she didn't have to spend the morning anxiously pacing and waiting for it to start. Peter Wright jogged from Kingston and across the park to find a small group of runners, mainly familiar faces from Ranelagh, in the car park. Matt Morgan remembers that it was fairly informal, with Paul explaining the unmarked route before sending them off. As Peter said, 'We all lined up and Paul said go and off we went.'

The tie for first place was not a coincidence. Chris Owens made a conscious decision to copy the finish of the inaugural London Marathon. 'I was running around and remembering that very first London Marathon. I thought that since this was the first one we should emulate and try to dead heat on this first time trial, and that's what we did. It was a way to mark the first event in a way that was not just about winning. That's always been one of the great things about Ranelagh: encouraging people of all abilities to achieve what you can, get the best out of yourself, not just focusing on the fastest few.' Matt's main memory of that first run is that decision of Chris's: 'Partway round I was hanging onto the back of Chris Owens and he asked me, "How would you like to finish together, hands held high as in the first London Marathon?" and I said yes, partly because he was going to beat me anyway!'

parkrun: much more than just a run in the park

What John Kipps remembers best about the inaugural event is not that he came in third but the fact that he set a 5K personal best (PB) there – and a five mile PB later that day at an event in Richmond Park. For Steve, who has run virtually all his life and competed in hundreds of races both in the UK and abroad, this time trial, on that first occasion and since, was 'a nice little diversion on a Saturday morning.' However, for Peter it felt quite a fast pace, as he was mainly doing longer distance races. He remembers turning left to come down the final avenue, out of breath and thinking that it seemed a long way to the end at this speed.

Rachel Rowan ran hard, as she usually did, so doesn't remember much except being tired and her finishing time, 20:01. James Russell, as an expatriate South African, was used to the idea of time trials and thought it was a good idea to have one in the UK. Asked what he'd thought of that first run, he pointed out that back then nobody realised what this simple time trial was going to turn into – they had just turned up for a timed run.

Karen Weir (née Broadbent) remembers lining up at the start in the car park 'with everyone poised to start their watches and no idea what was being created on that day'. She ran a 5K PB by twenty seconds, probably by pushing to keep up with Julie Drummond, as they finished together and Julie was a faster runner than Karen at the time. Julie remembers finding it competitive, even though it was not a race. She thought, 'Well, I might be able to catch them up!' As for the couple who came in last, for Simon it was an easy run around the park with his wife, but for Tanya that first Bushy Park Time Trial 'was a real triumph, just the fact that I could get round'.

The intention for this to be a weekly event was clearly indicated in Paul's report to Ranelagh runners after that first run:

Congratulations to all those who ran the inaugural event. Just like the first London Marathon we had a tie for first place. We also had a tie for last place. A new course record has been established and is jointly owned by Chris Owens and Matt Morgan at 18:47. Thirteen runners completed the course in crisp and chilly conditions.

Prizes were awarded to the first and last man and woman. Congratulations to Chris and Matt, Rachel, Simon and Tanya. I hope the Sweatshop vouchers come in handy.

A special thanks to those who helped marshal and organise the event: Duncan Gaskell, Alan Hedger, Robin Drummond and Jo Turner. As this is a weekly event we will be looking for helpers from time to time. Please contact me if you want to help.

1. Chris Owens 18:47
2. Matt Morgan 18:47
3. John Kipps 19:15
4. Andrew Lane 19:48
5. Steve Rowland 20:24
6. Peter Wright 20:41
7. Rachel Rowan 21:01
10. Karen Broadbent 24:56
11. Julie Drummond 24:56
12. Tanya Wolken 29:39
13. Simon Lawrence 29:39

The missing runners in the list were those who were not members of Ranelagh Harriers: James Russell (finishing eighth in 21:37) and Rachel Stanhope (ninth in 23:28).

Where are the pioneers now?

Chris Owens *has only run a handful of parkruns, and none from 2009 until May 2014. Not that he's been inactive – far from it, it's just that between work and training for triathlons (he took the V60 World Champion title for Olympic-distance Triathlon in 2013), Saturday morning has tended to be when he is feeling most tired and least like pushing himself running against the clock on a fast 5K.*

Matt Morgan regrets not having done more parkruns, but notes that he kept moving to areas without parkruns – first out to Croydon before any of the events started near there, later to Australia while it was still lacking in parkruns. When I spoke with him he had been unable to run for a while due to injury, but by June 2014 he was running at Alice Holt parkrun.

Having run BPTT on a few more occasions, **John Kipps** then got into cycling in a big way for a few years, but has now returned to running and is rapidly heading towards his hundredth marathon. He does not go to parkruns as often as he would like, 'because it's very hard not to race it and running that sort of pace is absolute agony – I'd rather run 26 miles at eight and a half minutes per mile than 5K in 19:15.' John has however discovered the joys of volunteering at parkrun, and, having sampled a few different parkrun venues and enjoyed that, thinks he might get into parkrun tourism a bit – once he's got his first hundred marathons completed. He also tells people about parkruns wherever he goes, such as at marathons, where he is amazed how many people still have not heard about parkrun.

Andrew Lane reached his hundredth parkrun in April 2011 at Bushy Park – the second of the original thirteen to do so. Having moved to Norfolk he has been having a good time touring all the local parkruns. He is also a member of the parkrun UK Board of Directors.

The existence of the informal BPTT spread by word of mouth and at first only very gradually. The second week there were fourteen runners, the third week only eleven. After that, the numbers started creeping up: more than twenty by the end of the month, more than thirty by January 2005, sixty-seven towards the end of September 2005. Looking back, this slow growth in the first year was a good thing, giving time for the results systems to be developed, with new systems for timing and recording runners being brought in; a time when mistakes could be made and learned from, when new ideas were tried out.

In the beginning...

Originally the course started at the Diana Fountain, near the chequered road markings, and headed clockwise, finishing down Chestnut Avenue. It was only when the Royal Parks planted trees across the old start area that it was reversed. Given the increasing number of participants this change was very useful, providing the kilometre along Chestnut Avenue to stretch out the field before getting into the narrower, more winding parts of the course. There were only two marshals in the early days, one at the Lion Gate, to make sure runners did not go out of the park, and one at the top of Chestnut Avenue to keep people from cutting off the corner.

For many of the early runners, the low-key nature of the event was one of the attractions. Chris Owens regarded it as a training run. Dave Symons of Thames Hare and Hounds Running Club noted that a side benefit of running in the early months was that there was less competition, giving a greater chance of coming high up in the field – or even first, as he did on more than one occasion (although with a PB of 16:05, he certainly didn't get those placings simply by turning up). Other very positive aspects, right from the start, were the emails of the results and the photos: 'everyone likes photos of themselves running!'

Steve Rowland, having run some of the time trials organised by running clubs in South Africa, never expected it to go beyond a few dozen serious club runners. 'That's probably all that Paul expected. I thought BPTT was a good idea and might peter out or become established, but nobody dreamt it would become what it has become and what it is going to become.'

Chris Wright, who later became parkrun's first employee, ran at Bushy for the first time in early September 2005. 'It was good, there were about fifty runners there, but it was nothing special; it wasn't obvious that it was going to be this huge success. But I came for my second run on 1 October, the first anniversary, and a whopping 155 runners turned up. That's when it started going nuts with this huge jump in numbers, and it's not looked back since then.' At that first anniversary run, Noel Pollock was first to finish in 14:39, with the Irish international runner Sonia O'Sullivan first woman home in a time of 16:58 and age grading (percentage of world record speed for age and sex) over 90%. Chris Owens's PB time of 18:01 at the anniversary, nearly a minute faster than a year earlier, now made him the seventeenth runner to finish.

The number of clubs involved also increased. In the early runs, most of the runners were from Paul's running club, Ranelagh Harriers, with a few friends from other clubs around London, particularly Stragglers. At the first anniversary, while Ranelagh Harriers, Stragglers, Thames Hare and Hounds and Thames Turbo Triathlon were well represented, participants came from more than twenty different running clubs, and there were considerable numbers of people who were not members of any running club at all.

By August 2006, 200 runners were turning up to BPTT and on 7 October 2006 for the second anniversary there were 378. Clearly there were a lot of runners who had found this new concept and liked it.

During all this time, Paul, Jim and Duncan were still meeting every few weeks and discussing where the Time Trial was going. Jim said, 'Numbers like 200, 300, and 400 were seriously discussed as limits, and if someone had suggested that Bushy Park Time Trial could one day handle 1,000-plus runners without problems I would have declared them insane.'

Duncan Gaskell saw the potential limits as challenges to be overcome: 'I thought that every time someone suggested something as a limiting factor, well, we'd just have to work out a way to make that non-limiting – and we did, and we carried on going with more and more runners.'

One aspect, which nobody had expected when those first Time Trials were held, was that not just club runners would participate. Club runners, committed and competitive runners, were coming, and plenty of them, to push themselves or check the progress of their training. However, Paul and Duncan received emails from people saying that they hadn't run for twenty years, but this had got them pulling their running shoes on again; that two months ago they had barely been able to walk round the course, and now they were jogging the whole way; that they were looking to see their time drop below thirty minutes – or forty – or an hour... Those emails, Duncan said, were what he found inspirational.

There is no doubt that parkrun is unique. Somehow, the core idea of the no-fuss, weekly time trials, which Paul brought out of South Africa, combined with the inclusive nature of running clubs such as Ranelagh Harriers and Stragglers, for whom encouraging runners of all abilities to get out there and try their best was important, produced a truly novel running phenomenon.

Chris Owens thinks that it is no coincidence that both the London Marathon and parkrun came out of Ranelagh Harriers. 'I think that the atmosphere at Ranelagh affected Paul's plans when he was planning his time trials, helped to shape the form that these took.' Chris sometimes helped at those early events, generally as a marshal. 'I always called out to people, encouraged them – not like some races you go to where the marshals just stand and point in the correct direction. I think that's an important part of the spirit of parkrun, that encouragement.'

Where are the pioneers now?

Steve Rowland said that he would probably parkrun more often if there was one closer to where he lives. He does like the fact that as parkrun expands, he can go to other parts of the country and there is a good chance there will be a parkrun to run on a Saturday morning: 'it adds something to your trip.'

James Russell continued parkrunning regularly, was the first of the original thirteen to reach one hundred parkruns and for a while was vying for the highest total number of runs, then other life events reduced James's parkrunning for a while. However, he's back parkrunning regularly, nowadays with his sons, and collected his 250-club T-shirt in November 2013.

At the time BPTT started, *Rachel Stanhope* was just getting into triathlons; she has continued parkrunning, mostly at Bushy Park, but only a few times a year. More recently, Rachel moved back into horse riding and eventing (which had been her main sport as a teenager, before she got into rowing and took that to Olympic level) and then back into rowing again. Although she does not parkrun very often, she thinks it is amazing and always runs at Bushy parkrun with her family on Christmas Day.

Peter Wright, having done the next four Bushy Park Time Trials, then got sidetracked by other things. A niggling injury brought on through training for a fast marathon encouraged him to turn to cycling, so as parkrun was taking off, he was dropping out. He did however keep following, online, the development of parkrun – helped by the fact that his son Patrick was parkrunning. 'I have enjoyed seeing the names of people I ran against reappearing in the parkrun lists and running pretty good times for runners in their fifties.' In September 2013, after falling off his bicycle, Peter was diagnosed with a brain tumour and he has been undergoing radiotherapy and chemotherapy following an operation. In January 2014, a two mile walk was exhausting, but he was hoping that the next round of chemotherapy would be a bit easier and he would be able to return to running. He said, 'The surgeon was very complimentary about my physical condition and it has helped with the side effects of the radio- and chemotherapy that I'm now undergoing. So I have a big incentive to start running again, with a parkrun as an initial target, hopefully in the spring.'

Starting to expand

During 2006, in the discussions held by the core team every few weeks, it became evident that at some time, if this new movement was to really take off, it would have to branch out to other locations. Initial discussions centred on two aspects: was this the right time; and where should the second event be held? Jim Desmond pushed for the new event to start as soon as possible, saying, 'if not now, when?' The two main venues discussed as candidates were Wimbledon Common and Nonsuch Park in Sutton, both situated in areas having strong local running traditions and both being relatively easy for Paul and Jim to get to for starting the new event. In the end Wimbledon Common was chosen for that initial expansion and Nonsuch didn't hold its inaugural run until September 2011.

In January 2007, Wimbledon Common Time Trial started. During the rest of 2007, Paul gained the first outside income for parkrun – £5,000 from adidas; formed a small company, UKTT Limited (UK Time Trials) to ensure that any money which he got from outside sources to put into development of the fledgling organisation could be properly accounted for; and started a further four events – Banstead Woods, Richmond Park, Leeds and Bramhall, with another five during 2008.

Throughout this period, Paul was putting in a huge amount of time, effort and his own money to make everything work. In addition to a full-time job, he was working maybe forty hours a week on the Time Trials/parkrun: processing results from the event which had just taken place, adding the details of first-time runners to the database, sending out emails and putting results and photographs online, sorting out errors due either to people mishearing names or the software struggling with characters and symbols in some names. At the same time, he was making preparations for the following Saturday, finding volunteers and working on software changes to solve problems and make everything run more smoothly. Additionally, he was searching online for ready-numbered disks to replace the old washers with their hand-punched numbers, looking at different timing methods, developing new software… and fitting all of this in around his normal job and his family.

Paul's wife, Jo Sinton-Hewitt, remembers the days when Paul would come home, in through the front door – and straight out the back door down the garden to the 'office' (a shed at the bottom of the garden). Heather Martingell, an early core volunteer, recalls that in those early years, often she worked with Paul until 6 o'clock or even later on a Saturday evening while they worked out what had gone wrong with the latest software change, and how to fix it and make the results work.

Everyone who has organised a local race for their club knows the amount of work that is involved. They know how much effort the event director puts in for a single event, even with delegation to other members of the club, to ensure that everything is properly organised, that it all goes well on the day, and that the results are produced quickly and accurately. From that perspective, the sheer effort that Paul put in, the perseverance and hard work to make the weekly format at Bushy Park Time Trial and the new events work in those early months and years, is nothing short of amazing.

Where are the pioneers now?

Rachel Rowan got into triathlons, doing a few sprint distance events before having her first child. She went back to BPTT a few times looking for a new PB, and got her time down to 18:48 in 2006. In 2011 she reached 81.30% age-graded. Her husband has also run it a few times, including running with a buggy, and their son, now four years old, has done Bushy juniors a couple of times, 'although he is a bit young yet and last time sort of gave up half way.'

Karen Weir, having managed a great PB at that first run, naively assumed she would be able to take off similar amounts each run; as she went back fairly regularly after that: 'I soon learned how hard it is to get a PB!' Karen moved over to Richmond Park Time Trial and became the Event Director, a position which she still holds today.

She also did a two-year stint as Event Directors' representative on the parkrun UK Members' Board.

*   **Julie Drummond** *ran several times in the early weeks, finding it conveniently close: 'I could jog there and run and jog back and still be home in time to get on with the rest of life on a Saturday.' Now in her sixties, Julie has been running much less in recent years.*

*   **Tanya Wolken** *became pregnant soon after the first BPTT and with one thing and another running took a back seat.* **Simon Lawrence***'s running was interrupted for a while after an ankle injury playing football for his company in 2008 required an operation and caused some misalignment. He is running again now, but for Simon parkrunning would just be for a change – if he wanted a race, he would go to the county championships. He thinks that the most important thing about parkrun is that the events are free ('and I can't think of anything else like that'), and that they are ideal for people who are starting running, to get out and run, 'without having to travel to a race and enter it and everything.' Tanya has also recently started training again, wanting to improve her general health and fitness. During winter 2013-2014, one of the goals encouraging her to keep running, even when unpleasant weather and dark nights made it hard, was the tenth anniversary approaching.*

What's in a name?

While Bushy Park Time Trial was growing and Wimbledon Common Time Trial, Banstead Woods Time Trial and the other early events were developing, discussions were going on behind the scenes about a universal name which would stand for all the events. Practical considerations came into this; the internet domain name had to be available, and it needed to be unambiguous: time trials are associated with several sports, particularly cycling, not just running. It also needed to be expandable, able to be combined with different names to denote the different events: BPTT, WCTT and BWTT were all very well, but there would soon be duplications of initials if many events started up.

Additionally, although anyone looking at the results would see that the Time Trials were attracting runners of all abilities, the name was a bit off-putting to many slower runners. As one parkrunner, Kevin Hann, said, 'I'd heard that Bushy Park Time Trial was going on, and the appeal was obviously that it was free, but the name "Time Trial" gave the impression that it was elitist, that it was for faster people. It gave no indication that it was also for slower or all runners. Even when Richmond Park Time Trial started, which was a bit nearer, I didn't want to go all that way to embarrass myself. But when it changed to being parkrun, that gave it a completely different image, because it's open to everyone, it doesn't give that elitist overtone. Because everyone's deepest fear when they enter their first race is "will I be last?" '

Stuart Lodge searched for appropriate domain names and found that www.parkrun.com and www.parkrun.org.uk were available to register. In discussions between Chris Wright and Paul about renaming the Time Trials they suddenly realised that this 'parkrun' Stuart had suggested for the URL would work as the new name. 'parkrun' summed up what the runs were about and was less ambiguous and more welcoming than 'Time Trial'. In May 2008 the website started to declare that 'parkrun organises free weekly timed 5K runs around the country'.

The original branching tree logo accompanied by 'BPTT' had been designed in 2006 by Danny Norman. It was used on 150 shirts which were sponsored by Sweatshop for distribution at the run on Christmas Day 2006, with the Sweatshop logo on the back and 'BPTT' on the front. In a further sign of things to come, 170 runners turned up on the day. The current logo, designed by Popcorn, retains that tree concept, with a fluffy tree incorporated into the 'k' of parkrun.

The pillars of parkrun

It was during these first couple of years of expansion that Paul formed what are now the pillars of parkrun: the weekly event of 5K, free to the participant, everyone being welcome, and the role of parkrun in helping to bring people together and encourage a community spirit.

Although we now all know that parkrun is a free, 5K timed run – not a race – at the same time every Saturday morning, and we take this for granted, initially the concept was not quite so fixed. Early discussions regarding Wimbledon Common as the second event considered a six kilometre course, rather than keeping to the 5K model. There were some runs not on Saturdays, such as the summer series at Middlesbrough's Stewart Park in 2009. Newsletters and reports quite happily referred to 'races' and 'wins'.

As parkrun developed its identity, and its relationship with other running organisations such as England Athletics, it became evident that there was a need to make a clear distinction: parkruns are not races. Additionally, to avoid other organisations getting concerned that parkrun would start putting on runs at different distances and on other days, Paul confirmed that parkrun is all about the 5K Saturday morning run (and more recently the 2K junior parkrun events for four to fourteen year-olds). The only exceptions are the Christmas Day and New Year's Day runs held by some parkruns and very occasional optional runs on special occasions such as the Queen's Golden Jubilee.

Meanwhile, numbers at Bushy continued to grow, and occasional famous names appeared in the results: Vivian Cheruiyot was first woman on 11 December 2004, setting a new women's course record. Mo Farah was first to finish on 19 November 2005, in 15:06. A variety of other international athletes ran the Bushy Park event while training at St Mary's College just around the corner.

In 2009, with more sponsorships developing, Paul took the next big step in the financial organisation of parkrun, splitting off parkrun Limited (UK) as a not-for-profit company, with responsibility for, and owning the assets of, all the UK parkruns, while UKTT retained the technology and the rights to parkruns outside the UK. A service agreement was set up between the two companies so that UKTT would provide the essential services such as results processing and other technological requirements, and the parkrun Limited Members' Board – originally consisting of Paul Sinton-Hewitt, Duncan Gaskell, Roger Wilson, Chris Wright, Jim Desmond and Hugh Brasher – would decide how much they would pay UKTT for this. All of this was carried out to make sure that nobody could take financial advantage of parkrun.

Onward

I asked Paul why he thought parkrun had been so successful. 'Partly,' he told me, 'the obvious – it's free. But also lots of other reasons – the social aspects, the encouraging, welcoming atmosphere for new runners, the simplicity, and because it's fun. More and more, it's because of the relationship with the community.'

There is one other essential aspect: the duplication of the event in other locations. The start was that first run in Bushy Park, but if Paul and his friends had stuck to just the one location, it would never have become what it is today.

Expanding out of Bushy Park enabled parkrun to enter a new chapter of its development.

2

Ten steps out of Bushy Park

What is parkrun all about? People of all abilities are welcomed and join in.

Christine Miles, Bramhall parkrun

parkrun has always grown organically. The second venue, Wimbledon Common, was carefully chosen by the BPTT team, but the development of each new event has been driven by individuals wanting a parkrun for *their* communities.

Step 1: Down the road – Wimbledon Common Time Trial (WCTT)
On 6 January 2007, Paul Sinton-Hewitt somewhat apprehensively left Bushy Park Time Trial in the hands of his friends and

set off to Wimbledon Common together with Jim Desmond, to see whether the Bushy Park Time Trial experience could be duplicated at a different venue. He need not have worried; the very first week, 51 runners turned up.

One was Ian Higgins, who notes that his being one of those first runners was pure luck. In 2005 he had been told that he would never run again due to a hip problem, but in late 2006 he thought the hip felt better and decided to restart. By chance, he went to the Thames Hare and Hounds (the oldest cross-country running club in the world) on the last Wednesday of 2006 and heard an announcement that WCTT would be starting on the first Saturday in 2007. So, on 'a damp, miserable Saturday morning' he went to Wimbledon Common, ran the time trial and enjoyed it, went back the next week and soon found that he was battling with three or four other runners each Saturday and he didn't want to miss a single week.

After a few weeks, Paul and Jim held a meeting to encourage some of the regular WCTT attendees to manage the event themselves. Ian Higgins had already expressed an interest but couldn't be at that meeting: 'That didn't stop me from being chosen as the Event Director.' A little while later, Paul and Jim left WCTT in the hands of Ian and his team, satisfied that the new venue was up and running well. Paul returned to Bushy Park, while Jim notes that he didn't go back to Bushy for eighteen months, as he got involved in starting up Banstead Woods Time Trial and then went on to facilitate the new events in Brighton & Hove and Basingstoke.

Originally the WCTT course was unmarked and the only sign that the run was being held was a couple of cones marking out the finish line. Then Ian marked the course with sawdust, but after a few weeks changed this to flour – one bag of cheap flour a week was all he needed to make a set of neat dots finished by a decent arrow, at each corner. The big advantage is that these course markings are rapidly biodegradable and do not need to be removed after the run – local ducks and dogs help to clear them up! On the rare occasions when there has been snow, he has used temporary marker paint instead. He acknowledges that the timing is critical, so the markers are still there when the run is held, and that they have been very lucky with the weather, not having to worry too much about rain washing the flour away – as he recalls, it never rained on a Saturday morning for about the first five years.

The original Wimbledon Common course crossed a major bridleway on the Common, and some of the riders became concerned, citing the potentially disastrous effects if a horse spooked and bolted when suddenly confronted by several dozen runners. Some of the runners didn't much like dodging horses either. Luckily, one of the WCTT volunteers was also a horse rider and arranged a meeting at which everyone could discuss the problem, which was resolved with a change to the run route. Numbers at WCTT soon settled to about sixty to eighty most weeks, jumped to 112 on 22 December 2007 and then exceeded one hundred more regularly from the summer of 2008.

Being the Event Director has not stopped Ian from running – far from it! He's a member of the 250-parkrun club, with more than 300 parkruns to his name, all at Wimbledon Common, and a PB of 16:59. However, for Ian, the biggest difference that parkrun has made is not in his running. 'It's the friendships and the people you meet, that's what's really changed. The community is the biggest thing.' He notes that if he walks through Wimbledon Village lots of people recognise him and greet him. Additionally, he's met and got to know a much wider cross-section of people than he would have done just as a club runner. 'I look around me in the café and there's a group of us, all ages from 15 to 75, chatting together – not what you would otherwise expect to see. It's also great because you go to parkrun on a Saturday morning and nobody is talking about work.'

Ian, who remained as Event Director until early 2014, tried to keep everything simple, with the minimum of kit. He's seen all the changes in the finish line equipment and registration methods, starting off with metal discs stamped with numbers and the long printouts of people's names which had to be searched to find each runner, through to the present system with barcoded finish tokens and athlete IDs.

Step 2: Heading out – Banstead Woods Time Trial (BWTT)

Next to start was Banstead Woods Time Trial (BWTT), near Coulsdon, Surrey, which held its first run on 16 June 2007, with 65 runners and Chris Phelan as the Event Director. Chris was a long-time club runner and Paul had previously suggested to him that he should get involved with BPTT, but the twelve miles from Carshalton to Bushy Park was just too far to travel regularly, taking more than an hour and a half each way by public transport. When WCTT had started up, Chris happily got involved in that – he loved the informality and minimalist nature of the event – and very early on Paul told Chris that he ought to have his own event.

Banstead Woods is owned by Reigate and Banstead Borough Council, and is a designated Site of Special Scientific Interest (SSSI). Before starting BWTT, Chris Phelan worked hard to get all the appropriate permissions from the landowners as well as endorsement and approval not only from the Council but also from English Nature (now Natural England). They were generally supportive but understandably concerned about the potential impact of so many runners on the paths, and whether there would be related problems with litter, or impacts on the wildlife areas. Although they gave permission for the event, the biggest potential problem was that they set a limit on the number of runners: sixty. For the inaugural run, 65 runners took part, although the second run had a more manageable 38.

While Jim Desmond and Paul Sinton-Hewitt were there initially, they left Chris to process the results alone as early as the third run – and he realised that yes, he did know how to do it! Chris notes that his achievements with BWTT were path-finding, because he was the first person to set up and manage an event who had not been part of the original team. By doing this, he showed that it could be done by other people, and that these events could be successful without the ongoing weekly personal involvement of Paul Sinton-Hewitt or Jim Desmond.

About four months after BWTT started, Chris held a public meeting and asked for more people to get involved, which was how he got his co-directors, starting with Kaye Benjamin as Volunteer Coordinator – 'a massive help, particularly since she really loved engaging with the community in that way'. Chris added that he couldn't have done this without Kaye, Dave Sinclair, Don and Sue Esslemont, Andy and Gill Stalley, Morgan Quinn and Linda and Steve O'Sullivan.

Because of the special location, right from the start Chris imbued the runners with a very strong ethos of looking after the woods, leaving nothing behind, and respecting the neighbours. He also developed an excellent relationship with the local newspaper, which helped the event to grow. Of course, with this growth the pressure on the woods also increased, which was a problem. Despite an increased runner limit, before it had even reached its second anniversary Banstead Woods parkrun had so many runners each Saturday that they were risking damaging the woods. This has become known in parkrun as 'The Banstead Issue': the problem of being over-successful and needing to find a way of managing that success.

To take some of the pressure off the park, Chris started working with the local authorities to find other sites nearby where parkruns could be set up. The first of these was Roundshaw Downs in Croydon, which began in July 2009 as the sixteenth UK parkrun, while Lloyd parkrun started in October 2010, Riddlesdown in July 2011 (finally making some impact on Banstead Woods numbers) and Nonsuch in September 2011.

Step 3: Heading North – Hyde Park Time Trial (HPTT), Leeds

Leeds, the first parkrun outside the M25, held its inaugural run on 6 October 2007 (Bushy's third anniversary) with fifteen runners. I've often wondered, 'why Leeds?' The answer? 'Serendipity.' In 2007, Tom Williams was working in the Sports and Exercise Science Department at the University of Leeds. He saw a race listing in *Runner's World* magazine for the free Bushy Park Time Trial and was immediately captivated by this amazing concept. Shortly afterwards, he was called to a meeting with Stewart Ross, Sue Jacklin and Paul Tilley, all from the university's Sports and Activity Department, which oversees the university sports provision, staff wellness programmes, intramural football teams and so on. They wanted to consider ways to get students to engage with the local community through volunteering and physical activity; did anyone have any ideas? Tom told them that he'd heard about this weekly event which took place in London. Why didn't they copy it?

A few weeks later, Tom was going to a triathlon in London, so he thought he'd hop over to Bushy and take part. London being London, and somewhat bigger than Leeds, by the time he'd got over to Bushy Park and done the run he had to dash back to the ExCel conference centre and didn't get to talk to anyone, 'but I was confirmed in my belief that this was a fantastic experience and Leeds ought to have one too!'

Back home, Tom called Paul Sinton-Hewitt to ask for advice about setting up something similar, expecting to get either some hints or a refusal to help. Instead, he received an invitation to join the family: they could set up Leeds parkrun (or 'Hyde Park Time Trial', as it was initially), and the Time Trial team would provide everything they needed – timing devices, stakes to make the finish funnel and so forth. They would even come up to help organise the first event. 'I thought this was crazy, too good to be true – but that I'd be mad to say no,' – so he and Paul Tilley drove down one day in September, met with Paul Sinton-Hewitt and he showed them the system and how it all worked.

On the volunteering side, Tom wrote the event into the curriculum for the Sports and Education Science Department. It worked really well, with one of the students becoming the Event Director during their third year (which the students spend working in sports development), and several students using the event for their fourth-year dissertations. While some other events have university backing, this is the only one with parkrun actually built into the curriculum.

Where are they now? Tom Williams became Event Activator for Northern England in 2011. In 2012 he became Country Manager for parkrun UK.

Step 4: Back in London – Richmond Park Time Trial (RPTT)

When Paul asked for people to attend a meeting about starting up Richmond, and was looking for volunteers, Karen Weir (née Broadbent), one of the original thirteen Bushy Park runners, was among those attending. Karen was relatively new in the running world, although she was friends with Joanne (now Paul's wife) and had been to several BPTT events, including the inaugural run. She thought that she would just be one of the volunteers at the new event, but to her surprise she discovered that Paul wanted her to step forward as Event Director – so she did. 'It wasn't quite jumping in at the deep end, or at least not unsupported, because Paul and Chris Wright and the team were around initially.' The first run was held on 20 October 2007 and during the first year Karen was at Richmond Park every Saturday. However, she gradually decided that this wasn't healthy in the long term, either for her or for the event, so she created the idea of a team of Run Directors, on a rota, together with a few committed volunteers each week – supplemented by additional volunteers from the mass of runners. 'It was a lot of work in the early days, and there were problems like trying to register people on the computer while trying to keep the laptop shielded in the rain, but it was great having this community, and giving something back.'

Karen has sometimes thought about stepping back from the Event Director role, but every time she thinks about it she realises she can't: 'It's such a large part of my life. It's great; I know practically every runner around here.'

Heather Martingell, a Ranelagh clubmate of Paul and Karen, moved over from Bushy Park to help Karen to manage Richmond Park Time Trial. At first, before any volunteer teams were organised, the first runner to finish was drafted to give out the tokens and the next handed the timer so that Heather could go and start registering people. She remembers that they made just about every mistake it was possible to make, from finish tokens being given out in reverse order to someone clearing the timer before the times had been downloaded into the computer. And she recalls the hours spent sorting out mistakes using every resource possible, including identifying runners, and the sequence they finished in, from the photographs.

The Richmond event team were also the guinea pigs on whom any new software changes or other innovations were tried out, since they were close enough geographically to Bushy Park and

Paul's house that they could meet to work through the glitches, while their numbers were small enough that problems were less likely to cause disaster than if they had happened at Bushy Park – where there were already 300 to 400 or more runners every week. It was so common for Heather to end up at Paul's house until 6 o'clock on a Saturday evening, trying to sort out the latest difficulties with the results, that she always did some baking and took cakes or biscuits with her so they would have something to munch on.

Step 5: Heading south – Brighton & Hove Time Trial (BHTT)

When John Doherty heard about parkrun from his colleague Jim Desmond, he thought that 'it would be right up the street for the good people of Brighton', so he went with Jim to meet Paul Sinton-Hewitt and Chris Wright, and started making the necessary arrangements: finding a suitable course, getting an agreement from the council and sorting out the logistics. They didn't see any rush to get started and they only advertised the event to runners in Brighton & Hove City Athletic Club initially; there were seventeen runners on the first occasion, 3 November 2007. While the Time Trial was in development the organisers went to Banstead Woods to see how Chris Phelan and his team did things, and Chris continued to support them, via telephone and emails, after their event started.

At this time, teams were still writing down everyone's names and entering their times into the computer manually. 'When we look back I wonder how we did it,' John said. Now they use four hand-held barcode scanners to process in excess of 400 runners weekly, and they can send the results to parkrun HQ electronically within an hour of the end of the run.

A potential problem at the beginning, caused by the limited initial advertising to members of the running club only, was the fast finish times of even the slowest participants; this made it a bit daunting for any potential new runners. That was solved when the wife of one of the runners started doing the run with her slimming club and it then became much more inclusive. John also found that the change in name from 'Time Trial' to 'parkrun' during 2008 helped make the event sound more welcoming to runners of all abilities – an impact that was noted at all the events.

John never expected the level of growth that the event has had; he thinks that they were really lucky to have selected a park which was able to cope with this number of runners and could take more if necessary, with wide paths and plenty of car parking. The start of another parkrun in Brighton, Preston Park parkrun in 2013, was useful in reducing the field a bit. John was very pleased to tell me that they really hadn't had any problems except for the need to increase the number of marshals around the course to give a polite warning to other park users that a horde of 300 to 400 runners is about to bear down on them!

Step 6: Into Wales – Cardiff Blackweir Time Trial (CBTT)

Phil Cook, an experienced steeplechase runner and Captain of Les Croupiers running club, was considering setting up a mid-week 5K winter series when a club member told him about an article in *Runner's World* which mentioned a set of 5K time trial events. He read the article, looked at the website and after getting some informal support from other runners in the club, proposed to the club committee that they might like to start one in Cardiff. At that point they were intending a monthly run.

After he contacted the Brighton & Hove and Hyde Park, Leeds Event Directors to ask them about their events, Paul Sinton-Hewitt emailed him, which led to a phone call, which in turn led to Phil visiting Paul in late December 2007 and staying with him over the Friday night before being taken to Richmond on the Saturday morning to see the sort of numbers that he might face initially. Phil had his laptop with him and showed Paul, and Chris Wright, the course he had chosen: flat, all on tarmac paths, an out-and-back route with a one kilometre loop at the far end, and finishing close to a supermarket containing a café for post-run coffee and socialisation. 'The next thing I knew I was travelling back to Cardiff with all the software on my computer, a TAG Heuer timer and all the other necessary bits of equipment needed for noting the places of the runners.' So he broke the news to the club committee that they were starting, weekly, in February, with a pilot in mid-January. After a dip down from the inaugural 56 runners on 16 February 2008 to 23 in the third week (due to a clash with a local cross-country league match), numbers stabilised, then started to increase.

'It was a bit unnerving to begin with,' Phil said, 'because I had been racing since 1980 and I was used to turning up for a race a good hour before the start and warming up and everything. Seeing the park still practically empty at 8.55 had me worrying that nobody was going to turn up, but I got used to seeing the runners flooding across from the car park in the last few minutes.'

For the first anniversary, 100 runners turned up, and soon Phil began to wonder how they would handle 150; they reached 200 and numbers kept rising. When they passed 400, then 500, the event still coped with no real problems, just minor changes being needed such as a longer funnel and more people registering runners.

Step 7: Into the north-west – Bramhall Park Time Trial (BPTT)

The next northern English parkrun to get started was in Greater Manchester. Rob Downs was a club runner with Wilmslow Running Club. He often ran around Bramhall Park and kept thinking this would be a nice place to organise a little local event, except that there would probably be a lot of paperwork involved and it might be a challenge to get the local council to agree. There was already a monthly race in the Manchester area, so he thought he could maybe set up a monthly event on a different date. Then Rob heard about the time trials at Bushy Park, Wimbledon Common, Richmond Park and Banstead Woods, and since he would be visiting relatives in London, thought he might try one of them. He emailed Paul Sinton-Hewitt to mention his idea, and the next thing he knew Paul was on the phone to him, being very encouraging.

At Richmond Park, he met Paul and Chris Wright after the run, and they were both very keen – although they did keep insisting that weekly would be better than monthly! In the face of their enthusiasm, and given that they had so much organised already, Rob began to think that just maybe this weekly format could work. Convincing his friends at Wilmslow Running Club to help with a weekly event was somewhat more difficult, as that did represent a rather large commitment, but he managed to persuade a couple of clubmates, Nick Bishop and Clare Stevinson, to help with the first few runs.

Rob found the council very helpful once he'd got the health and safety aspects sorted out, and he soon got permission to hold a weekly run with up to fifty people. At the inaugural run on 9 April 2008, there were 89 runners, and although it dipped to a low of 52 for the fifth run, it soon picked up again, passing the 300 mark in May 2009, 400 for the first time in May 2011 and more regularly in 2012, and 500 in April 2013, with 592 finishers for the pre-Christmas run in 2013.

Rob is not sure exactly why Bramhall parkrun was such a runaway success, but thinks it just provided the right formula to bring people together and create a community. When participants topped 150, the park managers contacted Rob and asked him what he intended to do to limit the numbers. His simple plan was to encourage the start up of other parkruns in the area: Heaton Park (inaugural run 20 June 2009) by Rick Bennett and employees at the Manchester Arndale Centre's Sweatshop store, Woodbank (inaugural event 22 July 2009) by Stockport Harriers, and, following the example of Leeds, South Manchester parkrun at Platt Fields Park, Fallowfield (inaugural run 14 November 2009) by Manchester University. These efforts were spectacularly unsuccessful in their original aim of reducing the numbers of people running at Bramhall parkrun every Saturday morning, but Rob is justly quite proud of the number of parkruns which are 'children' or 'grandchildren' of Bramhall, making the Greater Manchester area a hotbed of parkrunning.

As one of the first parkruns outside London, Bramhall encountered some issues which the organisers of Bushy and other Greater London area parkruns had never considered. Foremost was how to keep the laptops (at that time, needed for runner registration) dry when it was raining. Asking Paul and Chris whether they had a particular gazebo or similar portable shelter to recommend he was greeted with stunned silence followed by, 'but it never rains on a Saturday morning...' He also enthusiastically described the course: up this hill, then down here, then up this slope, and they told him it wasn't going to work because it was supposed to be a time trial, so needed a flat, fast course like at Bushy. Looking at parkrun courses now, flat and fast is far from being standard, but back in 2008, Bramhall was something of a trailblazer for the more undulating runs.

Bramhall also had the less-welcome distinction of being the first parkrun to have to cancel a run. Bramhall Park is in something of a dip, and on 10 January 2009, after heavy rain followed by a sudden drop in temperature, 'The whole park had turned into a big ice rink.' That was not something that had ever happened in south-west or south-east London!

Bramhall rarely attracts very fast runners nowadays as the two-circuit design in combination with some narrow paths and the number of participants reduces the potential for fast times. Rob doesn't mind this – there are plenty of other parkruns in the area for the fast runners to choose. The main changes have been the finish funnel, which has got longer and longer, and the need for a marshal/catcher at the end of the wooden bridge where runners have a tendency to come unstuck as they turn ninety degrees while moving from slippery wooden decking back onto tarmac.

parkrun has changed Rob's life considerably. He is very grateful to his daughters, who accepted that he would no longer take them climbing on a Saturday morning, and he is delighted that parkrun has become an important family activity. Both of his teenage daughters are running and even his wife, who was not very enthusiastic initially, decided to join in, and has earned her 50-club T-shirt. He now knows a lot more people in the local area than he used to, with many new friends and a very large number of parkrun-related acquaintances. Due to his parkrun work he had the honour of carrying the Olympic torch, which was an amazing experience, and he thinks that parkrun has also improved his running quite a bit.

Where are they now?

Rob Downs is still Event Director of Bramhall parkrun. He also runs it quite often: he's a member of the 100-club, has a best time of 16:11, highest age grading of 87.80%, commonly is first person back when he runs and ranks second on the first-finishes record board for the UK.

Nick Bishop, who agreed to help at the first few Bramhall runs, is still volunteering there five years later, while the other early helper,

Clare Stevinson, is now involved in the parkrun academic research programme.

Step 8: To the North-East – Albert Park Time Trial (APTT)

Andy Fisher was a regular runner, although not a running club member, when he heard about the Bushy Park, Wimbledon Common and Banstead Wood Time Trials. As an Assistant Headteacher he was often in London for meetings and kept meaning to try one of these events. But the meetings commonly ended late on Friday nights and he never seemed to get up in time on a Saturday morning, so he decided that the best way would be to start one back home in Middlesbrough.

He got in touch with Paul Sinton-Hewitt, who liked the idea of another northern event, then stayed with Paul overnight and talked about the idea more thoroughly. Having decided on the location he wanted – Albert Park – he contacted the park manager and the council's leisure services, and they told him to go for it! The first run was held on 31 May 2008 with 26 runners. Numbers grew slowly to begin with, as information spread by word of mouth, but they passed one hundred runners in April 2009 – a bit of a surprise to Andy, who had expected it to take three or four years to reach triple figures – with 143 for the first anniversary, 244 for the second anniversary and 300 in June 2011. The second Middlesbrough parkrun, at Stewart Park, started in July 2012, possibly helping to stabilise numbers at Albert parkrun. 'It was nice at the start, back when there were only thirty or forty people running, knowing everyone by name,' said Andy. 'That's not possible with the numbers now, but it's also nice to see so many new faces being part of this event you think is such a wonderful thing.'

In the early days, there was much speculation about the 'Mystery Marshal' who used to appear at a certain spot along the route and cheer people on – but was never seen before or after the run.

Alan Guy had been running and volunteering for a few weeks before he realised that he was the Mystery Marshal that people were talking about. When he was on early shift on a Saturday, he had been carefully ensuring that he was needed at the Teeside University Halls of Residence, just opposite the park, at the correct time to be able to cheer on his wife, Linda, and the other parkrunners.

'Starting up Albert parkrun is probably the best thing I've ever done or ever will do with my life,' said Andy. 'It's given me an introduction to a whole community of people who I would otherwise never have talked to. Five and a half years on, I still can't go into a pub in the area without someone saying, "You're the guy who brought parkrun here to Middlesbrough!" – it's been a wonderful experience on all levels.' He's also put in a lot of work, including processing results while away in Portugal: 'Albert parkrun was only maybe six or seven months old and I was going to be away. I had someone who was willing to get the files off the timer and scanner, but not to process things further, so I took the laptop with the necessary software on it with me, and he emailed me the files and there I was in a hotel lobby processing the results and uploading them. It was a lovely sunny day and I should have been lounging by the pool, but these are the things you do for parkrun!'

Andy started off managing the event mostly with family, then after a few months held a meeting to ask for volunteers, and started first two and later four core teams of six to eight people each, named London, New York, Amsterdam and Barcelona (after those cities' marathons), with each team taking on responsibility for the core volunteering roles one week in four. Still, he didn't get to parkrun himself very often in the early years. He only reached the 50-club in 2013 and he has his sights set on reaching 100: 'I want to run my ninety-ninth run in Weymouth, where I grew up, and the hundredth back at Albert parkrun.'

Early in 2011, as he and his wife moved away from Middlesbrough, he passed on the baton to Sharon Cadell (who went on to manage the second Middlesbrough event, Stewart parkrun). Later the former Mystery Marshal, Alan Guy, took on the role, with Tracey Quinn becoming co-director. All four of them have been honoured by being presented with a Mayor's Award by Middlesbrough Mayor Ray Mallon. 'Ray Mallon has been immensely supportive throughout; even when things got a bit difficult, with some problems with dog walkers in the park,' Andy said.

Step 9: Back south – North Hampshire Time Trial (NHTT)

Meanwhile, Euan Bowman had moved from Perth, Scotland, to work in Basingstoke in 2007, was looking for activities he could do at the weekends and found Wimbledon Common Time Trial on a website of free things to do in London. He really enjoyed the run, but it was a long way to go there and back, so when he saw an advert that the Time Trial organisers were looking to start more events he contacted Paul.

'I was new to the area and didn't know anyone, and I saw lots of runners around but no community.' Undaunted by his lack of backing from a club, and his total lack of experience with anything like this, Euan went ahead with getting it all organised. The biggest hurdle he encountered initially was navigating his way through the council. 'Finding out who to talk to, that was the problem; once I got to the right person they were very sympathetic, sent me a form to fill in. I wrote that there would be thirty-five to fifty runners.' Once he had the permission sorted, he visited Paul and, like others before him, was amazed to be handed all the necessary electronic equipment.

The remaining problem was volunteers. There were two local running clubs but they didn't know Euan, who could not even point to a previous running club for a reference, and, being resource-constrained themselves, were understandably reluctant to throw their weight behind him. So he asked a friend from work, Alex Naper, and he agreed to help. 'I'm incredibly grateful to Alex for his help at the start,' Euan said. Then Euan went to Basingstoke Volunteer Centre, which provided a couple of people. For the dry run (which was anything but, being held on a horrible rainy morning) a week before the event officially opened, Euan persuaded another work colleague to run one lap of the course. 'So I sent him off and he took a wrong turn, and I learned we needed to put out a few more arrows.' The next Saturday, 5 July 2008, Euan got up super-early wondering, 'What have I done?' and convinced that there would be no runners, since he hadn't done any advertising. He was pleasantly surprised to find he had 37 people, including Paul Sinton-Hewitt, Chris Wright, and a very early parkrun tourist, Roy Reeder, who was first to finish. 'I quickly learned how to stand up in front of people and speak to them, and it's surprising how many of those people from that first run I got to know well and became friends with.'

Getting enough volunteers remained a problem for some time. 'After a bit we started waiting for the runners to set off and then approaching the people who were still there and scouted them out as volunteers on the spot – that worked pretty well.' They also discovered that Paul had been right about encouraging people to come to the café after the run, as that did help to build the community, which 'just formed itself – a whole running community' once there was the parkrun around which they could focus.

After a low of just seven runners on the fourth run, numbers stayed pretty stable in the thirties and forties for the rest of the year then started climbing in January 2009, reaching 100 in April, and 142 at the end of June before levelling out again in the 100 to 150 range. In spring 2011 they rose again, passed 200 at the end of April 2012, reached 300 in April 2013 and a massive 462 runners on 11 January 2014. 'It's been very satisfying,' Euan said, 'I've met so many runners who have said, "If you hadn't started the run I wouldn't have got so fit and healthy." '

Step 10: Over the border – Glasgow parkrun

Richard Leyton had been running for a few years when he visited friends in London and they suggested that he should meet them at this free 5K event on a Saturday morning. He went, ran at Bushy Park, and thought, 'Well, that's quite good fun.' Naturally, he emailed Paul to ask if there was one in Glasgow and was disappointed to discover there were none in Scotland. Back home in Glasgow, he found himself gradually realising that he loved this wonderful thing called parkrun and really wanted one in his local park. From there it was a relatively small step to thinking, 'If I don't do it, who will?'

In London for another visit, he ran at Richmond, began to realise how basically simple the format was, and decided that yes, this could be done. At the time, the nearest events to Glasgow were Leeds and Bramhall, and the whole concept of parkrun hadn't reached Scotland. Undeterred, Richard set about finding a few other people who would be interested in getting involved. Helpfully, the council was very positive about it right from the start and Richard was introduced to the manager of the Glasgow Sweatshop store, Iain Brown, who was also enthusiastic about the idea. Working together they overcame obstacles such as changes in staff at the council, got the necessary permits organised, and, with a bit of a delay while Richard was sidetracked with getting married, things really started rolling.

Initially they planned to hold the run in Glasgow Green in the middle of the city centre, easy for people to reach by public transport and a really popular park. However, it was pointed out that the Green is really *too* popular to be able to accommodate a parkrun: the event would be being cancelled all the time for other events. So they looked again and settled on Pollok Park, which was helpfully not far from where Richard was living. Venue sorted, they got the approvals and Glasgow parkrun started up on 6 December 2008. Given the lack of understanding of how a free 5K could be organised, *every week*, in Scotland at the time, Richard was understandably relieved when 44 runners turned up for the first run. With the winter start, participation promptly fell, reaching a low of 22 for the third run before rebounding with a vengeance. 'Numbers just started snowballing, built up and up and up and up – the attendance graph is quite scary, really,' with 107 runners on 31 January and more than 200 in April, although it took a further year to pass the 300 mark. Amazingly, this rate of growth was just by word of mouth: people finding the run and telling their friends about it.

For Richard, it's the simplicity of the event that has always attracted him and he's tried to keep true to that philosophy at Glasgow parkrun. The volunteers turn up, they stage the event, the runners finish, people go to the café and go home, and the results are processed, with all equipment quickly packed up after each event, leaving no trace that the runners have been there.

The one thing that set Glasgow apart from the events further south was the later start time of 9.30. Richard admits that initially it was all about the café. 'With the run being held in Pollok Park and finishing near the Burrell Collection, their café would be the logical post-run meeting point – and they didn't open until 10 o'clock. With a 9 o'clock start the faster runners would never have wanted to hang about that long, but with a 9.30 start, it worked really well.' This set a serendipitous later start time for Scottish events, particularly useful for subsequent events further north in Scotland, avoiding teams having to set out courses while it was still dark.

People loved Glasgow parkrun, but runners having to travel some distance to reach it each week naturally wanted one closer to where they lived, so began asking how they could have their own events. That's how Edinburgh, Strathclyde, Falkirk, Inverness and Aberdeen parkruns began. It took quite a while for another parkrun to get started in Glasgow, as people wanted to keep coming to Pollok Park and meet all their friends, but eventually Tollcross was set up in the east end of Glasgow and Victoria parkrun in the west (Glasgow parkrun changed its name to Pollok parkrun in June 2014).

The start of new parkruns tends to lead to mixed feelings for Richard. 'You get to know people at parkrun, they become friends. Then they move and want to set up their own event, and you get to know them even more as you help them create their event and get them started. Then you don't see them again because they've got their own parkrun. It's definitely a mixed blessing, with the pleasure of seeing new communities and friendships, but at the same time losing contact with people you used to see all the time.'

3

parkrun goes global

parkrun is an event which attracts tens of thousands
of people across the world every week to do
something active and fun. parkrunners have the great
privilege of contributing to a wonderful community.

Nathan Warren, Cannon Hill parkrun, Birmingham

From one event with thirteen runners in a park in London,
parkrun has expanded to involve ten countries across the globe.
Besides the UK, there are now parkruns in Denmark, Australia,
South Africa, Poland, New Zealand, the USA, the Republic of
Ireland, Russia and Singapore.

Each Country Manager follows the same basic remit: to provide free, timed, traffic-free 5K runs at a fixed time on Saturday

mornings in communities which want one. Inside this framework they have freedom within which they can be inventive, in developing relationships with sponsors, for example.

One aspect which makes it easy for parkrunners to take part in local parkruns while on vacation is that they only need to register for parkrun once before running anywhere in the world. This wasn't always the case; back in 2009, it was necessary to let Chris Wright at parkrun HQ know you were planning to run in another country so he could share your athlete ID details with the parkrun organisers there, and he had to remind people about this in the parkrun newsletter. Now the database is truly global.

Expansion of events in the UK happened at least partly because individuals visited a parkrun then decided that their own community should have one. Similarly, global expansion of parkrun has developed mainly by individuals experiencing parkrun while visiting the UK, becoming hooked on the concept and returning home determined to bring parkrun to their own country.

Denmark

The longest-running parkrun outside the UK is Amager Fælled parkrun in Copenhagen, Denmark, which started on 16 May 2009 as the twelfth parkrun event. There were twenty runners, fourteen local, while six had crossed the North Sea in order to participate in the first parkrun in continental Europe.

Paul Sinton-Hewitt candidly admits that if it hadn't been for Jonathan Sydenham, who set up Amager Fælled parkrun and spearheaded the development of the other Denmark parkruns, parkrun might not have developed into an international organisation.

Jonathan started parkrunning at Wimbledon Common on visits to the UK, back when there were only the Bushy Park and Wimbledon Common events, and was soon planning his visits around parkruns. He decided he had to have one in Copenhagen, so he talked to Paul Sinton-Hewitt about it. The initial idea was just to have the single event as an offshoot of the UK parkruns, but discussions with Paul and an early core volunteer, Roger Wilson, led to the suggestion that there could be more than one. As Jonathan said, 'That opened up a whole new can of worms, thinking about changing everything into Danish, with the database not capable of coping with words including letters not in the English alphabet.' Even the format of numbers provided plenty of potential for confusing errors, since where English speakers put commas to break up numbers, continental Europeans use decimal points. The experience of the team in tackling the challenge of translating parkrun to Danish was very useful later while setting up the Polish and then Russian events. In fact, there were many other lessons learned about starting parkrun in a new country, lessons which were helpful in all the future expansions.

The first winter, Amager Fælled parkrunners ran at 20 degrees below zero, on ice (carefully) and though snowstorms. Jonathan had a special T-shirt designed and gave them to runners who came at least monthly, December to March.

In the next couple of years several other events started. Jonathan notes that there are considerable cultural differences between the UK and Denmark, which has affected parkrun Denmark. While a much higher percentage of the population run, many of them neither belong to a running club nor want to be involved in any organised form of running. Also, there are many other free running events, such as marathon training events advertised by local newspapers, than there are in the UK. Additionally, Saturday mornings in Denmark are 'family time' during which, whether or not you have children, you have a leisurely time with the family then go and do the weekly shop. That has not stopped people who love parkrun from turning up, but might have affected attendance. Jonathan has also noticed that the Danes are much less likely to run a parkrun, even just jog round it, if they are running a race the same weekend, which is in contrast to many people in the UK who might take it easy but still parkrun.

Australia

Tim Oberg first heard about parkrun when living in London, as a whisper of a 'fun run' he could take part in with his dog. He went along to Wimbledon Common and tried it, forgetting his barcode the first time, but gaining his first official time on 24 July 2010. He thought this was 'pretty cool'. Later that year he was moving back to Australia and wanting to shift from a travel-related career into one associated with health and fitness. Contacting parkrun by email, he asked if they had thought about moving into Australia. A couple of meetings later, and it was agreed that Tim could start up parkrun Australia with a franchise agreement drawn up. 'This was really a step into the unknown,' Tim said. 'I hadn't been an Event Director or anything like that; I hadn't had any chance to see behind the scenes before I left for Australia. It was a real leap of faith on both sides.'

On his way to Australia, Tim stopped in Cape Town and told his wife's family what he was intending to do. In one of the lucky coincidences which have surrounded parkrun as it developed, it turned out that his brother-in-law's best friend worked for adidas and was able to put Tim in touch with the Melbourne-based manager of adidas for the Pacific and Asia region. Since Tim was moving to Gold Coast, about an hour's drive south of Brisbane in Queensland, he contacted the Gold Coast Council and found out that he needed to talk to the senior Active Parks Officer, a woman called Samantha Hughes. Samantha turned out to be a marathon runner, was interested in the parkrun concept and would support it. Additionally, the then-mayor of the city was Ron Clarke, a famous long-distance runner from the 1960s and 1970s, who was happy to become parkrun Australia's Patron.

From the start, Tim was more interested in managing the development of parkrun Australia than any individual parkrun, so he needed to find other people to be the event directors. Meanwhile, he set up a not-for-profit organisation, which in Australia means an incorporated association, parkrun Incorporated, which trades as parkrun Australia. Having identified a potential event location at Main Beach in Gold Coast, he soon found a couple of people who were interested in taking on the event director role. During the same period he met with adidas, expecting a big meeting and finding that he was giving his PowerPoint presentation to just two people. However, he did find that adidas were looking for something running-related in which to invest in Australia.

While sponsorship negotiations were in progress, Tim continued working in other jobs, but in his spare time he developed parkrun Australia and financed the start up of the first few Australian parkruns himself. Main Beach held its first run on 2 April 2011 with 108 runners. Most had heard about parkrun either because they were British ex-pats or via a few local running clubs. With minimal promotion, growth was slow initially. The second Australian parkrun started at New Farm, Brisbane, in September 2011, initially with just 42 runners, and dipped to a low of just twelve for the fifth run, but then rallied and grew to become the largest parkrun in Australia, commonly attracting more than 300 runners.

This was followed by Albert parkrun in Melbourne in November 2011 and St Peters parkrun, Sydney, in January 2011. Sponsorship from adidas worked out and provided the operational costs; Tim continued managing the development alongside other jobs. In the middle of 2012, with a couple more sponsors on board, he took a deep breath, tightened his belt a notch and started managing parkrun Australia full time – and to good effect. By the end of 2012 there were eighteen events attracting more than 1,600 runners a week. A year later and that had grown to 56 events (38 events launched in a year!) and more than 7,000 runners on a single Saturday. In October 2013 the first 'home grown' parkrunners, Brian Peters and Hans Juergen Grollius, reached the 100-club.

It's not always been plain sailing. At all events there have been occasional problems and technical hitches. Tim reminds all new event directors that there is no expectation that they are going to be perfect. 'The sooner something goes wrong the better, really. Then they learn that they can cope with it, and it reminds the runners that we're not the London Marathon, each event is managed by volunteers and at the end of the day it's just a fun run.'

As in the UK, there is a core team managing parkrun Australia: in addition to Tim, there's an operations manager, a communications manager, a sponsorship manager and a technical support manager – all except Tim being volunteers.

Poland

When I asked Jakub Fedorowicz what had led to the development of parkrun Poland, he explained that he started parkrunning while living in the UK, going to Newcastle parkrun. 'I thought it was great. Then I got a new job back in Poland, where there was nothing like parkrun. I thought that it would be great to have parkrun in Poland, so I contacted Paul and asked him about starting parkrun in Poland.'

In October 2011 Gdynia parkrun started, with just five runners and a team of three volunteers – Jakub and two friends. The weather was relatively good, but cold. The runners said they enjoyed it – then Jakub told them all that it would be there the next week, and the one after that. Numbers stayed low through the first few weeks, reaching a high of just 25 for New Year's Eve and Jakub started to worry that it wasn't going to work. However, in March, numbers suddenly started increasing, as word of the event spread and runners started travelling from Gdańsk for the parkrun. Next, the Gdańsk city council asked Jakub if he'd consider an event there – and he said yes, but that there was no money for it – so the city council said they would pay the costs. That made two events and the number of runners continued to increase, faster in Gdańsk than in Gdynia. Łódź parkrun started in June 2012 and Poznań at the end of July.

By the end of 2012 there were 2,500 runners registered. 'We had no sponsors, no media support, it was all done locally, based on true community involvement and word of mouth,' Jakub said. 'I never thought that people would look at what we were doing and take it back to their home cities and do all the work for us, for themselves, but they did – there's something magical about parkrun, you start off not knowing anyone, but you make new friends. I'm still in touch with all the Event Directors, still calling them all every week to check they're okay and ready for their parkruns.'

The breakthrough that Jakub had been waiting for came when a runner came to Gdynia parkrun, returned to Warszawa (Warsaw) and contacted him saying that she'd really enjoyed the parkrun and would he start one there? This was important because not only is Warszawa the biggest city in Poland but it contains all the key people and large companies. Warszawa-Praga parkrun started up on 11 May 2013, with 82 runners at the first event and suddenly growth of parkrun Poland rocketed. The number of people registered passed 10,000 by the end of 2013; Kraków, Wrocław, Szczecinek, Żary and Leszno also started up in 2013, with Cieszyn, Konstancin-Jeziorna, and Warszawa-Żoliborz added to the list of events in the first four months of 2014 (bringing the total to thirteen). By early July 2014, more than 10,000 people had run a parkrun in Poland.

There has been a great response from the city councils, particularly in the smaller towns where otherwise there would be no running events at all, and attendance is increasing every Saturday. parkrun is getting more and more interest from Polish national television and the newspapers have been getting interested. parkrun is a novel concept in Poland, not just for being a free event, but because of the way it is community-based and volunteer-based.

parkrun has changed Jakub's life. He's made lots of new friends, and gained something very special from the parkrun community. He admits that it is also a lot of work, so that sometimes he doesn't get to spend as much time with his family as he'd like, nor to run his parkrun as often as he'd like to. He's working on getting more people involved, to build two or three teams of volunteers covering Saturdays in rotation.

South Africa

Bruce Fordyce, nine times winner of Comrades Marathon (a 56 mile ultramarathon) in South Africa, had known Paul for many years – Paul had actually been one of his seconds at Comrades in 1990. When Bruce came over to run the London Marathon in 2011, Paul suggested that he should come to Bushy parkrun the day before. Bruce had no idea what he was about to experience and he was absolutely gobsmacked by the 800 runners, a handful of whom, like him, were running the marathon the next day. Bruce finished eighteenth overall and first in his age group. However, what really impressed him wasn't the fast runners, 'but that thirty minutes after I finished, people were still coming in. I saw the magic.'

After that one experience Bruce was a firm convert to parkrun and what it could do for people, and he was determined to bring parkrun to South Africa. By November 2011, the first parkrun had started up, Delta parkrun in Johannesburg, with a start time of 8 o'clock to avoid the worst of the heat. As the parkrun South Africa Country Manager (assisted by his wife Gill), Bruce decided to develop things slowly to begin with. There were three or four 'dress rehearsals' for that first event and Paul Sinton-Hewitt travelled to South Africa to train everyone how to use the equipment. At the first run there were 26 people, at the second, thirty. Participation built very gradually initially then increased steadily to pass 100 runners after six months, 200 in June 2013 and 300 in October 2013.

Meanwhile David Ashworth and a couple of other people said they wanted a parkrun closer to home, so Roodepoort was started up in Johannesburg in April 2012. Designing the course took a while, with several test runs in the lead up to the inaugural event. On the day there were 42 runners. Bruce Fordyce was there, as was regular Delta parkrunner Tracy Rankin, and they were first man and first woman home. Like Delta, Roodepoort stuck at about thirty runners for a while, then rose to 84 at the end of October 2012 and, after an absolute low of six on 24 November, 117 on 12 January 2013. Numbers really started climbing in the middle of 2013.

Bob Norris is the Event Director for the parkruns in the Eastern Cape, starting with Nahoon Point. Bob, himself a former Comrades runner, admits that when Bruce came back from London in 2011 and started enthusiastically telling him about parkrun and saying he had to start one up in East London, Eastern Cape, Bob didn't have a clue what he was talking about and frankly was not interested. Bob had been in the road racing world for many years and was tired of running and runners and people wanting other people disqualified and so on. Bruce told him this was different. 'How different can it be?' asked Bob. 'Trust me, it's different!' Bruce told him; Bob remained sceptical.

Bruce called again in February 2012 to say that he was coming to East London for the Surfers Challenge (a race which started as a challenge event between local surfers and runners and which is also a natural obstacle course, with sand, boulders and rivers to be negotiated on the way) and he wanted Bob to take him round and show him three or four possible 5K courses. Bob and Bruce had been friends for a long time so Bob agreed, if only to stop Bruce nagging, and showed him five potential courses – with Bruce immediately being very much taken by Nahoon Point. Six months later, Bob found himself the Event Director of the Nahoon Point parkrun, which started on 11 August 2012, with Bruce and Gill there, and 81 runners. He thought that it would then get smaller, but the next week there were 111 runners, by week five there were more than 200, and apart from a dip to 63 in some bad weather at week eleven, the number of people turning up just kept growing, passing 300 in January 2013 and 400 in February.

Bob discovered that Bruce had been completely correct about it being different. 'It's been a revelation. I was involved at all levels of road running and at parkrun... everyone says thank you!' He likes the whole community, the way it's got such a relaxed atmosphere, so outgoing, how everyone talks to everyone else. parkrun has also taken people who used to be competitive runners and didn't know how to get back into regular running as they got older, and not only shown them how to run again but enabled them to enjoy their running. And it has brought whole families out running together, which he thinks is great.

Bruce didn't want to expand too quickly. For one thing he likes to be present for each inaugural event, so he would prefer not to have two starting in the same week. However, 2012 ended with six South African parkruns established and by the end of 2013 there were 23 parkruns and more than 42,000 people registered, with the weekly total of runners topping 3,700. By the end of June 2014 there were 32 parkrun locations.

The explosion of numbers at some of the events has been phenomenal. North Beach in Durban started in November 2012 with 74 runners and by mid-2014 was regularly attracting 500 to 700 participants; Modderfontein Reserve began in January 2013 and now attracts similar numbers to North Beach. In contrast Summerfields, situated just outside Kruger National Park, has the distinction of having the smallest average number of runners of any parkrun: highest 28, lowest just one, average 9.5.

With the increasing number of runners at Nahoon Point, some congestion developed and Bob became concerned about the possible environmental effects on the nature reserve where the run is held. So he decided to start up some more parkruns to give people alternative events to go to. In a piece of serendipity, someone approached him to ask about starting one at Sunrise-on-Sea, a location Bob had been thinking about. Then he started an event at Kidd's Beach, followed by one at St Francis and another at Hobie Beach, Port Elizabeth. As has happened in several other areas around the world, the new parkrun events have got even more people running, but not actually reduced the number of runners at the parent event – where 521 runners finished for International parkrun Day on 7 October 2013 and 611 the following week! There's naturally a bit of friendly rivalry between the events, with lots of checking of results each week to see if any of the other events have managed to beat Nahoon Point for numbers of runners.

As in most countries, there had initially been some resistance to parkrun in South Africa from running clubs and other organised events. 'The traditional running clubs were a bit suspicious at the start,' Bruce told me, 'they thought that parkrun was a threat, but now they've realised it's a kindergarten – and some people who start running with parkrun are going to graduate to running with them.' Some of the race organisers were also a bit concerned, and asked Bruce if he could change the parkruns to Sunday. 'They didn't get the whole global thing, how it's Saturday in every country, and how important that is,' but now they've accepted that parkrun is in South Africa to stay, and they might as well adapt, move their runs to Saturday afternoon or Sunday, and benefit from the additional runners developed by parkrun.

Bob agrees that while some clubs have been very supportive, others have been grumbling into their coffees about parkrun. His response is to encourage them to come and see parkrun for themselves, get involved, use them as a recruiting ground. Meanwhile, a whole new running club has been blossoming out of parkrun South Africa, called Born to Run, to provide a running club environment in which people coming from parkrun can feel comfortable as they take their next steps to running more, and longer distances.

While I was talking to Bruce, his mobile rang and his wife, Gill, answered it for him. 'Another random person asking about the parkrun,' she explained after the call was over. 'They get Bruce's number and they call him – to ask where the parkrun is, when it is, and how much it costs – they can never quite believe that it's free.'

I asked Bruce what were the best bits about parkrun for him personally. 'The letters I get, the emails, people saying thank you, telling me how parkrun has changed their life. Those are pretty good. And when I've been injured and I'm walking around the course with the people near the back, chatting, instead of running fast near the front, I get to see the park, and how welcoming everyone is.' Then he grins. 'And then there are the Root 44 parkrun birthday parties – instead of mums hiring a bouncy castle or taking the children to the zoo or a playground, they all run the park-run and then they settle down to eat their cake and everything – a healthy alternative birthday party, and it's free! They've had three of those so far. And when I see a parkrun event turning a year old and starting to give out red shirts [for those who have reached fifty parkruns] just after – it's great.'

Bruce thinks that parkrun is one of the most exciting develop-ments in running for many years, appealing to a huge section of the population who would never normally participate in a sport-ing event. He also notes that the loyalty that many people have to-wards 'their' parkrun is amazing: 'There may be other runs which are more picturesque, with lovely beaches, such as Nahoon Point parkrun, and fantastic views, but when you're running your home run everyone knows you, and that makes it special.'

New Zealand

New Zealand parkrun started through the efforts and enthu-siasm of two families: the McChesneys and the de Charmoys. Richard McChesney and his family had been living in London, Richard running with the Stragglers and running lots of parkruns (particularly Richmond Park, but also at least one run at most of the other parkruns around Greater London). Meanwhile his son Zac had been a regular at the Bushy juniors 2K events, winning their first year's points league, as well as running the Saturday parkruns. At the end of 2011, Richard and his family decided to move back to New Zealand, but he didn't want to be without the parkrun he had grown to love. parkrunning on New Year's Day, Richard bumped into Paul Sinton-Hewitt and told him that he wanted to start one up in New Zealand. Paul thought it was a great idea; he was already talking to his old friends Noel and Lian de Charmoy about taking on the role of Country Manager for New Zealand.

Noel recalls that he was a bit sceptical at first. When he'd been a keen runner back in the 1970s, a 5K didn't really count as a run: he had friends who wouldn't even consider they'd had a run if they'd been out for less than thirty minutes. However, he gradually realised the value of the 5K distance in getting people started in running – while providing a nice bit of speedwork for the more experienced runners.

While Paul was setting up the agreement with Noel and Lian to manage parkrun New Zealand, Richard was busy training alongside Rachel Elliott and the rest of the team setting up Newbury parkrun. Three months after Richard and his family arrived in New Zealand, Lower Hutt parkrun near Wellington started up on 5 May 2012 with 84 runners, including Zac. Numbers settled to around fifty runners per week for the next few weeks then began to increase, with 96 runners for Christmas Day 2012, and passing the one hundred mark in January 2013.

It was not all plain sailing. Just after Richard had found a pleasant course and arranged permission from the council to use it, a couple of days of heavy rain led to the route being flooded and he had to rethink, resulting in the course that Lower Hutt parkrunners now use. Also, just nine weeks after the event started, Richard's work took him away for four weeks, so he needed to get a team in place who could manage the event without him. Luckily one of the first people involved, Kent Stead, was an experienced events manager, and agreed to take it on.

Noel and Lian's own event, Cornwall parkrun in Auckland, started on 28 July 2012 with 35 runners including both Richard and Zac. The next event to begin was Barry Curtis parkrun south of Auckland on 25 May 2013 with 36 runners, including Zac. Porirua, just down the road from Lower Hutt, started on 6 July 2013 with 71 runners, 43 of whom were first-time parkrunners, and Hamilton Lake parkrun started on 19 October 2013 with

59 runners including a few 'tourists' such as Paul Gordon (who normally runs at Lower Hutt), making five parkruns on the North Island. The first event on the South Island, Dunedin parkrun, started on 11 January 2014 with 68 runners. A fantastic 55 of these were locals who had never run any parkrun previously; the tourists came mainly from the North Island, but also from Australia and even the Czech Republic.

Noel and Lian have found that they can always spot the first-timers: they're the people holding an A4 sheet of paper flapping in the wind, which they think they need to give in before they can run. 'One guy had actually pinned his to the front of his shirt, like a race number,' said Lian.

USA

Rick Brauer, Country Manager for parkrun USA, first heard about parkrun in an online newspaper article he read in 2011. He wrote to the author, saying what a great concept this was, and unexpectedly got a reply from Tom Williams thanking him for the kind words and support. Tom added that Paul was out of the country but would respond when he got back. Paul did respond and an email correspondence started, in which they discussed whether Rick thought that parkrun could be viable in the USA, followed by a meeting with Paul in February 2012 and the start of parkrun USA. For Rick, one of the funniest parts was how long it took him to realise that the Tom Williams of parkrun was the same Tom Williams he had previously listened to on *Marathon Talk* podcasts.

Rick gets fantastic support from his wife, Lori, who sorts out all the IT and database-related aspects, including processing the results for Livonia parkrun and helping the other USA events whenever they have problems.

At this time there are just three parkrun events in the USA. Rick and Lori's event Livonia in Michigan started in June 2012. Clermont Waterfront, along the shore of Lake Mineola, Clermont in Florida (not far from Orlando) started in April 2013 with Karen Bowler, formerly a southern England parkrunner, at the helm. Durham NC in North Carolina was started in June 2013 by Julie Messina, formerly a Brighton & Hove parkrunner. These three events have been very successful, but despite expressions of interest from more than ninety communities, progress on starting other events has been slower than expected.

Nevertheless, Rick and Lori are hugely enthusiastic about the difference parkrun is making to people's lives, the community spirit it engenders and the people who have started by walking, progressed to run-walk and are now running the course and racing each other. Then there are the international visitors. 'We have people who are visiting the US from the UK, New Zealand, Australia, and they have business maybe in Boston, Philadelphia, Chicago or DC, and they will fly, or hire a car and drive the 250 miles or so to Livonia to parkrun. It's great for the runners here.'

Ireland

The first event in the Republic of Ireland, Malahide in north Dublin, began on 10 November 2012, two years after the first event had started up in Northern Ireland (Waterworks parkrun in Belfast). Matt Shields had initiated Waterworks parkrun and had become involved in managing the parkruns in Northern Ireland, effectively becoming a parkrun Ambassador for the region before there were such posts officially. Taking on the role of Country Coordinator (later Country Manager) for the Republic of Ireland was a natural development.

Growth of parkrun in Ireland has been rapid, with events in the Dublin area quickly attracting large numbers of runners: 200

at Griffeen, over 300 at St Anne's, over 500 at Malahide and 600 at Marlay after just a year. Those elsewhere in the country have been somewhat smaller. All, however, have been very firmly community led rather than being started by running clubs – an interesting difference, Matt finds, from the events in Northern Ireland, many of which are closely linked with a running club.

By the end of the first year of parkrun Ireland there were six events and 9,450 different runners had participated; six months later there were eleven events and more than 16,000 runners, and by the end of June 2014, fourteen events and more than 19,000 runners. As Matt said, 'it's really beginning to rock.' Both the Irish Health Service (HSE) and the Irish Sports Council have become very supportive. Past and present Irish running heroes have also showed their support, with Irish international Sonia O'Sullivan running at Malahide and at Castle Demesne, while both John Treacy, former World Champion cross-country runner and Olympian, and present head of the Irish Sports Council, and the Irish International track and field athlete David Gillick helped to present the prizes at Marlay parkrun's first anniversary in March 2014.

Russia

In spring 2013, a popular Russian running site published an article about parkrun. Some runners were so inspired by the idea of free, weekly timed runs that they decided to organise something similar in Russia, with the first unofficial run on 20 April 2013. For the eighteen runners and four volunteers this was the beginning of a long road to bringing parkrun to Russia.

Soon after, Maxim Egorov and Semen Serikov contacted Paul asking for help to bring parkrun to Russia officially. Paul was delighted that parkrun was so inspiring, but hadn't had any plans for starting up parkrun in Russia and didn't think it would be possible in the near future. So the Russians continued to gather together for Saturday mornings 5K runs, using not the name 'parkrun', but a word-for-word Russian translation of it ('parkovye zabegi' – 'runs in parks').

In July, Paul and Jo went to Moscow and took part in one of the runs. After three days in the company of Moscow runners dedicated to parkrun, Paul was a convert to the idea of parkrun Russia. Preparations for the launch took about eight months: translating the main site into Russian, preparing event sites and support pages, migrating the existing base of parkovye zabegi runners to the parkrun database and so on. Meanwhile, the parkovye zabegi events continued, through the rainy autumn and cold snowy winter, with a time shift to 10 o'clock for winter, and shoes with spikes needed in the icy conditions.

On the first day of spring 2014, parkrun officially started in Russia with two events (a global first – all other countries started with just one): Severnoe Tushino, Moscow, with 39 runners and Kolomenskoe, Moscow, with 64 runners, including one visitor, Catriona Paterson from Black Park parkrun. Just over two months later, the third event started, at Gorky Park. parkrun staff Paul Sinton-Hewitt, Richard Leyton, Alan Dempster, and Jane Niven were among the 45 runners, as well as committed parkrun tourists Paul Freyne and, for his 200th parkrun, John Matthews. By this time, Meshchersky parkrun was taking registrations and their first run took place on 31 May 2014 with 32 runners. Many of those who came on that rainy spring morning to the first event are currently directors of the parkrun events in Moscow.

Singapore

East Coast Park parkrun started on 21 June 2014 with 29 runners and seven volunteers. Eight of the runners were visitors, including Tim Oberg, a few Australian parkrun tourists and dedicated international tourist Nneka Okonta.

The ones that got away

*The very first parkrun outside the UK was Rolf Valley Time Trial (RVTT) in Harare, **Zimbabwe**. This started in 2008, after a runner came from Zimbabwe for an extended trip associated with the Commonwealth Games, experienced parkrun, thought it was fantastic and wanted to take it home. At the time, there was no thought of setting up parkruns country by country, it just happened. The event was very successful for a couple of years, but sadly following national political upheaval the organiser dropped out of sight and the parkrun has never been restarted.*

*Elliðaárdalur parkrun started on 29 October 2011 in Elliðaárdalur valley in Reykjavík, **Iceland**, noted for having an actual forest of trees, a rather rare thing in Iceland. The Country Manager and Event Director was Smari Josatatsson. A group of about forty runners hopped over from the UK and Denmark for the inaugural run, with a start time of 11 o'clock and seventy runners in total tackling the beautiful course – down along a river and beside waterfalls, then a loop through the trees before ascending again back along the river. Neil Reissland, then a regular at Banstead Woods parkrun, finished first, in 17:35 after a very fast initial downhill mile of about 5:20, although he points out that, 'The lead cyclist (and Event Director) actually abandoned his bike, ran the course rather than cycled, and did it faster than I did,' and highest age-graded. The tourists were definitely taken with the thermal pools close by the finish and thought those should be organised at every parkrun! Originally this event was intended to be run all year, but it closed down for the winter after the ninth parkrun and restarted at the beginning of March 2012. There was another group visit from the UK on 26 May 2012, but unfortunately the event closed for good after the 32nd event on 28 July 2012.*

*A special mention is due for Camp Bastion parkrun in **Afghanistan**, organised under the banner of parkrun UK, and 'open to runners of every age, nationality, rank, cap badge and civilian contractors'. This event, set up by Lance Corporal James Barnfield, began* *in October 2011, with the unique start time of 6.30 am, averaged some fifty runners per week and had an average run time of 23:10, probably the fastest of any parkrun. With Camp Bastion gradually closing down, this parkrun was last run on 11 January 2014, the 111th occasion of the event.*

4

From beginners to Olympians

parkrun is for EVERYONE, every single runner, jogger, buggy-pusher or walker that crosses that finish line really matters and that's why parkrun is so perfect.

Alexandra Watson-Usher, Roundhay parkrun

parkrun is for people of all ages and all abilities; for many participants, this aspect of the event is very important. parkrun provides an environment where you can run fast, push yourself and race other runners if you want to, but it doesn't matter whether you're fast or slow, whether you want to run, jog, or walk. It really is for everybody. It is, perhaps, particularly important for beginners, for whom opportunities for running in company can be harder to find, but it's clear that parkrun is also being used by fast (and slower!) club runners, veteran runners and even international athletes.

From the young...

The youngest age at which children are allowed to register to parkrun is four years, and small numbers of four and five year olds are found completing parkruns alongside their mother or father, mixing running and walking, and having fun. Six year olds are rather more common and can be seen trotting across the finish line with a huge grin on their faces while their accompanying parent says, 'I never expected him (or her) to finish!' – and several months later wearing their 10-club T-shirts with immense pride. Some of the older children, even those not yet in their teens, are quite speedy.

It's fantastic to see children running in this supportive environment alongside parents and siblings. At parkrun they are not only enjoying the run, but are taking responsibility for themselves, such as lining up to have their barcode scanned, and are learning to help others, for example stopping to check if another runner is okay after tripping.

It's not only the very young who are embracing parkrun. The demographic chart of parkrunners shows that sizeable numbers of teenagers are also parkrunners.

Carmen Goncalves (age 12) told me that she couldn't really run before she started at Delta parkrun. Now she's running cross-country races for her school – and winning them. She was the first junior parkrunner to reach the 50-club in South Africa and she's on the parkrun South Africa 'most events' leaderboard alongside her father, Carlos. Carmen likes the fact that parkrun isn't pressured, that it's a race against your own time, not against other people, as well as the family aspect and the fact that you can bring your dog.

Heart beating fast as I wait for the horn. When that klaxon goes I know it's just me against the time, and it goes... Halfway through the run and I aim for a tall woman in front. Only two laps to go and I smile; I know I'm on my way to completing my first ever parkrun! Coaches, parents and friends taking part and watching – what an amazing event! I push on until my last lap and then I go! Speeding round the course I know I can do it... You can add a sprint finish to that as well, even strangers encourage me towards the line and when I take that leap of faith I am a winner and we all are! Us Carlisle parkrunners are unbelievable – we encourage others and push on when it gets hard... JOIN IN THE FUN or lose out.

Holly Howson, Carlisle parkrun (under-13)

A Midlands parkrunner said, 'I started running parkrun in April 2013 when I was nineteen. My first time was 39:33, I carried on going and have managed to get my time down to 29:06. This April I will be running the London Marathon which is something I had never dreamt of doing and parkrun is where it all started. The friendly people at parkrun helped me to realise that you don't need to be an athlete to run – anyone can do it.'

Gavin Irvine, a student at St Andrews University, has found parkrun sufficiently motivating that despite typical student Friday nights out, he gets up on a Saturday morning to walk the three miles to Craiftoun Country Park and run St Andrews parkrun. He said, 'Upon completing my first parkrun I felt euphoric, I didn't realise running could provide such a feeling!' Nearly a year later he had run thirty parkruns and a half-marathon and was contemplating his first marathon. He has also encouraged some of his fellow students to start parkrunning. For Gavin, 'The small sense of achievement I get every Saturday morning never wanes and this is what brings me back week after week. My eternal thanks go out to parkrun because without it I would be on my butt playing video games.'

...to the veterans

Amazingly, there are a few people still completing parkruns in their nineties. While the numbers parkrunning in their seventies and older are relatively low, time and time again I hear that parkrun has given runners of all ages new goals, often after they thought their competitive running years were behind them.

Helena Tobin, now in her thirties, had previously trained as a middle-distance runner. When she happened upon parkrun, 'I hadn't trained or competed seriously for some time; parkrun has been great for helping me rebuild my lost confidence.' She had rarely run over 3,000 metres and found it refreshing to have this new goal. Jo Quantrill, in her late fifties and heading towards another year at the top of the Banstead Woods female points table said, 'Being in the twilight of my (twenty year) running career it is so nice to have something I can do reasonably well at and not feel like an old bag.'

For Henry Hopkins, who is in his late fifties and runs at Eastleigh and surrounding parkruns, 'I can't believe the other running disciplines and events I've got involved in that ultimately came through meeting people at parkrun, from 100 metre sprints and triple jump (somehow ranked in UK top ten for age group!) to half-marathons and team relays.'

When I chat to friends, I use the language of 'it's only 5K' or 'it is only about a half hour' (my average) run and it is really fun. I emphasize the latter: 'it is really fun'. But I also add that when you are running it, it is a bit 'different', it is real and not just talking about it and can be a bit challenging, yet fun. I am only 65+ but can't understand some of my age group's resistance to trying it. I repeat 'fun' because it really is when you see more than 300 and even 400 people, some younger than you and others older, and every one running at their own pace, so encouragingly recorded and reported to you.

A north-west England parkrunner

Keith Booth, in his seventies, said: 'It keeps you fit, doesn't it? It's something to aim for on a Saturday morning. And you meet some nice people, and some nice dogs – and you get a sticky bun at the Lloyd Park café afterwards!' He added, 'And when I get too old to do it I might just come along for the sticky bun.'

Danny Ousthuizen, a veteran ultrarunner with 22 Comrades Marathon and nineteen Two-Oceans Marathon finishes (90 and 56 kilometres long, respectively), was encouraged to start parkrunning by his son, Gavin, and it's since become a way of life. There are many people of all shapes and sizes walking the Ebotse parkrun, he told me, with club runners running it and a lot of older, ex-Comrades runners getting out every Saturday, meeting at and enjoying the parkrun. For Danny, one of the best things about parkrun is that 'we're getting so many juniors out who would never have run if it wasn't for the parkrun.' People plan their life around parkrun, he said, adding, 'I think it's the best thing since sliced bread!'

Bill Marks started running in his fifties and 'retired' in his sixties. Shortly before his seventieth birthday, someone told him about parkrun – and Walsall Arboretum was just starting a few miles away. 'I have just done my eightieth run and am very proud to be a part of this great family of parkrunners,' he said. 'Don't say you can't – say "I'll try." You won't regret it.'

And further proof that age doesn't need to be a barrier to parkrunnning is demonstrated by people such as John Taylor, age eighty, who completed his first fifty parkruns at Kawana in November 2013, and Norman Phillips, also a Kawana regular, who only started running in his sixties – although he admits that at age ninety, 'It is getting a bit harder now.'

From beginners...

What is perhaps most amazing about parkrun is the way in which it has inspired people who were not, and never wanted to be, runners.

We have never been into running as we'd always imagined it to be for serious athletes and runners. We used to see runners in Lister Park in Bradford on a Saturday morning while walking. We did ask about the event, however it took us about a year to pluck up the courage to finally attend. Since December 2013 we have done around 95 runs between us and are getting very close to that magical fifty mark. Something we would have never ever imagined in our lifetime. Like many people we are a little hooked on the event and look forward to it every week. The occasion is great, we've met many people and just as we have supported people, there are others who have supported us.
Mohanlal & Urmila Mistry, Bradford parkrun

'I'm not a runner,' said Lindsey Martin. 'My daughter had suggested that I should try parkrun but I wasn't interested.' Then one Saturday morning they were cycling though Bushy Park as the run started. 'It was the most moving sight,' she said, 'this sea of people coming towards us with this look of delight, determination... and the lovely mix of people, including really serious runners, people with kids, older people, dogs.' She added that parkrun brings out the best in people, such as when she fell and two other runners stopped to help her. 'It's fantastic. It does so much for people. I never miss it when I'm home, ever. I've got to be ill to miss it, or away.' In November 2013, about three years after she first ran with that 'sea of people', she was awarded her place in the 100-club, although she still insists that, 'I'm not a runner, really.'

I'm the guy at school never picked for teams and written off at sport generally. This year I will reach my 250-parkrun target. A friend of mine, Pete Golton, suggested we try parkrun a few years ago to get our sons' football team a bit fitter. They gave up but I was hooked. Whatever had happened during the week, at 9am I was on a start line and by 9:30 I was drinking coffee and chatting with new friends. Now I'm training for the fifth Brighton Marathon. parkrun (and Pete) are to blame/thank for this. Running has helped me mentally and physically. It's a community event that's slowly making great changes. It's making running open to all, inclusive and inspiring. I thank it for the change it has made in me. It's a superb concept and an even better reality.

Paul Zara, Brighton parkrun

Susan Harvey, in her early forties, was not a runner at all when she first watched her husband running Frimley Lodge parkrun, felt inspired and decided to try it. The next week she tried to run it with her nine-year-old daughter, only to discover that 'fit' for tennis and aerobics and 'fit' for running 5K were rather different and 'by 200 yards my daughter was going off ahead'. Susan could only manage one lap initially, but in September 2010, she completed both laps for the first time, finishing in 39:11 (and not last, as she had feared she would be). The next week she *ran* both laps; by July 2013 her PB was 28:10 and a few months later she was acting as the pacer for 32 minutes. She has now reached the 100-club, joined a running club (Cove Joggers) and run several 10Ks and a half-marathon.

I saw an advert for a beginners jogging group, and thought I could start jogging. They told me about parkrun but I thought I would never be able to run five kilometres. By week four or five my confidence had built enough to give it ago. My first parkrun I was so nervous... I ran, walked, ran, walked but it didn't seem to matter. No one judged me for walking (other than myself) they were just supporting me doing it and being out there. The volunteers were very supportive even in the few moments you saw them as you jogged past. I now run a few times a week.

Amy Exeter, Sedgefield parkrun

Dorothy McDonald was 56 when she started at Temple News-am parkrun, Leeds. She said, 'My first event in April 2012 was hard, but encouraged by my niece and her eight-year-old son I returned the following week, knocked over three and a half minutes off to get my first PB.' Inspired by parkrun, she's joined Kippax Harriers and now runs two or three times a week. For Dorothy, the encouragement from volunteers and other runners is crucial, particularly for the final push to the finish line: 'To hear cheers of "well done, you can do it, keep going" – well, I just feel I have to work harder to deserve the praise.'

> *The first time I went I was a nervous wreck but I was pleasantly surprised at how easy it was to fit in. People of all shapes and sizes, at different fitness levels. I now enjoy going every Saturday and improving my PB. I have gone from 45 minutes with some running and walking to 33 minutes just running. At the end of the run people cheer you on, which is encouraging.*
>
> *Poppy M, Darwin parkrun*

...to Olympians...

There are also many very good runners who run parkrun occasionally or more frequently. There's no doubt that having several fast runners at the front of the field can bring a particular buzz to the parkrun, particularly when there's the possibility of a new course record being set, and at parkrun you never know when you're going to be running alongside county, national or even international athletes.

> *I started running in May 2007 and came to the very first Leeds parkrun in October of that year. I've lost weight; got fitter and improved my health. I've met hundreds of truly inspirational lovely people including Olympic and Paralympic medallists. I've gone from believing that 5K would be the only distance my little legs could cope*

with to having competed in the London Marathon in April 2013. To share the same ground with the fittest and the fastest is awesome but to see the ordinary become the extraordinary is so inspirational. I love meeting new parkrunners and watch them improve, get confident and then fly! I love the fact that parkrun celebrates achievements no matter how great or small. I love the courage and persistence in people whether it's to just get to the start line; to simply put one foot in front of the other and then to finish the course. It really is a beautiful, heart-warming, soul-lifting experience!

Jaz Bangerh, Leeds parkrun

Looking through the results, particularly at Bushy parkrun, it is possible to pick out the names of a number of present and past top-class middle-distance and long-distance runners, including Sonia O'Sullivan, Mo Farah, Justina Heslop, Andrew Baddeley, Gladys Chemweno, Craig Mottram, Katrina Wootton, Bernard Kiptum, Charlotte Purdue, Alistair Brownlee, Jonathan Brownlee, Liz Yelling, Richard Nerurkar, Vivian Cheruiyot, Ron Hill, Paula Fudge, David Moorcroft and many others.

Irish international Sonia O'Sullivan has been parkrunning since the early days at Bushy Park, finding it conveniently close to home. Usually, she would run a lap before the start, in eighteen minutes, then run the official run in under seventeen minutes and finish with another sub-eighteen minute lap. Her record of 16:22, set on 18 June 2005, stood for nearly three and a half years. Sonia remembers that in the beginning not many elite runners came, but then they started to see how useful it could be as a training run – helped by the Bushy Park course being flat and fast – and for the elite women, there were plenty of men to run against. At the same time it was pleasantly low-key – you could turn up, run and go home, or stay and socialise a bit as you pleased.

I asked Sonia what she thought was the most important thing about parkrun and her answer was instantaneous: 'The most important thing is that everyone is welcome and respected, whether they are the fastest or the slowest, they are recognised for what they are able to do. I think that's why people keep coming.'

Originally from Cork, Sonia sometimes parkruns in Ireland when she's back home. In September 2013 she ran at Castle Demesne parkrun, finishing first woman in 20:14, before going back along the course, as the weekly run report noted, to run with fellow runners and encourage them along. Now that she is getting older and inevitably not running quite so fast, Sonia admits that it's more fun to go to the smaller events where she still has a good chance of being in the top ten. For other athletes, when she's helping them with their training, she recommends parkrun as a good place to test themselves, then use their parkrun time to calculate their training times. She also thinks that the 2K junior parkruns are a great idea: '5K is too far for the children really, especially if they are trying hard. 2K is better for them.'

Mo Farah turned up unannounced at Bushy parkrun to run round with his wife on her first 5K run in 2011; he had previously run there in 2005. Dan Robinson, one of the top British marathoners and winner of the bronze medal for the marathon at the 2006 Commonwealth Games in Melbourne, has run at Wimbledon Common parkrun, while a couple of weeks after the Olympic Games in 2012, the rower Sophie Hosking (who won gold with Kat Copeland in the women's lightweight double sculls) turned up there. 'I announced that she was here, and there was spontaneous applause from the assembled runners for several minutes,' said Event Director Ian Higgins. 'Afterwards, she stayed for more than two hours, let people try on her gold medal and be photographed with her. She was fantastic.'

For Liz Yelling, parkrun has been many things. While she was running at elite level, incorporating parkrun into her training, 'added a really nice dimension to my training. I got to socialise, be with others, get a really good workout in the middle of a training session.' She has been recommending parkrun to top runners for training for years, and continues to do so, considering it to have an important role. 'It offers a great benchmark for fitness, so you can rock up and find where you're at without the pressure of a formal race, and it's consistent, so you can do it on the same course week after week.' The simplicity also makes it easy to incorporate into serious training, since you can just turn up, run and return home with no messing around.

Now that Liz has retired from elite sport, parkrun is a non-pressure situation where she can jog if she feels like it, or run as hard as she can, or push the buggy with her twin sons in it. 'It's liberating – a very nice environment to just run as I please.' As she told me, 'That's the great thing about parkrun, we can go down as a family and Ruby can play in the park afterwards. Now we have the twins in their buggy as well, as a family we can still get out and be active and join in the running community at parkrun. I don't have to sit at home and look after the children and take it in turns to go out and run.' She added, 'It's great seeing people getting a buzz from it, being competitive with themselves. parkrun is for anyone and everyone. Because a lot of people say to me, "oh I'm not built for running," and I think if you want to run you can run, and parkrun gives those people the opportunity to do that.'

Andrew Baddeley has run at Bushy parkrun on several occasions. It's become something of a tradition in his training group to run on the last Saturday or first Saturday of the year as a good transition between the winter cross-country season and heading off to Australia for the early track season.

He appreciates parkrun for many things: the atmosphere, friendliness and the café after the run; the fact that children and teenagers are there with their families on a Saturday morning; that the volunteers give their time for everyone; that you know you can turn up at any parkrun at the start time and have people to run with. He likes that there's no entry standard and everyone can have a go – that slower runners get a chance, therefore, to watch faster runners, learn from them how to warm up, for example, and perhaps be inspired by them. 'If you look down the results of Bushy parkrun, see all the international athletes who have run there: Mo Farah, all the Kenyans... It's got to be inspiring.' Also the fact that the parkrun is there every week means that you can use it in training: you know the course, the distance, and it's timed for you; you can test whether you've got the timing of your pre-run snack right, or see how much you were affected by the previous night out. And if a niggle sets you back a week, you can just go the following week instead.

Justina Heslop has used both Bushy parkrun and Wimbledon Common parkrun, where many of her clubmates in Clapham Chasers run, to test her fitness and achieve faster times. She said, 'I can never really push myself hard enough in training and the race-like conditions of the parkrun really helped me push on to improve my parkrun times and therefore my 10K times in road races.' Apart from the training benefits, she notes, 'I've enjoyed every parkrun I've been to, I've always been struck by the warmth and enthusiasm of the people. My twin sister has done a couple and my twelve-year-old niece has started running the Newcastle parkrun and is loving it.' She added, 'I love that it's not just about fast times – it's totally open to everyone. I've had ex-work colleagues and old friends who I wouldn't associate with running at all contact me to say they had done their local parkrun and had seen that I had the record for Bushy.'

I am 23 years old. I am an Olympian. I have Aspergers and an intellectual impairment which I don't let stop me enjoying sport. I belong to the Special Olympics. I recently competed in the Asia Pacific games in Newcastle, Australia, winning gold in the 1,500 metres and silver in the 5,000 metres. I did my training at Sandgate parkrun. Every Saturday I am at parkrun and I love the friends I have made, the friendships I have developed, the achievements that have only come because of parkrun. My confidence has grown over the past year and I run with my parkrun friends on Wednesday night and Sunday afternoon when I can. I love the wonderful acceptance and encouragement I get when I don't do as well as I would like and the way I am cheered on when I run well. Another Special Olympian also does the Sandgate parkrun and although he walks there is always someone there to cheer him over the line. parkrun improved my life and the lives of my family.

Shaun McKee, Sandgate parkrun, Queensland

Ultramarathon runners also parkrun. Marathon and ultrarunner Steve Way was third Brit in the 2014 London Marathon, finishing in 2:16:27, and set a new British 100K road record at the National 100K at Gravesend three weeks later. Steve was 'well chuffed' when Poole parkrun started just two miles from his house in 2011, providing a great speedwork opportunity where he can run hard, trying to hit specific targets, with other runners around. On his journey north to the Commonwealth Games in Glasgow in July 2014 (where he ran 2:14:16, breaking Ron Hill's British over-40 marathon record set in 1979), he ran the undulating Heaton parkrun as a marathon-pace run in 15:42. Steve loves that parkrun is always available for a final flat-out 5K the week before a marathon. He also loves that he can meet his clubmates there and run with them, and the relationship that he's built up with the Poole parkrunning community: 'It's a fantastic community, and they're my biggest supporters.'

Sharon Gaynor started off in her twenties literally unable to run a mile because she was so unfit, but worked her way up to representing the UK at 100K and 24-hour races. She's also a committed parkrunner. Sharon got hooked on parkruns in 2007 when, returning from injury and wanting a race to run at short notice, she read in *Athletics Weekly* that there was a free 5K race, 'well, they called it a Time Trial, but it sounded like a race to me,' in Hyde Park, Leeds. It was eighty miles away, but she drove over there. 'It was great. I got home and there was an email telling me my time! And I went the next week and the email told me I had run a PB! So I kept going and found it a really useful way of gauging my fitness.'

Sharon still uses parkrun as an essential part of her training. She runs a fast, hard parkrun on the Saturday before running a training marathon the next day, and is certain that this has helped to improve her ultramarathon performances. Further, parkrun has obviously worked its magic on her. Not only does she run in all four of the parkruns within about fifteen miles of home, but also really enjoys running different parkruns, actively looks for parkruns wherever she might be going for her ultra races, and volunteers if she's injured and can't run.

Other elite athletes also make use of parkrun. In Australia the women's national field hockey team, the Hockeyroos, use park-run in their pre-season conditioning programme. As Adam Commens, their coach, explained, 'As with most people, elite athletes find it difficult to motivate themselves sometimes. It is especially difficult for athletes that enjoy the team aspect of our sport to go out and complete the required physical training when they are off in their home location without the support of their teammates.' parkrun has proved to be excellent: each member of the team can get out amongst a group of great people wherever they are on a Saturday morning, complete a 5K conditioning run, then let the Hockeyroos staff know their results.

...and everyone in between

The global parkrun demographic chart shows that all age groups are parkrunning. The results also show that runners of all abilities are taking part. Graphical displays of the finishing times for any individual parkrun generally show a bell curve, the peak varying in position (faster on the flatter parkruns), and with a long tail if there are a lot of walkers.

For many committed running club runners, who have club training runs and plenty of local and regional races to choose from, parkrun may not have changed their lives, but it is still useful. As Shane McDermott, an early and fast runner at Bushy said, 'It's convenient and reliable; you know it's going to be there, on time and with no fuss. You can just turn up, run and leave, or go for a coffee afterwards if you want to.' David Symons was another fast early adopter, finishing first at the third Bushy Park Time Trial, and he agrees. Now, he says, 'I still try hard when I go out there; it's a personal challenge, but not the same tension as paid-for events.' He added that, getting slower and training less, the coffee and camaraderie is becoming more important.

> *When I started running in the summer of 2010, parkrun was the first timed event I encountered. I soon became hooked and found the confidence to enter a 10K race. At Cardiff parkrun I was introduced to Les Croupiers RC – I joined them and started running more competitively. Within the year I ran my first marathon and haven't looked back since. I have volunteered at parkrun just as many times as I have run it, and now act as one of the Run Directors in Cardiff.*
> *Amanda Thompson, Cardiff parkrun*

Paul Sinton-Hewitt wants everyone to have access to a parkrun if they want one, and that includes considering access for disabled athletes – for example wheelchair athletes, registered blind and hearing impaired runners. Often, very minor adjustments can enable runners with disabilities to take part. Alan Burrell at Wynnum parkrun notes that for a deaf runner he simply provides a written summary of the pre-run briefing, particularly safety aspects.

On wheels...

In addition to the male and female age-grade categories, categories have been created for male and female wheelchair athletes to make it easier to compare performances. Some wheelchair parkrunners are quite fast, particularly if they use racing wheelchairs, which can make a huge difference in speed. Obviously, not all parkrun courses are suitable for wheelchair athletes, just as not all are suitable for running with buggies.

Ari Seirlis ran Comrades Marathon in 1985, for a bet, shortly before a diving accident left him quadriplegic and in a wheelchair. When Ari discovered North Beach parkrun in Durban, South Africa, he was delighted. Level, fully paved, it's ideal for wheelchairs – even everyday ones like Ari's. His work as CEO of the Quadriplegic Association of South Africa (QASA) involves a lot of travel; when he's home he wants to keep to a routine and part of that is parkrunning with his sister.

'I really enjoy the exercise; with my volume of travel, it's very important to get that hour of exercise every week,' Ari said. 'And I get a chance to chat with my sister. I usually try to get one friend to come each time as well, to catch up with them. I've probably recruited a dozen or more people to parkrun that way.' He notes that the parkrun is very friendly, he always looks forward to it and he's enjoyed it every time. Additionally, 'always someone will come over, tell me I've inspired them. And just occasionally I overtake people and I see them pick up their speed a bit!' His only problem is that he usually bumps into someone who knows him and wants him to stop for a chat. 'Maybe one of these Saturdays nobody will stop me and I'll get another PB.' For Ari, every North Beach parkrun is also a trip down memory lane, as the route takes him past the site of his accident and past the hospital where he did his rehabilitation. 'I'm glad I did Comrades when I did,' he said.

'But since then I've completed the New York marathon using a handcycle, twice – and I'm a parkrunner!'

...or with a little help from your friends

For visually impaired runners, all that's needed is a guide – another runner who runs with the visually impaired person, warns them of obstacles and is usually linked using a strap or a hand on an arm.

For Tony McEvoy, who runs at Ormeau, parkrun provides the opportunity for him to run with everyone else in the community rather than boringly on a treadmill, and to take part in an event that's about running, not about blindness or disability. He runs with a guide who can warn him verbally about corners coming up, or obstacles, as his 5% remaining vision doesn't allow him to see hazards such as dogs, benches or a child cutting in front. He said, 'Like everyone else I want to run a PB, and most of my guides encourage me to do so, to run the best I can.' Coming from a rural area, parkrun has also helped him to break through the relative social isolation of city life, where people just don't talk to each other. He's joined a running club; he's discovered that a near neighbour is a parkrunner and a member of the same running club, so they can travel together; he's met old work colleagues and re-formed friendships; he's taken part in a marathon relay, running 5.3 miles; and he's looking to do 10Ks and even a half-marathon.

Katie Kelley continues running at Darwin parkrun, despite gradually losing her peripheral eyesight (making running in crowded spaces particularly challenging) and has previously guided a blind friend at Newy parkrun. She said 'I will just keep making adjustments to whatever my situation is.' An excellent example that blindness does not need to be an obstacle to parkrunning is Derek Coughlan, a blind regular Wimbledon Common parkrunner, who in December 2013 reached his hundredth parkrun. It was noted in that week's run report (appropriately titled 'Derek's Day') that 'on a course which presents many obstacles in the shape of tree roots, uneven ground and the like' he had fallen only once – rather less than many of the fully sighted runners.

And Susanne Laustsen, age 54, who ran marathons before losing her sight, now runs at Amager Fælled parkrun with her husband Kim as a guide around the twists and turns and the puddles in the gravel paths. Since 2010 she has completed more than 175 parkruns and often comes in as first woman. Susanne said, 'parkrun is very important to me. It gives me the opportunity to maintain my training and still participate in competitions. I have got a lot of new sport friends that I meet every week, it's like having a big family. parkrun is a really nice event, well organized, not too big and not too crowded, it fits a blind person very well.'

5

Volunteers:
paid in smiles

I love parkrunning; I love volunteering even more. I think parkrun breaks the mould, you can get out more than you put in. Just volunteer and you'll see exactly what I mean.

Andrew Bennett, Event Director, Corby parkrun

Volunteering is at the heart of parkrun. Without volunteers to fill the roles before, during, and after the run, from course markers to token sorters, run directors to report writers, the free, weekly parkruns could not take place.

The very first parkrun volunteers were Paul Sinton-Hewitt, Jo Sinton-Hewitt (then Jo Turner), Alan Hedger, Duncan Gaskell and Robin Drummond. When Paul started the Bushy Park Time Trial he was injured and couldn't run so was happy to volunteer weekly. As the event grew, many people who ran the event regularly started taking a week out occasionally to make sure that everything went smoothly – and to ensure that the event could be held every week. Ian Callander, Emma Gray, Orlando Pellicano (who helped with the tech side as well as at runs), Jane Martin and Paula Sheridan were amongst the early volunteers.

There are many different volunteering roles and just as many different reasons for volunteering. Martin Yelling notes that one of the strengths of parkrun is that, 'You can offer as much or as little as you wish; you can run every week, volunteer every week or a bit of both.' In Chris Wright's opinion, 'It's most successful when you get that feeling that it's not a group of volunteers and a group of runners, it's just a group of parkrunners.'

Although parkrun did not set out to be an opportunity for volunteering – it was an opportunity for running – it has also come to provide a fantastic opportunity for a wide range of people to volunteer, and many do. For example, on 3 May 2014, in addition to 72,129 runners, joggers and walkers, there were 4,884 parkrun volunteers worldwide.

Management teams and core volunteers

For each parkrun to succeed, there has to be a core of dedicated individuals who are prepared to give their time on a regular or frequent basis to set up before the run, to help during the run and to help clear everything away afterwards. Beyond that, there are many parkrunners who volunteer both in roles where they can run and in roles where they take a break from running. For those of us on parkrun management teams, volunteering at our parkrun is a major part of our parkrun experience – and part of our way of life: parkrun is what we do on a Saturday morning and it feels rather strange to go on holiday and *not* be volunteering, even if you visit another parkrun and run there.

Many people find that when they start up a new event or take over as Event Director, for a while at least they don't actually *run* their parkrun very often. They are busy getting everything sorted, sometimes meeting specific people and talking to them during the run – chatting to other users of the park to ensure good relationships with the wider community, or giving guidance to someone who will be holding a charity run or walk in the same park. However, as the team builds up and more people come forward to volunteer, this should change, and many parkruns set up rota systems so that key roles are covered by teams – for example four teams on a 'two weeks on, six weeks off' basis. Even if the Event Director is not running at all, perhaps due to injury or other health problems, it is important to develop the volunteering teams and train enough people for the key roles that the Event Director can take a holiday or visit another event knowing that their parkrun will still go ahead without major problems.

Of course, some people manage to both volunteer *and* run, even when short handed. Rob Downs, Event Director at Bramhall parkrun, has been known to initiate the run, run it himself, finish first and then time everyone in. Occasionally, he admits, he's intended to do that but one or two runners have overtaken him and got to the finish first and they have had to sort the times out afterwards – fast runners like that are usually recording their own time on a sports watch, so it's not too difficult.

For many parkrunners, being on the management team or being a core volunteer simply means they have some days when they are happily volunteering as the Run Director or taking on another non-running role, and other days when they are just as happily lined up with the other runners. Also, being part of a parkrun management team doesn't mean that you have to be in the management team for ever – it's perfectly normal for someone to be in a role such as Event Director, Volunteer Coordinator or regular Run Director and then, whether due to other things in their life altering, or just because they want a change, step down and let someone else take on the role and learn what being a core volunteer can do for them.

Volunteering roles

The volunteering roles can seem a bit daunting initially, but really they are all quite straightforward. Many people start as a marshal, which is really easy: stand out on the course, making sure that people go the correct way and, in the rare event of something going wrong, make sure the runner is okay and let the Run Director know.

One of the great things about marshalling is getting to see all the different styles of running. Many first-time marshals comment on this, and the enjoyment they get from watching everything from the apparent effortlessness of some of the fastest people, through the comfortably chatting joggers, all the way to the slowest runners determinedly pushing their way through the 5K and the walkers enjoying the fresh air. Runners also greatly appreciate the encouragement they get from the marshals: 'Come on, only one K to go and it's all downhill from here!' 'That's right, just a push up the hill!' 'Well done, looking good!'

> One of my favourite volunteering jobs is to marshal at the top of a climb and direct the runners around the boating lake. I am normally a very quiet and reserved person but here I let myself go and cheer all the runners up the slope with, 'You are doing well, the hard bit is done, now go for home.'
>
> John Robert Richardson, Norwich parkrun

parkrun: much more than just a run in the park

Some parkruns only have one or two marshals, while others may use many more, and some do not have any but have a tail runner.

Tail runners were initiated at Richmond Park by Karen Weir. When the park was busy it could be difficult, with their undulating, single-lap course, to know who was the last runner and therefore when the finish funnel could be packed up. Karen said: 'When there's a tail runner, nobody ever finishes last – well technically the tail runner does, but they have volunteered to do so. Also, while sometimes the person who would otherwise be at the end just wants to be left alone, often they're very happy to have someone to chat to them, encourage them when they're finding it hard on the uphill section, maybe give them some training tips.' It has proved to be a popular volunteering role: 'It's the first volunteer position that gets filled each week; they say they get to hear lots of stories about people's efforts and what it's taken them to get this far, and that's really inspirational.' Steve Way was tail runner at Poole parkrun the week after winning the 50K World Championship in 2012. Poole named that week's parkrun 'Beat a World Champion Day' – and laid out a red carpet for him at the finish.

Some events also have a lead bike to inform other park users that the runners are coming or to guide runners along the route.

Another running volunteering role is pacer, assisting other people to reach their particular goals, whatever those goals may be. Pacers pride themselves on finishing on time and they get a lot of satisfaction when they help someone to reach a previously-elusive target.

I love being a pacer and trying to encourage runners to get around in a time that is just a bit faster than they have done before.
Nathan Smith, Harrogate parkrun

Volunteers: paid in smiles

At the finish, typically there will be one or two timers, one person handing out finish position tokens, and a number checker, plus at larger events a funnel manager and a numbers assistant. Other volunteers register the runners by scanning their personal parkrun ID barcodes and the finish tokens.

Then there are the roles for before or after the run, such as setting up the course, briefing new runners, clearing up afterwards, writing the run report, managing the volunteers, processing the results and storing the equipment.

Why volunteer?

parkrun is important to me because it can be so many different things. If I need to do a long run then parkrun can provide a welcome spot of company in the middle. When I'm pushed for time or am on a drop-back week a parkrun is just enough to get the endorphins flowing without pushing me too hard. If I'm feeling particularly good parkrun is an excellent test of my speed and a new PB is always very satisfying. When I am injured, feeling under the weather or just knackered I can go along to volunteer and still see my friends and have fun.

Gemma Rathbone, Leeds parkrun

A common source of volunteers, whether for one week, several weeks, months or even years, is injured runners. Every time a runner is injured, and rather than staying snuggled up in bed on a Saturday morning goes down to their parkrun to volunteer, they are, whether they know it or not, walking in the footsteps of Paul Sinton-Hewitt. For Paul, 'Those early years were wonderful because our systems were so basic that I used to record every finisher by hand. This meant that I got to know about 250 people personally and I made a lot of friends. Many of these people are now my closest friends.'

parkrun: much more than just a run in the park

Volunteering at parkrun is hugely important for injured runners as it gives them a way to stay involved with running and to keep in contact with the running community while they're injured. Time and time again people tell me that volunteering has given them something positive to focus on while they couldn't run. For some, it's a push into a whole new world.

Peter Harvey started volunteering due to a knee injury when he had only been parkrunning for a few weeks. His wife Susan said, 'I think it helped us to get to know everyone at Frimley parkrun, his volunteering.' Jo Quantrill, who started off at Wimbledon Common and moved to Banstead Woods once that started, said, 'When I was out of running for three months with an injury, volunteering kept me sane.' Having had a similar experience, I really know what she means. Additionally, once you have been parkrunning for a while, it becomes a habit, and not getting out of bed on a Saturday morning to go to parkrun feels strange. Getting up and going to volunteer gives you most of the parkrun experience and is enjoyable, even if it does not quite make up for the frustration of not being able to *run*.

Donna Speirs at Barrow parkrun said that their volunteering team sometimes looks like a scene from an Accident and Emergency ward, with casts and crutches everywhere. Similarly at Lloyd, one day when we had been one marshal short and an injured parkrunner turned up offering to volunteer, I looked at the finish line crew (all in various stages of injury recovery) and had to ask, 'Okay, who feels capable of walking over to the second marshalling point?'

For Jennifer Greve, who runs at Livonia parkrun in Michigan, USA, having the opportunity to volunteer is one of the big strengths of parkrun. As a new, rather than an established runner, who developed an injury, she said, 'If I had been running on my own and run into this injury problem, I might not have gone back to it again, but the fact that we're still getting up every Saturday morning and we have a place to go and we have people we know, means that I still have the camaraderie and support, which means that once I can get back to it again it's not going to be so hard, because that structure is still there.'

Many people volunteer for several weeks in a row while injured and then return to running – sometimes rather sooner than their doctor has suggested, as with Liz Mason running the undulating Banstead Woods course, with her broken shoulder and collarbone supported by a sling, after being told that she could run for up to 200 metres on a flat surface. 'We're all like that here, we're all a bit mad, aren't we?' she said, laughing. 'Yes, volunteering is great to help you keep sane while you can't run, but after a while...'

Club runners and other competitive runners often volunteer when they are saving themselves for a team cross-country on the Saturday afternoon or a race the following day. This can lead to a sudden bump in the number of volunteering offers for the day before a local 10K or half-marathon, which is great, with runners really appreciating the extra marshals encouraging them around the course.

Susan Harvey usually volunteers when she's got a race the next day. 'It's an eye opener how spread out the field gets even on the first lap. I get a lot of enjoyment from watching people, cheering them on – I try to do that by name, because I know how great it is when you're running and get acknowledged by name. It always amazes me how tired the first finishers are, everyone pushing themselves to the line.' She added, 'I really enjoy it; I don't feel like I'm missing out at all. In fact, I think that the people who never volunteer, they are the ones who miss out, they don't get as much out of the parkrun.'

Probably the most common reason why people start volunteering is to give something back: to their parkrun in particular, to parkrun in general, or to the running community.

Neil Reissland admitted that he had not volunteered all that much when he started parkrunning, being too focused on pushing himself to see what he could do in getting his time down and his age grade percentage up. But after he was awarded the monthly prize by Roundshaw Downs in March 2011, he felt a need to give more back and started volunteering regularly, including as Run Director. 'It took me a lot longer to go from fifty runs to one hundred than it had to get to fifty, but that's all right.'

Cass Castleton started volunteering because of the website message suggesting volunteering three times a year and because he realised that without the volunteers there could be no parkrun. However, since he was running for his health, and he really did not want to drive an hour to the parkrun in order to not run, he looked for a way he could volunteer and still run. So he offered to do Brighton & Hove's token sorting after the run (no mean task with 300-400 runners most weeks), and he now takes that on regularly, including demonstrating the best way to carry out the task to other people who are doing it for the first time.

Trisha Cue has a unique volunteering role at Banstead Woods parkrun, taking monthly photographs to check no excessive damage is occurring in the woods. The day I visited, she was on registration. 'It's great that we all volunteer and do our bit, but I admit I prefer to volunteer if I can still run as well – so I'm a selfish volunteer!' She paused to scan in a runner, then added, 'It's nice to volunteer [and miss a run] occasionally, you get a completely different aspect and you get to chat to new people. But the people who volunteer all the time are just amazing.'

Wendy, also at Banstead Woods, agrees that it's good to give something back by volunteering 'because other people do it for you,' plus there are additional benefits: 'The atmosphere between the volunteers is lovely, and I just love seeing everyone finish.'

Gill Stalley was introduced to parkrun by her husband Andy and now manages the volunteers at Banstead Woods. Initially, when her husband was parkrunning on a Saturday and marathon running on a Sunday she found it frustrating, but she started coming out just to enjoy the woods, then started walking the parkrun, then running it. 'Everyone knows me as the volunteer coordinator. I enjoy doing it, sorting out the little puzzle to fill all the spaces. Managing the volunteers is my hobby. And when I was injured it was great that I could volunteer, because I was still able to be involved in it all. And it's such a great atmosphere; if I can be involved in one way or another then I'm happy.' parkrun has become a big part of her life. 'Saturday morning isn't Saturday morning if I haven't done a parkrun. I've made so many friends. It's so nice coming down in the morning, saying hello to everyone; everyone's in such a good mood, which gets even better if you get a PB.'

Another Banstead Woods volunteer, Steve O'Sullivan, likes volunteering because it gives something back; he likes helping at the finish: 'I get a lot of enjoyment watching them, whether it's the first person or the last person. You get to know the faces, and then the people and then their stories, each person's little challenge.'

Volunteering at parkrun can be a way of giving back to the wider running community. Chris Phelan has put a huge amount of time and energy into Banstead Woods over the years and I asked him what had been his motivation. He explained, 'I was well into running, I'd run competitively and really appreciated the support given to runners both at cross-country and road races. Setting up Banstead Woods Time Trial was my opportunity to put something back into running.' He added that every time he calls out to people while they're doing the parkrun, tells them 'well done', greeting as many as possible of them by name, he sees what a difference it makes, how people really value this support. 'So many people come up to me afterwards at the parkrun and say thank you. In fact, it's not just at the parkrun; I can be in the local supermarket shopping and someone in a smart suit will greet me by name and make some comment about Banstead Woods, and I'll realise they're a parkrunner, but often I don't recognise them, when they're not in their running gear!'

Sarah Barfield is a runner, but has only run a parkrun once. Her running schedule involves Friday and Sunday runs, with Saturday as a rest day, so when she heard on *Fetch Everyone* that Leamington parkrun was starting up she thought this would be a great opportunity to volunteer. She's been volunteering since about the second event, both as a means of giving back to the running community and because she enjoys it so much. 'Sometimes it's hard to get up on a Saturday morning and make the twenty-minute drive over there, but I always feel better for having been there, and I've made so many friends. I like the camaraderie, the atmosphere. Those of us volunteering always have a good giggle; it's a very friendly place to be, and it's interesting to watch how people are progressing in their running. I get a very positive vibe from the parkrun and it really sets me up well for the rest of Saturday.'

Andy Morgan-Lee at Eastleigh parkrun said: 'It's great, volunteering, you meet lots of people. When you're running you're more focused on what you're doing; you get more time to chat when you're volunteering and you get to cheer everyone on.'

For non-running partners, parents or children of runners and sometimes for friends, volunteering provides a great way to get involved and is much more fun than simply standing around at the start or finish, or sitting in a car, waiting for the runner to return.

Beware however! Volunteering at parkrun is so rewarding that you might soon find yourself heading off to 'your' parkrun even if your teenager has decided to have a lie-in this Saturday morning or your spouse is heading in a different direction!

Jenny Booth isn't a runner, although her husband Keith, now in his seventies, still runs. However, she's been volunteering at parkruns since soon after they started, first at Banstead Woods and now as part of the management team at Lloyd Park in Croydon.

Michael Lee is a permanent volunteer at Eastleigh parkrun. He has a bad back and can't run. After he turned up to support his wife, it was only a matter of time before one of the Run Directors suggested he could give them a hand. Wearing a great tutu (for International Dance Day – any excuse for dressing up at Eastleigh parkrun) he was obviously enjoying himself: 'It's a great team, a happy family,' he said. 'And what else can I do on a Saturday morning?'

Joyce Dearing used to enjoy a lot of walking but now has severe rheumatoid arthritis and cannot join her husband, Mike, in parkrunning. However, she gets a lot of pleasure from marshalling regularly at Hull parkrun: 'Watching the youngsters go past, and the mums with their pushchairs – it's magic.' Additionally she really enjoys the social side, being part of the group. And Helen Cordona, who has a prosthetic leg, started volunteering at Lloyd parkrun because some of her friends were there. She likes the community and watching the different people: 'Today I've seen two people running with their dogs, I've seen a little boy running in the first ten... I think it's amazing, just brilliant.' She also has every intention of running it herself sometime.

Matt Shields has found that non-running volunteers are an important part of parkruns and it can become an important part of the volunteer's life: 'That's true of my own wife, for a start,' he said, 'she's heavily involved in managing Waterworks parkrun now, loves the community feel and loves to see the kids running.' Phoebe Riddle, age nine, whose parents and brother run, said, 'I like to volunteer because it's fun and it helps people out. I like being involved in the running of the parkrun. I like watching the runners come in and talking to other volunteers. I love watching the dogs that come and run, and of course I love it when we can go for a hot chocolate after everyone has finished.'

For a growing number of teenagers, parkrun is providing an excellent forum in which they can do their required volunteering towards their Duke of Edinburgh Awards in a friendly, healthy environment, probably one they already know as a runner. Here they can take on a variety of tasks, increasing in level of responsibility, with some young people graduating from marshalling through giving out finish tokens to timing, scanning barcodes and all the way up to Run Director. At Riddlesdown parkrun, situated close to two schools and with a school teacher as the Event Director, there are often several such volunteers at any one time. When they want to run (to fulfil the physical activity requirements of the award) they carry out volunteering tasks such as course set-up, sorting equipment between runs, and writing run reports.

parkrun also gives veteran runners the chance to remain part of the running community after their own running days have finished. Ron Trodd at Eastleigh parkrun does a great job ringing a handbell for each runner to let them knew when they start their third and final lap, and ensuring that they head for the finish funnel, not the main course, at the end. Before a heart problem stopped him running, Ron, a veteran runner now in his eighties, had completed eighteen consecutive London marathons and 78 marathons in total, and was heading towards the 100-marathon club. Coming to the finish funnel after the last person had safely finished, Ron said, 'I've run for over forty years, but I can't run any more, so it keeps me in touch with everybody.' Similarly, regular volunteers Peter Meloy, Maurice Day (a former ultramarathon runner, now in his eighties) and Percy Jordan at Tilgate parkrun are all veterans who are no longer running. Peter was heavily involved in a West Sussex Fun Run League club but when unable to run he had dropped away from the running community altogether. Volunteering at parkrun has given him a route back into the community and an opportunity to give something back to running.

parkrun volunteers can be truly amazing. Chris Phelan shared the story of Jim Cartwright, a regular Banstead Woods parkrunner, who telephoned from his hospital bed to apologise for not being able to make it down to the woods that Saturday to volunteer. When asked why, he explained he'd had 'a little stroke'. Unfortunately a second stroke left him with more severe paralysis of his right side, and affected his speech, but he worked hard at his speech therapy so he would be able to return to calling out the half way times to parkrunners: that was a major goal for him.

Benefits of volunteering

What people get out of volunteering at parkrun also varies, although one of the amazing things, as Garry Wells from Blackbutt parkrun said, is that, 'You get out much more than you put in – not just directly at parkrun but also in your working life and friendships.'

Most runners discover, once they volunteer for the first time, that it's fun: commonly, acting as a marshal for the first time, they come back to the finish area positively bubbling with enthusiasm about how many runners had smiled at them and thanked them, and talking about how fascinating it was to see all the runners and their different running styles. James Moore, a regular parkrunner at Lloyd parkrun, noted on a muddy winter morning that volunteering 'is as much fun as running, but much less hard work.'

Many people have found that volunteering at parkrun has changed their lives: they have discovered that they can lead people or motivate people – or both; they have had a go at being Run Director and discovered that yes, they can stand in front of a hundred or several hundred people and talk to them – so they can do public speaking; have had the opportunity to write run reports and discovered an aptitude for writing that they didn't know they had.

'It's given me more confidence,' Paul Bissett, Ardgillan parkrun Event Director said. 'I'm quite shy normally and if someone had told me two years ago that I'd be standing up in front of a crowd making speeches I'd never have believed them. But now I have to do that and organise the team.' Mick Turner, one of the Roundshaw Downs Event Directors, agrees. 'Nicky [fellow Event Director] and I absolutely hated the speaking but it's really helped us. After a while you no longer get fazed by speaking in public and now I'm not even nervous about giving my wedding speech.' He added, 'You do worry at first if you miss something out of the pre-run announcements, but after a while you relax.' Mick also noted that in addition to meeting Lorraine, who he's since married, through parkrun, 'I've made a lot of very close friends through parkrun, fantastic people. I love the volunteering aspect, helping people to do their runs. I'm very inspired by people who start off with very little experience of running and then get fitter, lose weight, become a glowing picture of health and look so happy – it's really lovely to think I've helped people like that along the route. Some parkrunners get heavily into running, others just do the parkrun once a week, but whatever they want to do, you help them.'

Volunteers: paid in smiles

Gill Stalley, Volunteer Coordinator at Banstead Woods, also found that her role has improved her confidence: 'not only from the running, because I know that I can do that, but I'm more confident in front of people and that's helped me at work.' Danny Norman thinks that the improvements in confidence come because when you stand up there and tell dozens or hundreds of people what to do, you're doing it for the right reasons, to make sure that everyone has an enjoyable and safe run.

Nat Glenn, Event Director at Larne parkrun, considers that the best thing about volunteering is the pleasure of watching people who were not really into running getting into it: setting and reaching their own goals, initially just to finish the course, then going for their parkrun PBs and even going on to longer races. 'Watching them talking about their next goal, and seeing how parkrun is central to that.'

Julie Messina, as an American living and working in the UK several years ago, found that volunteering at Brighton & Hove parkrun helped her to become a part of the community. 'I started going along to run, though 5K was a long distance to me as a novice runner, and began volunteering. I ended up on the volunteer committee and after a while I stopped being "that American lady" and started to be just Julie, which was great.' Naturally, when she and her husband returned to the USA, she wanted to have a parkrun there – and organised the Durham, North Carolina, parkrun.

I try to volunteer a few times a year and have found the experience to be very rewarding. It's great to see all the different running styles and I love to see the effect that encouragement gives to those near the back of the course. I've got to know more people and can turn up each week now and find someone I know to chat to rather than standing on my own.

Paul Chapman, Cardiff parkrun

You've volunteered *how* often?

Late in 2013, volunteering statistics started being displayed on the profile page of each parkrunner, so now you can see how many times you have volunteered and how often in each volunteering role, which is rather nice. Also, each week's volunteers are now displayed at the bottom of each weekly results page.

Additionally, there are many people who assist unofficially but don't expect their contributions to be captured by the volunteering forms: the runners who stay after they have finished their own run, cheering in all the other runners; those who make special efforts to bring food for anniversary parties and other notable events; the people who help pack up the equipment and carry it all back to the storage cupboard or someone's car. Then there's the parkrunner who gets up extra early to pick up other people and take them to a different venue; the runner who acts as a pacer for a friend; the one who finishes their own run and then goes back and encourages another runner over the final section; and the one who coaches other runners on the way round, giving them tips about pumping their elbows backwards and taking short steps to get up the hill.

Mentors and Ambassadors

From very early in the history of parkrun, as new events started up, the people taking on the challenge of managing a parkrun have been assisted by those that have been through the process before them. When I was settling into my role as Volunteer Coordinator and then Event Director at Lloyd parkrun, I was helped hugely by Nicki Clark. Nicki had done her 'apprenticeship' at Banstead Woods, learning all the volunteering roles there, as well as, said Chris Phelan, improving their standard of photography. She was Lloyd parkrun's Volunteer Coordinator during the time when she was preparing to start up Riddlesdown parkrun. Nicki took me through the intricacies of the computer systems for managing volunteers and results and patiently answered my concerned queries on Saturday mornings as I met each results-processing problem for the first time.

As the rate of expansion of parkrun has increased, the role of such local mentors has become ever more important and in 2013 an official parkrun Ambassadors scheme was set up. Ambassadors are parkrunners who are usually already involved with managing their local parkrun but have offered to assist further, often by providing advice and encouragement to new teams as they go through the process of setting up a new parkrun. Starting in 2013, parkrun has held an annual Ambassadors' Conference to enable ambassadors from all around the UK to meet, share experiences and learn from each other.

When all else fails...

Runners like to have their results; volunteers like to produce those results and take a certain pride in doing so quickly and efficiently. On occasion, volunteers have gone a long way above and beyond their normal duties to bring people their results.

At Barrow parkrun, where the core volunteers take it in turns to look after the essential equipment each week, one week the volunteer in question happily came over to parkrun – and nobody realised until 8.45 that the timer, the barcode scanners and the laptop were not at the park. 'We did have the finish tokens,' Donna Speirs said, 'so someone did the timing on their mobile phone and several people sat in the bandstand where we usually register everyone and did all the registration by hand – writing down the runners' IDs and finish positions – then it all got transferred to a computer later the old-fashioned way. If we can manage that we can manage anything!'

And one day in spring 2011, the Lloyd parkrun timer decided not to work. With runners' names and positions recorded but no times, Nicki Clark waited for the query emails to come in, all along the lines of, 'Why don't I have my result yet?' To each runner, she responded with a request for them to send her their time, if they had been wearing a running watch. Then – in a process which would be enough to try a saint – she went through her finish line photos and estimated all the times, based on the time stamps on the pictures, those times from people who had been timing themselves, and the distances between the runners in the pictures.

As the number of events and the number of runners has grown, Paul and the various Country Managers have recommended that volunteer teams not go to such lengths. Really, what is the very worst that can happen? Runners get to have a great run in the park with their friends, chat with friends and go home feeling like they have had a great time – and simply don't actually get an official time and finish position. And there is always another parkrun, same time, same place, the next week.

However, it's not just in emergencies that volunteers have gone the extra mile to make their parkrun work. At Delta parkrun, as the number of participants grew, some of the paths were getting rather congested, particularly where runners had to use a bridge over a stream. One of the volunteers, who happened to work in construction, decided that this problem, and some other bottle-necks, could be solved. Having spotted some massive concrete pipes abandoned in the parks, he contacted the park authorities for permission, then asked the construction company if he could borrow a crane. With a bit of assistance he sorted everything, including moving the pipes and using them in making a new bridge – problem solved!

6

The numbers game

I like the fact that your time is recorded and available online within a few hours, as this gives you an indication of how you are doing and a challenge to improve each week if you can.

Tony Price, Wolverhampton parkrun

When I ask people what they like about parkrun, alongside the fact that it is free and friendly, runners usually mention the near-instant feedback. You run a parkrun for the first time and, generally within an hour or two, your time is sent to you, together with your age grade. The next time you parkrun, you get not only time and age-grade percentage but also, if you were faster, congratulations on having run a PB – a Personal Best time. Beginners commonly get a lot of PBs in the first few months of parkrunning, which can be a massive psychological boost.

Times, PBs and record breakers

Many runners, whether novice or experienced, are obsessed with their run times, using sports watches to check their mile or kilometre splits (time for each unit of distance), noting their overall speed, whether they managed a negative split (faster on the second half of the run) or if they hit the sprint times they were aiming at. Alan Burrell from Wynnum parkrun, Queensland, provides a lot of statistics for parkrun Australia and is known as 'The Prof'. As he has noticed, 'Running does attract people who like stats and competition.'

The rapid feedback provided by parkrun is an incredible bonus not usually provided by fun-runs of this distance. Gavin Oosterhausen, who runs at Ebotse parkrun in South Africa, said that this aspect is even more of a draw in South Africa than in the UK. 'Runners are number crunchers; we like looking at the numbers, the seconds count to us, the position we came. That's all immediately available at parkrun, you don't have to wait two or three weeks to get the results, which often happens in South Africa.' He's definitely a competitive runner and considers that both the community and the competition drive him: 'You see the same guys every week and you run alongside them or just behind them trying to catch them, so it's really that competitive nature that comes out; I really like it.' Gavin appreciates not just the times but all the stats that come out of parkrun.

My first parkrun was in November 2013 and I finished in 33rd place with a time of 29:15. This first run got that competitive spirit back that I had lost so many years ago. It also got easier to run every time as I got fitter. I must admit the bug got me hook, line and sinker and I started training secretly. Now I'm running an 18 minute 5K

and I'm getting close to a 1 hour 16 minute half-marathon time. Who could believe that would happen?
Jacques Joubert, Hamilton Lake parkrun

Because parkruns are timed runs with a fixed distance, people often become self-competitive and strive to reach specific time goals. For the faster runners, this might be sub-twenty, sub-seventeen or even sub-sixteen minutes. For many others it might be breaking the 22, 25, 30 or 45 minute barrier. Of course, once that target has been reached, there is always another, harder goal to aim for, to try to take off another thirty or sixty seconds.

My first experience of parkrun was a struggling 5K. Getting my first time was motivation for me to come back the next week and beat my time. Since then I have completed over sixty runs, been the first female to finish seventeen times (and counting), have run my first half marathon and in September 2014 I will be running the Sydney Marathon; I have parkrun to thank for helping me to achieve this huge goal. parkrun has become a part of my life now, has given me the opportunity to meet some great people who are now friends and is still continually motivating.
Gooya Mozdbar, Cornwall Park parkrun

parkruns sometimes provide official pacers – runners who volunteer to complete the course in a set time, so that anyone who is aiming to reach that time knows that if they just keep up with, or ahead of, the pacer, they will reach their target. At Bushy parkrun the pacers turn out one week per month, alternating between odd- and even-numbered minutes, carrying little flags stating their goal pace, and dressing up in a theme. At Conkers parkrun, the pacers aim for 20, 22½, 25, 27½, 30 and 35 minutes, while at Eastleigh, they periodically ask people who are wanting to beat a particular target to let them know, and try to match those runners with appropriate pacers.

parkrun: much more than just a run in the park

Even at parkruns where there are no official pacers, faster runners will pace a slower friend to a given time target, pressing the other runner to maintain the required pace and encouraging them if they start to flag. And people sometimes run with and encourage another parkrunner they don't even know – just because they've realised they are trying to achieve a special goal such as sub-thirty minutes.

Whether or not there's a nice round time target as a goal, there is always a PB to aim for and there are always cries of, 'I got a PB!' from runners as they half-collapse in the finish chute, or, 'Did I get a PB? I think I did...' followed by a nervous wait for the official results.

I talked my hubby, Mark, into parkrun and before long it became our Saturday morning 'date'. It gives us a chance to catch up and chat as we cycle there and back. And then there's the suspense and wait for the results email... I love getting this to see what we achieved. Eighteen parkruns later and both of us have set numerous PBs. It's simply the best way to end a week and start a weekend.
Susan Cameron-Davies, Darwin parkrun

parkruns are definitely not races, and are not predominantly about fast times. However, there is no doubt that having local, regional, national or even international fast runners coming to run can add a little extra something, with everyone wondering whether a new course record will be set, be it male, female or age-graded.

At Bushy parkrun, which is pretty flat and has the advantage of being close to St Mary's College, where many international runners train, there have been several notable reductions in the course records. For the men, after Chris Owens set a benchmark of 18:47 in the first run, David Symons ran 16:39 two weeks later. Kevin Quinn dropped the record down to 16:10 on the ninth event, and Dermot Cummins reduced it to 15:54 in March 2005. The next step down was 15:04 by Bernard Kiptum in May 2005, then Phil Sly ran 14:54 in September 2005 and Noel Pollock ran 14:39 two weeks later. The Australian 5,000 metres specialist Craig Mottram reduced the record to exactly fourteen minutes in June 2006 and this stood until middle-distance runner Andrew Baddeley ran 13:48 in August 2012.

Andy Baddeley's record breaking win in 2012 was very special for him. In August 2012 the London Olympics were in full swing. Andy's training had been interrupted by injury; he went into the heats for the 1,500 metres feeling that he was about a week behind his peak form and just missed out on a place in the final. Six days later he decided to make use of his top fitness by going for the parkrun record. 'I had it all planned to come in just under the fourteen minutes,' he said. 'My coach had my sports watch and was going to pace me on his bicycle through the gravel path section. So I came off the grass of the avenue, swinging onto the trail, and I was running hard, really hard, wondering whether I'd gone off too fast. He swung onto the path about thirty metres in front of me calling, "this is the pace, this is the pace!" and I was running as hard as I could, managed to catch him up and keep with him while he kept yelling at me, "this is the pace." I continued up the final grass section, crossed the line and somebody told me how fast I'd run and I was thinking, "How did that happen?" I spoke with my coach after and he admitted, "Oh yes, I was just guessing! But I looked at you and you looked all right, so I just kept telling you that you were on the pace." '

For Andy, that day was a lot of fun: it was a lovely sunny day, the Olympics were on and everyone was in a good mood, and many people hung around to talk with him about it afterwards. 'It's funny,' he said, 'because so many people do parkrun, they understand it more than they do elite athletics. I've met a lot of people who are way more excited about my being the parkrun record holder than about anything else I've done in running – because they can see more how the 13:48 for parkrun relates to their time, while they don't really grasp the speed involved in running a sub-four-minute mile.'

Rachel Rowan set the women's benchmark the first week at 21:01, with Kate Symons running 19:57 two weeks later. At the eleventh event, in December 2004, Vivian Cheruiyot ran 17:52, and this record stood until Sonia O'Sullivan ran 16:38 in May 2005 then 16:22 three weeks later (both times being the first finisher overall). This stood until Katerina Wootton ran 16:20 in January 2009. Gladys Chemweno finished in 16:11 in May 2010 and Justina Heslop ran 15:58 on 22 October 2011. That remains the fastest women's time on the Bushy parkrun course, but the female world parkrun record was broken by Hannah Walker, a top GB cross-country and 5,000 and 10,000 metres track runner, who ran 15:55 on 27 July 2013 at St Albans parkrun.

Justina Heslop told me about the day she broke Gladys Chemweno's record: 'It's honestly one of my proudest achievements. It's a long story but that was a really special day for me. I was caring for my ex-boyfriend who had terminal cancer and that was one of his last outings before, sadly, he died shortly afterwards. I have a lovely picture of us taken just after I'd finished. I think I was running fast to get back to him as I was always worried about him. He was a huge supporter of my running so I was so happy to do it for him!'

Even though parkruns are timed runs, not races, it's part of the nature of running that many people will try to catch up with and overtake the runner who is just in front of them. Sometimes the runner being chased doesn't know it, other times they do, and fantastic races for the line can be seen for 126th versus 127th place in a field of 140. These little competitions also bring people together; it's great when someone thanks you for (usually quite unknowingly) pushing or pulling them to a new PB.

I was introduced to parkrunning by a friend. My first run was on Christmas Day. Afterwards a complete stranger came up to me in the car park. 'I just wanted to thank you.' Puzzled, I looked at her quizzically. 'I chased your pink shorts all the way around and managed to run a PB!' Sometimes it's about your goals. And sometimes it's about helping other people reach their goals.

Sarah Aldington, Porirua parkrun

At the same time, the fact that a parkrun is not a race, that there's no cut-off time, and that the last people get cheered into the finish chute just as much as the first, is really important. Suraj Valand, who designed the Greenpoint parkrun course in Cape Town, said, 'I tell people to come along, there's no cut-off, so if on that day you don't feel like running, just don't run. You can jog, run half or just walk through the park and enjoy looking at the sun shining off the water and onto the flowers – it's there to be enjoyed.'

And because your results are stored and remain available online you can easily look back and see how your running has progressed. As Nicola Forwood said, 'Your parkrun stats track your running journey, particularly if your first run was a parkrun. I love that.'

Age grading

Age grading is a calculation which converts your time to a percentage of world record speed for your age and sex for that distance. It lets you see how you are doing in relation to other people of your age and it provides another set of standard targets for runners to aim for, whether you are trying for over 80%, over 65%, over 50% or any other goal.

Age grading takes on a particular significance for veteran runners. Beginners, of whatever age, tend to see improvements in both their time and their age grade during their first weeks and months of running. In contrast, for people who have been running for many years there is, inevitably, a slowing down as you pass through 'senior' to 'veteran' and then up the veteran age groups. Eventually, the day comes when you realise that you are never again going to achieve the speeds you could when you were younger, or that the time goal you were striving towards is always going to be out of reach. Age grading, however, provides a different opportunity: trying to maintain or even improve on your age-grade percentage, rather than your time.

Age grading also makes it much easier to compare performances among people of different ages. On the parkrun event websites, if you click on the Age Grade column of the results you can sometimes see that veterans in their fifties, sixties or seventies may be finishing some distance down the field by time, but be right up at the top when you look at the results by age grade. While the majority of course records by time are held by people in the 20-40 age categories, quite commonly, people holding the highest scoring age-graded run for a particular parkrun are those who are in the veteran age categories – and often in the older categories within the veterans.

The wider picture

If you like not only to analyse your own runs but also to look at the wider picture, there is plenty to keep you occupied on the parkrun websites. You can view and analyse results from your home parkrun, your country, and even global data. parkrun websites are, as Martin Shute said, grinning, 'a great time waster!'

Just considering the results from a single run at a given event, you can order these not only by time or by age grade but also by name, age category, male and female, gender position, total number of runs for each participant and even the notes, which shows you quickly who got a PB and who is a first-time runner at the event. Ordering by club is useful for those interested in following the progress of their clubmates, and when calculating the results of competitions within a club or between clubs.

There are even more data points available for those who want them. On each event page, at the bottom of the page there are the overall statistics for the event, such as male, female and age-grade records, highest and average attendance, the number of PBs which have been run and (I find these really fun) the total hours people have spent participating and the total distance they have all covered.

Additionally, for each event, under the Results tab, you can see not only the complete list of results for each occasion that the event has been held, but also clubs which have been represented, age/sex category records, the male and female points tables and lots more.

On each country's website, at the bottom of the pages you can look at the number of parkruns, number of runners, number of runs (more than five million in the UK to date, for example), female and male record holders and, again, the total distance run and the total run time. Similar information is held on the bottom of the global parkrun web pages.

There's additional information for each country under the Results tab; some for just the most recent week and others cumulative, such as attendance records for each event; the clubs with the largest number of parkrunners, and how many runs those athletes have completed in aggregate. There's also the one the parkrun tourists follow: the Most Events league, listing parkrunners who have attended a large number of events or a lot of inaugural runs.

For some countries there's also a demographic chart showing the age and sex of runners. In Poland so far there have been rather more male than female runners, while in Australia and even more so in South Africa, the reverse is true. Again, similar information is provided on the global parkrun website (www.parkrun.com) including the demographic chart, which overall shows quite a balanced sex ratio and parkrunners from 4 to 99 years of age.

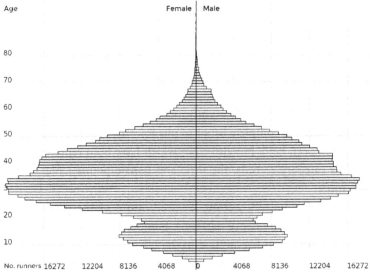

Demographic chart showing age (left axis) and number of runners (bottom axis)

For the Australian parkruns, 'The Prof', Alan Burrell, produces a set of statistics each week, making it available on the Facebook page of *the parkrun show Australia*. For each event the table includes an absolutely amazing range of information including not only the percentage of first timers and of PBs, the number of volunteers, the percentage finishing in under twenty minutes and the highest age-grade percentage but the 'number of AUS laps': the total number of kilometres run at the event divided by the length of a circuit around Australia!

Graphical growth

The best way to see at a glance just how fast parkrun has grown is the amazing global historical chart. This provides a week-by-week display of the number of parkrunners and of events – and growth has been nearly exponential. Country-specific versions are also available. The charts also demonstrate the seasonal changes in parkrunning and even give some indication of what the weather was doing: a sudden large drop in the both the number of events and the number of people parkrunning on a particular Saturday strongly suggests extreme weather conditions.

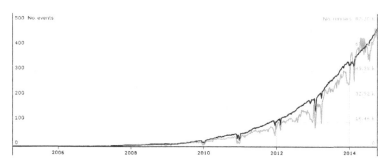

Historical chart showing weekly totals of parkrun events (left axis, black line) and number of runners (right axis, grey line)

The number of people registered to parkrun passed the one million mark worldwide in May 2014. parkrun South Africa grew from 22 to more than 100,000 registered parkrunners in just over two and a half years and a South African, Tracy Unsworth, became global parkrunner number 1,000,000. More than fifty events have in excess of 5,000 registrants each, Bushy parkrun topping the chart with more than 25,000 runners registered. However, it's important to remember that parkrun is not about how big each event can get, but whether the event is serving its community: Kingscliff parkrun, well into its second year, averages about forty runners and has only about 750 people registered – but that's fine!

Anniversary totals
First run, 2 October 2004: 13 runners, 1 event
First anniversary, 1 October 2005: 155 runners, 1 event
Second anniversary, 7 October 2006: 378 runners, 1 event
Third anniversary, 6 October 2007: 681 runners, 4 events
Fourth anniversary, 4 October 2008: 1,315 runners, 10 events
Fifth anniversary, 3 October 2009: 2,913 runners, 20 events
Sixth anniversary, 2 October 2010: 5,718 runners, 46 events
Seventh anniversary, 1 October 2011: 11,428 runners, 95 events
Eighth anniversary, 6 October 2012: 23,676 runners, 176 events
Ninth anniversary, 5 October 2013: 48,254 runners, 311 events
Tenth anniversary, 4 October 2014: 77,694 runners, 477 events

parkrun clubs – rewarding persistence

When Paul Sinton-Hewitt set up Bushy Park Time Trial, he never expected that people would run it every week. 'When I was marathon training,' he said, 'I would have made use of a time trial like BPTT maybe four times in the final six weeks of training, to sharpen me up and judge my progress. I never thought that people would run the course week after week, all year round. I blame it on the T-shirts!'

The T-shirts, and the parkrun clubs which they indicate, were never planned. The first acknowledgement was for Darren Wood when he'd completed one hundred parkruns. Darren hadn't been on the start line on 2 October 2004 because, although he had heard about the first Bushy Park Time Trial in an email from Ranelagh Harriers, he had thought it was just for the fast runners, and he didn't go – for which 'I kick myself every day'. He did decide to give it a try on the second week, and thought it was brilliant: low key, relaxed, and very useful for speed work.

Asked how he'd ended up running so many, he said, 'It was just a habit! I didn't want to miss things. It was a release to do the runs, so I'd organise our holidays to avoid missing a run, just because I loved the runs, loved the community feel, running every Saturday, and the first Christmas Day run.' When he reached one hundred runs, he was surprised at the fuss people made; this included giving him a black fleece jacket with 'BPTT' on the front and his name embroidered across the back.

This was the start of the 100-club, although parkrun didn't believe that very many people would join this club. Chris Wright said, 'One of my tasks at the time was to put in regular orders to an embroidery company to stitch the name of each new club member on the back of the fleeces. It makes me shudder to recall this, when I consider how many members of the 100-club there are now.'

Darren continued parkrunning and in January 2010 became the first person to reach 250 parkruns. He passed 400 during 2013, continuing even when he had to make his way slowly around the course on crutches after a foot operation. He reached 450 at the inaugural Rushmoor event, 3 May 2014, and anticipates running his 500th parkrun in spring 2015.

Originally there was only the 100-club, which evolved from the fleece jackets to black T-shirts and running jackets with '100' on the back rather than the runner's name. In 2009, Nike's Simon Charlesworth decided that 50-club T-shirts, and 10-club shirts for juniors, would be a good idea. Simon had been introduced to parkrun by Hugh Brasher, and for Simon, coming to Bushy Park, 'The main thing was observing how much community spirit had galvanised around the run, and I could see how addictive it was. But the first recognition of consistent attendance came at the 100-runs point, which needed at least two years of parkrunning.'

Simon was really excited about encouraging people to run more. 'So I said to Paul, how about making some of the achievements more achievable, bringing down the barriers to showing your commitment to parkrun? The T-shirts helped identify people who are committed to parkrun, and also helped people to hold a conversation, which assisted in building the idea of community more and more.'

These clubs have given every runner a reachable goal regardless of their speed. 'You can see it in the results,' Paul said. 'People start off and they often dip in and out for the first few months, maybe running ten times or so in that first year. But when they get within tasting distance of that first shirt, their behaviour changes and they start to turn up every week. You see it again as they work towards the hundred – from about ninety, they do every run. Even when they get to fifty, people start planning which date they want to run their hundredth – it's a psychological hook which we had never planned, but is very effective in changing people's behaviour.'

Runners value their parkrun club T-shirts very highly and many wear them proudly practically every time they participate.

Bruce Fordyce loves it when South African events start gaining their own home-grown 50-club members, usually just after their first anniversary. The first home-grown South African 50-club parkrunner was Tracy Rankin, closely followed by Dieter Meyer. In October 2013, Carmen Goncalves became the first South African junior runner to achieve this status. South African parkruns make a big fuss of people reaching the 50- and 100-clubs, ushering them over the finish line with large flags or banners. Willem Loison, who started at Bushy Park and racked up his first 75 runs there before returning to South Africa, became, on 15 June 2013, the first person to celebrate his hundredth parkrun in South Africa, running at Roodepoort. The organisers made a big effort to celebrate this. Ann Boniwell got up at 5 o'clock to bake a chocolate cake with '100' iced on it, and Willem was ushered into the finish by a large black flag proclaiming '100'.

The first member of the 50-parkruns club in the USA was Jennifer Greve, who reached this milestone towards the end of 2013.

The numbers game

Jennifer had been a total non-runner before she started at parkrun. At first she walked the course and then began jogging it. She reduced her time to about 33 minutes and ran her first road races. Running through snow and on ice in the winter was something she had never thought she would do before parkrun.

By the tenth anniversary of parkrun, there were:
- *20,220 members of the 10-club*
- *21,279 members of the 50-club*
- *5,272 members of the 100-club*
- *147 members of the 250-club*

7

Café and
community

Just running isn't reason to join to this idea. The most
important is running with people and meeting them
before and after the run. Great vibrations, smiles and...
endorphins!

Tomek Bagrowski, Gdańsk parkrun

Once the last runner has crossed the finish line, the event isn't
over. Obviously there's packing away the equipment and sorting
out the results. But much more important is the local café.

When Paul Sinton-Hewitt started expanding parkrun he knew
he wanted every parkrun to have a social focus, which is why each
event is encouraged to nominate a café, coffee shop or local pub
where parkrunners can congregate after the run. Here, people talk

about the run, sort the finish tokens, manage the results, drink tea, coffee or hot chocolate, perhaps eat an iced bun, a bowl of chips or even a cooked breakfast.

Every Event Director I've spoken with agrees that parkrun is more than just a running event; it's a community, a place where people can socialise, catch up with old friends and make new ones, congratulate each other, encourage each other, commiserate with each other when a run has not gone as well as expected.

Nat Glenn, the Event Director of Larne parkrun, said that the best aspect of his event is 'the community; it brings the community together.' He added, 'It's seeing the faces of people as they cross the line, people who could only run five or ten minutes when they came for the first time, now running the whole way, getting faster, growing in stature, more confident in themselves, volunteering.' Additionally, 'It's the way people come to parkrun on their own, not knowing anyone, and they make friends, and it doesn't stop at parkrun, it continues on into their private life – that's what parkrun is about.'

Sandhya Drew, a regular Banstead Woods parkrunner, is adamant that the social side and the inclusivity is extremely important: 'At 9 o'clock on Saturday you either give your time and volunteer, or run, and it doesn't involve money and you're doing something social.' She noted that as a bonus, it takes you to some beautiful places.

> *parkrun has been a huge source of joy for me over this year; it has given me one of my best friends.*
> *Sarah, Dulwich parkrun*

A repeating theme in emails to parkrun, some of which are published in the newsletters, is how well supported runners – particularly slower runners – feel. Similarly, practically every parkrunner I've talked to has mentioned the feeling of community, how even as a first-timer you feel welcomed, and that as a regular you get fantastic support from the other parkrunners, including around the course from the marshals, who are usually parkrunners themselves, and in other weeks have run alongside you.

> *parkrun epitomises everything that is good about running. It's all-inclusive – elite runners, runners with dogs, walkers with buggies, kids and pensioners share the trail every Saturday morning. Runners on their way out shout congratulations to runners already on their way back and the runners on their way back encourage those still on the outbound leg. Friends high-five each other as their paths cross. And all around the world runners are doing the same thing every Saturday morning.*
>
> *Sarah Aldington, Porirua parkrun*

The social aspect means that while their actual run may take less than twenty minutes (or as long as an hour), many people find they spend most of Saturday morning at their parkrun – and they wouldn't have it any other way.

For many, that feeling of community, of being part of 'their' parkrun is very strong. It keeps them coming back to the same parkrun week after week, running into the 50-club, 100-club and even 250-club all, or almost all, at one location – even if there are other parkruns within just a few miles. The familiarity, the routine, the fact that you just have to turn up on a Saturday morning and you know what will be there – means, as Andrew Lane, one of the 'original thirteen' said, 'it couldn't be easier' to just turn up, rather than not.

This community spirit crosses boundaries. For the most part I have no idea what my fellow parkrunners do for a living, and they don't know what I do – we're all parkrunners, and that's what's important. Franz Werndle, who was involved with Richmond parkrun very early, agrees: 'It doesn't matter whether you're a mechanic or a lecturer or a town councillor.'

I had turned forty, happy but wanting to get fit, and a friend told me about parkrun. I decided to give it a go and I was hooked immediately! Every Saturday rain or shine, I and my friends would be there wanting to run. I started telling more people about this fantastic event, and met some fascinating and amazing people there. I love volunteering as much as I do running (well nearly) and am totally addicted to running now. I have signed up for my first half marathon having completed a 10-mile a few months ago. I am also very proud to be involved in Southampton junior parkrun. Thank you parkrun, you have changed my life! My husband now runs regularly at Southampton with me and helps out every Sunday at junior parkrun. We are a healthier, fitter, happier family.

Sarah Shave, Southampton parkrun

Jennifer Greve, at Livonia parkrun, Michigan, said, 'The social aspect is so important for helping you stick with something new like running, especially something that you don't necessarily *want* to do but know is good for you.' It was the development of the core group, going out for coffee after the run, and finding that she and her family were making a whole lot of new friends that made the difference. She found herself running through the winter, which she had never thought she would do, and went on to complete her first road race, a 5K, raising money for cystic fibrosis – which Jennifer's daughter has. 'There were seven of us parkrunners there, and it was a great way to do my first race. Since then I've gone on to do four or five races and I'm just looking forward to getting through my present injury problems and going on to do the races I've signed up for during next year.'

After running for years in Cape Town, I moved to Gauteng for work and could not find a nice place to run besides the gym until I found out about parkrun. Going there for my first run after not running for about three years, I realised why I love it so much and I can't actually do without a run in the open for more than a week. It's the perfect way to keep fit and healthy and a great way to meet other runners. Thanks parkrun, you guys are doing great things for the communities.

Robin Philander, Roodepoort parkrun

A Leeds parkrunner told Tom Williams that before she started parkrunning, she was sure that if she died, nobody would go to her funeral. Now, she knows that there would be lots of people there. By that time they knew each other well enough that Tom quipped, 'at least unless it was held on a Saturday morning!'

In Russia, Maxim Egorov said, even in their first winter, before officially becoming part of the parkrun family, 'what delighted us most, after the running all our participants stayed at the finish line to express their feelings and thoughts with each other, even when it was below minus 20 degrees in Celsius! It became a tradition in Russian parkrun community, to bring food and hot tea from home and share them with fellow runners after the event. And that friendly atmosphere kept us warm even in the severe frost.'

I discovered parkrun in October 2011. What initially struck me was the fantastic organisation, the camaraderie between the runners and the community spirit. I've enjoyed all of my ninety runs so far and the encouragement and advice of my fellow parkrunners helped in my quest to train for and run the London Marathon in 2013. parkrun has changed my running so much. Saturday mornings will never be the same again and we now look to see if there is a parkrun when we plan holidays, so we can be parkrun tourists! Thank you parkrun.

Kevin Tomkinson, Brueton parkrun

The community feeling is also expressed at more sombre events.

In summer 2009, a sudden death shocked Richmond parkrun. Dr Stephen Instone, a lifelong runner, had been a member of Ranelagh Harriers since his teens. Through hard training he had brought his 10 mile time down to 54 minutes, and his dedication to running was such that when he fell off a ladder and broke his ankle he was soon out doing laps of Richmond Park on his crutches. Stephen ran the first ever Richmond Park Time Trial, finishing in 19:54 and tenth overall, with the highest age grading, 75.29%. He ran there nearly every week thereafter, winning the first points prize and being presented with a trophy at the first anniversary. During the second year, he built a commanding lead in the points, but in July 2009 he tragically drowned while on holiday in Switzerland.

Clubmate Steve Rowland wrote of him, 'Rarely can the loss of a member have been so keenly felt not only throughout the club but also in the running community in general.' Runner and author John Bryant, who often met him while training in Richmond Park, wrote: 'It seems trite to say that I shall miss him in the park. But Stephen was a fixture there. We shared a mutual respect that only hard-core runners understand – it needed no explanation, no justification.'

In Stephen's memory, Ranelagh members bought a new trophy and at that second anniversary Stephen's widow Shelley Instone was given the original trophy while she presented the new Stephen Instone Cup to that year's winner, Duncan Brown. It is a tribute to Stephen's combined running talent and dedication to Richmond parkrun that his points total for that second year was only overtaken by Duncan in September, a few weeks before the anniversary.

Since then, many other parkrun communities have expressed their appreciation for runners after their deaths. One in particular stood out for UK Country Manager Tom Williams: Arthur James at Bradford parkrun.

Arthur started at Leeds parkrun then became a regular runner at Bradford parkrun, also introducing his daughter-in-law and grandson to parkrun. His motto was 'run because you can!' Not only was he well known locally for his sprint finish, but, Event Director Linda Bussey said, 'He would encourage anyone and everyone to come to parkrun, making an effort to chat to everyone and really welcome anyone new, often running or walking with them to make sure they finished the run and got great support.'

In May 2011 Linda was proud to present Arthur, then aged 79, with his 100-club T-shirt and jacket: 'It was the first 100 that I ever got to present at Bradford and the cheers from the other parkrunners and Arthur's family who attended especially for the occasion were just fantastic.' That night, Arthur unexpectedly died in his sleep. On the Saturday following Arthur's funeral, Bradford parkrun celebrated Arthur's life. 'We invited everyone who knew Arthur to come along to that Saturday's parkrun and run, walk or support to celebrate everything about Arthur. His daughter-in-law ran wearing his 50-club shirt and his grandson ran wearing his 100-club shirt. Lots of money was raised for Marie Curie, the charity that Arthur both volunteered at every week and raised money for every race he completed (and he did hundreds).'

This celebration has since become an annual event at Bradford, and every year his family choose one parkrunner to receive a trophy, 'The Arthur'. Tom Williams, attending this celebratory event in 2014, wrote in the parkrun newsletter afterwards that Arthur was: 'A shining example to all of us that if you're going to do something you might as well have a jolly good time while you're there.'

When I started parkrunning a few months ago, I had no idea what a wonderful, awe-inspiring, emotional experience it would be. I will

always remember 2013 for some of the best and worst times of my life – the best for discovering parkrun and my life finally beginning; the worst for my dad's life ending suddenly a few days before Christmas. parkrun gave me amazing support and focus through this time. The sense of community is astounding – I love the buzz, the colour, the positive feeling in Shrewsbury Quarry Park on Saturday mornings. Without parkrun, I think I would have given up – not just on running; I would have given up on life; but parkrun has restored my faith in humanity. All this from a free, weekly run in the park.
Margaret Connarty, Shrewsbury parkrun

While parkrun has helped to create communities, it's also very true to say that it has grown so far, so fast and with such robust strength *because* it's such a community. If people didn't feel this community spirit, that they were a part of something, not just participants in a timed run, they wouldn't be so enthusiastic about it. They wouldn't turn up in sun, rain, or snow; wouldn't blog about it so passionately; wouldn't encourage and cajole their friends, relatives and work colleagues to parkrun; and wouldn't give so many hours to volunteering at parkrun – from the Event Directors and core volunteer teams to the regular runner who volunteers on a few Saturdays through the year. I don't know any Event Director, nor any member of the parkrun HQ team, who doesn't consider the community aspect of parkrun to be extremely important.

Online, also, the parkrun community is visible. In 2009, Paul set up a parkrun group on Facebook. Called very simply 'parkrun', it covers all events. Additionally, Facebook pages have been set up for each individual parkrun event. More recently, people started tweeting about parkrun.

Facebook groups are gradually becoming used more in the UK; they are already an extremely important part of parkrun's social fabric in most other parkrunning countries. Facebook is being used widely by parkrunners for sharing anecdotes and pictures, congratulating people on reaching milestones, and letting them know about other local running events. Both Facebook and Twitter supplement use of the event website pages and optional volunteering emails to call for volunteers, explain delays in results and give notice of special events or event cancellations at short notice. They are becoming extensions of their parkrun communities.

The relationship with a local café can develop into something special. There are a couple of cafés which have given repeated donations to their parkruns. At Barrow parkrun, the café enjoys being involved with the parkrun so much that they offered to open up for the Christmas Day run, although the offer, while greatly appreciated, was firmly refused.

Amanda Woodham said that the café used by Brighton & Hove parkrun 'has been voted the best parkrun café in the UK'. She added, 'It's really fantastic – and they do very well out of parkrun!'

There was no café nearby when Larne parkrun was starting up, but Dixon Hall, home of the Sea Cadets, was close, and the council approached Robin Alexander of the Sea Cadets, who turned out to be a big supporter of parkrun. Post-parkrun coffee and socialising now take place in the Sea Cadets' large hall. As a bonus for the Sea Cadets, this has led the wider local community to realise that the hall is available for use by the local running club, dog shows, fitness classes and the like, which brings in a bit of income for the Sea Cadets.

Eastleigh parkrun is well known for providing cakes every week – such that two of the runners suggested that at best if you ran the event you would be 'calorie neutral' at the end of it. They also go to the sports centre, just a couple of hundred yards away, after the run, for results processing and further socialisation.

Jane Luxton and Warwick Bilham told me about a nice tradition amongst runners in the company Legal & General in southeast England. They run at a variety of parkruns, depending on where they live; when one of them reaches a milestone – fiftieth or hundredth run – they invite colleagues to their parkrun and then to their house for breakfast afterwards.

> *What I like most about parkrun is its enormous success as one of the best community sport ventures in the UK. I've made many friends through parkrun and love to encourage others in their running. We have so many success stories to tell. Social media – Facebook and Twitter in particular – help us connect as one large happy parkrun family.*
>
> *Amanda Thompson, Cardiff parkrun*

Community in the parks

parkrunners come into contact with many other users of the parks, cycle tracks or trails where the events are held. These range from dog walkers to Nordic walkers, golfers to disc golf players, personal trainers and their clients to British Military Fitness groups, horse riders to bike riders and many others. There is, inevitably, the potential for disagreement when disparate groups are using the same park at the same time, but there are also fantastic opportunities for building links with other communities.

Other events close to the parkrun course can sometimes provide extra entertainment; Craig Boon said that at Launceston parkrun in Tasmania they have been treated to views of equine events and a national competition among firemen.

Tilgate parkrun has formed a good relationship with the golf club in the same park. The golf club reserves tables especially for parkrunners on a Saturday morning and provides a pleasant venue where runners and volunteers can enjoy a post-run coffee, and the results can be processed.

Sometimes negotiations are necessary to minimise conflict with cyclists, horse riders or other groups. Usually, if approached in a positive spirit, something can be worked out. Always, in the pre-run briefing, Run Directors remind parkrunners that they share the parks and must be courteous to other people. A smile, nod or gasped 'good morning' is generally reciprocated!

In Australia, where many parkruns are held on cycling paths, it is important that parkrunners remember to keep left. Claire Anderson from Bunyaville parkrun in Queensland said that they have a great relationship with the local cyclists, who often stop and cheer on the runners.

A perennial area of potential conflict is car parking. As numbers of parkrunners grow, car parks can get quite congested early on a Saturday morning. This is an aspect where every individual parkrunner can help by considering whether they could run, walk, or cycle to the park, or take public transport or carpool. Public transport options do vary hugely depending on the parkrun location – Lloyd parkrun is blessed with a tram stop just yards away from the start line.

High-fives

In the UK, many courses are two or more laps and it is traditional for faster runners and slower runners each to encourage the other with quick phrases such as 'well done!' and 'keep going!' while overtaking or being overtaken. In Australia and New Zealand, where many of the courses are out-and-back, so that runners spend much of the middle section of the run passing each other in opposite directions, this has translated into a huge amount of mutual encouragement and high-fives between runners. This aspect has become so important that when the trial route for Blackbutt parkrun did not include any sections allowing this ritual, Scott Northey cunningly suggested a route change which not only avoided a downhill section with a bollard at the bottom but also incorporated a 700 metre stretch where runners passed each other, allowing the high-fives to take place.

parkruns and charities

Because parkruns are readily available (and free!), some groups use a local parkrun as their challenge fundraising event, with people turning up, usually with newly printed barcodes in their hands, to run or walk the course for their particular charity. Sometimes this is as part of a series of challenges, other times just the one event.

Some parkruns nominate a charity, usually one local to the area, and raise funds for it. At Barrow parkrun, after local girl Alice Pine died from non-Hodgkin's lymphoma, they held a 'purple parkrun' to commemorate her. The opportunity for participants to give donations was there, but discreetly, with no pressure on anyone to do so. The money they raise goes to support families with terminally ill children to go on holiday, by providing a luxury mobile home for them to stay in.

The wider parkrun community

Everywhere, parkrun provides an instant community and a ready-made topic of conversation.

When Willem Loison moved back home to South Africa after several years in the UK, he didn't know many people outside his family, but parkrun soon provided the opportunity for him to get to know people. Most-prolific parkrunner Darren Wood attended a friend's birthday party in Plymouth, was sitting by someone he didn't know at all, and wondered what they would find to talk about. They started by exchanging names and the other person asked, 'Are you *the* Darren Wood?' Darren admitting that he was, the other person replied, 'I run Cardiff,' – so they talked parkrun throughout the meal and had a great time. Darren has also found parkrun to be a talking point with work colleagues and even with the estate agent when he was selling his house.

An interesting parkrun community link has been formed between Bradford parkrun in the UK and Launceston parkrun in Tasmania which are 'twinned' and keep in touch with what each other is doing. They even have one parkrunner, Chris Reynier, who lives part of the year in each location, which obviously assists with this.

As parkruns have expanded across the UK and globally, parkrunners have discovered that wherever they go to parkrun, they will be welcomed and surrounded by people who – although they've never met before – are nevertheless members of their community. parkruns have also become a deliberate place for runners to meet up.

In 2013, Richard Evans, who runs at Wimbledon Common parkrun, decided to ride a recumbent bicycle around the world during 2014. I asked him if he would be doing any parkruns along the way. His route went close to quite a few parkruns and he thought that was a great idea, but he didn't think it would be possible: he was travelling very light and wouldn't be taking any running shoes. I asked him what his shoe size was, and after a few emails to the relevant parkrun organisers giving approximate dates he would be visiting, I was able to confirm that everyone had enthusiastically agreed to make sure that when he turned up, a pair of running shoes would be available. The first parkrun he reached was Warszawa-Praga in Poland, who were very pleased to host him for a run on 12 April 2014.

While Richard's cycling tour is unusual, parkrun tourism has taken on a life of its own. A parkrun barcode has become is a passport to friendly communities in a growing number of countries and event locations worldwide: parkrun tourism is BOOMING.

8

parkrun
tourism

Whether you are running around the village common at Mulbarton in a field of sixty odd runners or around Bushy Park with a thousand plus runners, you will always experience the same warm atmosphere.

John Robert Richardson, Norwich parkrun

For many parkrunners, one of the pleasures of parkrunning is turning up at their local parkrun every week and meeting up with friends for a chat before, after or during the run. Some 'parkrun passionistas' never run at a parkrun event other than their home parkrun. However, some runners make a circuit of several local parkruns, many parkrunners visit other parkruns as an important part of their vacations, and some runners are dedicated 'parkrun tourists' seeing how many different parkruns they can run. Running inaugural parkruns is a special goal of many of the dedicated tourists, with the result that, despite the group having no single home base, nevertheless they tend to bump into familiar faces again and again.

While dedicated parkrun tourists may not be a large part of any single parkrun event, and may not even consider themselves to really have a home parkrun, they are very far from being outside the parkrun community. They also form their own community, making good use of social media to keep informed about each other's parkrunning activities, to swap information about inaugural parkruns, how to get to them and where best to stay if an overnight trip is required. The level of dedication shown by some parkrun tourists is amazing: Gill Fordyce remembers one runner who arrived at the inaugural Upington parkrun in South Africa having driven for nine hours to get there after missing his booked flight.

Additionally, tourists act as cross-links between different parkrun events, helping to build up connections between the different communities and assisting in the development of the worldwide parkrun community. Bruce Fordyce noticed in the early days of parkrun South Africa how much parkrunners visiting from overseas were appreciated, and particularly the motivation provided by occasional visitors wearing red 50-club T-shirts before there were any home-grown parkrunners in that club.

By June 2014, in the UK, more than 600 people had run at least twenty different parkruns or five inaugural runs. In Australia there were already seventy people who had run at least twenty events or attended at least five inaugural runs. In South Africa, nineteen people had run at fifteen or more events or at least five inaugurals; in Denmark, 25 people had run a minimum of four events or three inaugurals; in New Zealand, 61 had run at least three events and in Poland, eight people had run at least five events. The rate of expansion of parkrun has for some time made it impossible for anyone to run all the events.

UK parkrunners sometimes set their sights on becoming 'regionnaires': running all the parkruns within a given region – Wales, Scotland, West Midlands, Northern Ireland or wherever. Those who manage all the events in Greater London describe themselves as 'Lon-Done'.

Roy Reeder was possibly the earliest parkrun tourist; he has run more than 260 parkruns at more than 90 different events. Roy started parkrunning on Christmas Day 2004, when he was first to finish and Paul Sinton-Hewitt provided champagne and mince pies – Roy considered this an auspicious start! He ran a few times in 2005 and 2006, getting his time down to 16:22. He volunteered in the early days at Wimbledon Common parkrun, eventually ran there a few times, and also helped when Banstead Woods started up, running there on a number of Saturdays in 2008.

Roy was present on the start line of the inaugural Leeds parkrun because he happened to be in Barnsley that weekend, so he hopped over to run it. When Cardiff started, he got a lift with Paul so went to that inaugural event, and he made it to the first Brighton & Hove, although he never set inaugurals as a personal goal; he attended the sixth running of Bramhall, while Albert parkrun, Middlesbrough, he reached only for event 46 in 2009. This made him the first person to have run all of the available parkrun locations (eleven at that time). Toward the end of 2009, when there were 26 events, he had run at 21 of them and was top of the leaderboard for the most different parkruns. Then his enthusiasm for constantly going to new events waned and he was overtaken by Chris Cowell. Roy still enjoys running at different courses, as seen by the ten different events he attended during the first three months of 2014.

Chris Cowell admits that it was actually his wife Linda who first got him started running. Originally Chris, then clinically obese, accompanied her on a bicycle, but soon he started running and 'I never looked back.' He heard about Bushy Park Time Trial in February 2008, tried it and loved it – but it was 25 miles away, so when Basingstoke started (a mere seventeen miles away) he began running there and persuaded Linda to join him. They have maintained that as their home run even though several other parkruns are now closer. Chris's real tourism started due to the coincidences of getting injured (so being unable to chase PBs) and noticing the Most Events table on the parkrun website. First he tried the closest ones – Richmond and Wimbledon – then travelled further, to Brighton and Cardiff. 'Then it got somewhat manic,' he said, as he flew into Glasgow, and got up at 'stupid o'clock' on Saturday morning to drive to Bramhall one week and Leeds another week – struggling to find the venue while navigating with an out-of-date map. However, 'I absolutely loved the adventure of it and Saturdays became the highlight of the week. Still are.'

He and Linda also enjoy parkrun tourism as something they can do together. They soon started to book ahead for inaugural runs and plan holidays around them, including a cycle ride on the Lands End to John O'Groats route incorporating Forest of Dean and Strathclyde parkruns on the way. They use travelling to parkruns as excuses to visit family and friends and to see sights such as Ely Cathedral (Norwich parkrun), the Scottish Assembly (Edinburgh parkrun), and the National Memorial Arboretum (Conkers parkrun). Chris's main regrets are missing the only running of Morden Hall parkrun, and not getting to the Iceland event – often passing through Reykjavik while delivering aircraft, but never managing a Saturday layover. However, one week he did get stuck overnight in Copenhagen due to heavy snow. Having packed his running shoes 'just in case,' he made his way to Amager Fælled parkrun on the Saturday morning and ran it – very carefully.

Chris was the first parkrunner to run at one hundred different parkruns, leading to the naming of the 'Cowell Club' – membership being gained by parkrunners reaching that goal (and 'a half-Cowell' for those managing fifty events). Linda, despite delays due to injury, was the first woman to one hundred events. For Chris, one of the most important things is that: 'They are all different and yet at the same time all the same... you know what you are getting... it is addictive and non-judgemental.'

Paul Fielding started parkrunning to get fit to return to orienteering; he was looking for a local race to enter when he discovered the Basingstoke Time Trial. Having watched one and discovered that there were plenty of slower runners in the field, the next week he and his wife ran it. Paul finished in 31:21 and decided to run it once a month, to check how his running was progressing. When Reading parkrun started he went to see what that one was like, after which he realised that if he ran five more different courses, he'd be listed on the parkrun Most Events page (the qualifying number of events was only seven at that time) – and it all went on from there.

Paul reaches nearly all the parkruns by public transport, often running from the railway station or bus stop to the parkrun and back again, so he needs to keep his gear down to fit into a small rucksack, but he makes a point of carrying spare footwear if it's forecast to be wet and muddy. For Paul, planning the journey is part of the fun; he researches the best way to get to each event, often starting very early in the morning to make the parkrun into a day trip. 'I get some odd looks when I'm the only one getting off the coach or train at a remote station in the middle of nowhere,' he said, 'and some more odd looks later from the same driver when I'm getting back on again at the same station, but I love seeing bits of the countryside which otherwise I would never see.' Running between the station and the event can extend the parkrun into a longer training run, which helps with his marathon training. Asked how parkrun has changed his life, Paul notes that he now runs a lot more and weighs a lot less. Also, 'as a result of parkrun I now run marathons, which I would once have thought impossible or at least highly improbable.'

Nneka Okonta's journey into parkrun was rather gradual. A member of the Datchet Dashers, Nneka first heard about Bushy Park Time Trial in 2008. She ran it a couple of times that year, once in 2009, and then, starting running again after an Achilles tendon injury, gradually became more and more obsessed. 'I guess I was a slow burner,' she said.

Nneka's first parkrun tourism experience came when she was sent to South Africa for work and arranged to fly in on the Friday and run Long Beach parkrun on the Saturday. Just before the Olympics she was in Australia for three weeks, so she made her way to parkruns in Brisbane and Sydney. Next, work transferred her to New Zealand for nine months; the nearest parkrun was four hours' drive away but soon she was taking every opportunity to drive over for the weekend to a race in the area and to do the parkrun as well. She became the first person to run in all three Southern Hemisphere parkrunning countries. Back in the UK for a while, she flew to Poland to parkrun in Warszawa: 'the park is really beautiful and the people really friendly. Somehow I managed to drive the hire car into the pedestrian area of the park, and had to get out again over the pavement and start late, but I still did the parkrun, of course.' She visited Livonia in Michigan on Labor Day weekend 2013, when most of the regular runners were away and there were only ten runners – giving Nneka her highest finish position (first woman and second overall), which she enjoyed, 'although it was a bit quiet.'

Nneka readily acknowledges that parkrun has changed her life. She now always has something to do on a Saturday morning, and it has opened her up to new experiences: 'If I'm going somewhere new to parkrun, I think, "what else can I do while I'm there?" I've been to places that I wouldn't have thought of going otherwise. And I've met so many fantastic people, and we can have a chat while we're pootling round the parkrun, and then I get to meet so many wonderful volunteers!' Nneka's impact on her parkrunning friends in New Zealand is evidenced by the fact that, two months after her return to the UK, the Lower Hutt run report congratulated 'our favourite parkrun tourist' on reaching the 50-club. In April 2014, Nneka added Kolomenskoe parkrun in Russia to her tally, then, having returned to New Zealand, flew to the inaugural East Coast Park parkrun in Singapore in June.

Louise Ayling started parkrunning in January 2011 when she'd just about reached being able to run thirty minutes without a walking break, and had signed up for 'Janathon': running every day during January and blogging about it. She turned up somewhat early and rather nervous at Wimbledon Common parkrun, sure she would be the last to finish, ran the whole course and thought she was going to die! Just at the end, a woman overtook her, she tried to out-sprint her and lost the fight for 198th place. 'That's how I learned the first rule of parkrun: that you will be beaten to the finish by someone in their eighties, an eight year old and someone pushing a buggy – get over it.' Finding out about the 50-club, and reading in the parkrun newsletter how few people had run more than fifty events, she wondered whether she could reach both of those goals before the following Janathon. Louise managed to run her first fifty parkruns at fifty venues, her fiftieth being at Bedfont Lakes on New Year's Eve 2012, although she has repeated venues occasionally since then.

parkrun: much more than just a run in the park

Louise can't remember the last time she turned up at a parkrun venue and didn't know anyone: 'There's always someone I've met before at another parkrun, or who I've chatted to online, and who will look out for me. That's one of the great things about parkrun, that despite rarely running in the same location twice, I'm still part of a community.' She's even volunteered at inaugural parkruns when injury or illness has meant she wouldn't be able to run but she didn't want to miss the fun. She joined the Cowell Club at Tonbridge parkrun.

Since she started working her way up to ultramarathons (races longer than marathon distance), Louise looks for parkruns which she can turn into a longer trail run. 'It was parkrunning, and particularly parkrun tourism, that led me to ultrarunning.' Louise said. 'It might sound a bit silly to say I'd travelled hundreds of miles for a 5K parkrun, but it was much easier to justify driving that far for a marathon or ultra – and I could just run a new parkrun on the day before whatever long race I was entered for.' She's worked out that the next time she goes to see her sister in Canada, if she changes planes in Toronto it wouldn't be *that* difficult to drive from there down to Livonia parkrun in Michigan. She took her husband to Iceland for his fiftieth birthday (naturally managing to run the parkrun there). 'So when I casually asked him, "have you been to Singapore?" he replied, "There's a parkrun starting there, isn't there?" He knows me too well!'

My running club paid a club visit to a local parkrun, Bedfont Lakes on 25 June 2011. Because I enjoy variety I suggested that the club should visit a different parkrun every other month – so Bushy in August, Black Park in October and Gunnersbury in December. Christmas 2011, visiting relatives in Melbourne, I ran Albert Park parkrun whilst on my way back to the airport – so I'd done five different parkruns for my first five parkruns and I had become a committed parkrun tourist. My New Year's resolution was twenty in twenty; I achieved that with Eastleigh on 4 June 2012. Checking the map I decided that fifty in fifty was achievable. 2 March 2013 found me running my fiftieth at Concord in Sheffield. I did two more to make my total 52 including fifty UK parkruns, then returned to Bedfont Lakes to collect my '50' shirt. I'm still a parkrun tourist but I do enjoy running additional times at my favourite parkruns.

Roderick Hoffman, Bedfont Lakes parkrun (3 runs out of 92!)

John and Joanna Cassells, both in their mid-seventies, first read about parkrun in the *Scottish Running Guide* when looking for things to do while on holiday in Scotland in January 2012. Since they had booked to stay in Edinburgh starting on the Saturday, they decided to drive up to Strathclyde on the Friday and run that parkrun before continuing to Edinburgh. Back home, they found that their nearest events were 38 miles in one direction (Braunstone) or 39 in another (Sheffield Hallam). Undaunted, they registered with Sheffield as their home event and on 22 January were going to run there – but discovered that Barnsley was starting up, so went and ran that inaugural event instead. Then they got to Sheffield Hallam, after which they did another event – so four locations in their first four parkruns.

John and Joanna are well known in parkrun circles, particularly among tourists, because of their T-shirts: homemade matching shirts which, when put together, say 'I love parkrun'. Originally they were only going to wear them once, for a Valentine's Day run at Valentines parkrun. However, they wore them for Worsley Woods inaugural run a couple of weeks later and the T-shirts soon became famous in their own right, with people wanting to have their photo taken standing between the two halves. They were all set to retire them once they had earned their 50-club shirts, but there was such a fuss about it that in the end they had another set made. This time they wore the opposite sides, so it was fun seeing whether people noticed the change. The shirts also have a message spelled out across the back: 'Oh yes we do!' Now they wear their 100-club shirts when running a course they've visited before, and the message shirts for new parkruns.

Paul Freyne originally used Bushy parkrun as an additional incentive to get himself up and running on a Saturday morning during his marathon training in 2007. He first set out to get on the Most Events leaderboard in 2010, when that only required seven venues: 'I'd never been on a leaderboard for running, so I set out to manage this. I ran my seventh event, Roundshaw Downs, on Christmas Day, went back onto the website expecting to see my name there on the leaderboard – and they'd changed it to ten events minimum!' Naturally he went out and ran a few more, with Richmond being his tenth on 8 January 2011. That goal reached, he set himself another challenge: the 38 parkruns south of London. Paul spent the next three months travelling to different parkruns. 'Before I knew it I was doing one every week, going all over the place and having a great time.' Paul's wife, Susan, works in central London, so Friday afternoon she hops on a train and Paul picks her up at an appropriate railway station for whichever direction they're headed. They also try to do something extra at each location, whether that's watching an ice hockey match, visiting the pandas at Edinburgh Zoo, or seeing a show at a theatre.

Paul regrets that he missed out on the first Bushy parkrun. 'I ran my first Berlin marathon in September 2004, then went to the Stragglers' end of month handicap race and ran my fastest ever 5K. Three days later there was the first ever parkrun – and I didn't know about it.' Despite heading the UK and global Most Events leaderboards, keeping a reserve list of parkruns most likely to be reachable in bad weather conditions, booking accommodation well in advance and heading for lots of inaugurals, Paul insists that he's not obsessive at all, 'it's just what I do on a Saturday morning.'

parkrun tourism

Charles 'Cass' Castleton started running to lose weight and improve his fitness after a check-up showed that not only was he overweight (20 stone or 127 kilograms) but he had developed diabetes. He was looking for goals to keep him running and one of his friends said, 'Why don't you parkrun?' To which he replied, 'What's parkrun?' Living in Tonbridge Wells, he drove to Brighton & Hove parkrun one Saturday morning, arriving at 8 o'clock to find nobody there. By 8.40 the first dozen or two fast-looking runners had turned up and he said to his wife, 'I'm going home; no way am I running with these!' By 8.50 suddenly there were more like 400 people there, of all ages and sizes, so he joined them for his first parkrun – and he didn't even come last! He went back the next week, got a PB and 'this world opened up in front of me.'

Meanwhile he started to develop more goals: 10K, half marathons, even running the Two Oceans Half Marathon in South Africa, where he learned that he was two weeks too early to run the Cape Town parkrun. Well, that was it! He decided not only that he needed to come back and run a parkrun in South Africa, but that he would challenge himself to run a parkrun in every country where there was one to run: England (Brighton & Hove and several more), Wales (Newport), Scotland (Glasgow), Northern Ireland (getting up at 4 am to fly over and run the inaugural Antrim event), Ireland (Malahide), Denmark (Fælledparken), USA (Clermont Waterfront), Poland (Łódź), back to South Africa (Big Bay), then to Russia for Severnoe Tushino, Moscow. He's planning a big trip to Australia and New Zealand.

Cass alternates running at Brighton & Hove with running at other venues. He notes that one of the great things about parkrun is how friendly everyone is. He's particularly grateful to the management teams and parkrunners of Łódź parkrun in Poland and Severnoe Tushino in Russia who made sure he got to and from their parkruns safely.

parkrun: much more than just a run in the park

Becky Thurtell initially used Bushy parkrun as a monthly benchmark of her running progress, then started going twice a month and then weekly. She began visiting other nearby parkruns such as Richmond, Wimbledon, Kingston, Bedfont Lakes and Crane Park, and found that she enjoyed going to new places: 'It's like a little mini adventure, as you are not quite sure what you'll find when you get there'. Presently heading for the Cowell Club, she now shares the driving with two other parkrunners, and she enjoys repeatedly bumping into other tourists. She also likes going back to Bushy: 'it's like "home from home" as I see all the regular runners from the early days.'

In Australia, with the long distances between parkruns, most tourists set themselves the goal of becoming a statesman or stateswoman (completing all the parkruns in their state) rather than covering the whole country; Kathy Rae was the first to reach this goal for New South Wales. Some do manage to travel to neighbouring states or even go further afield occasionally. The first person to parkrun in all states and territories was Brendan Peel; other people reaching this goal therefore join the 'Peel Club'. As of the end of June 2014, Alan 'The Prof' Burrell and his wife Roisin topped the Most Events leaderboard in Australia, both on 41 events, with Roisin one inaugural run ahead of Alan (fifteen versus fourteen); Neil Barnett (Sandgate parkrun) has also managed 41 events. There's something of a battle between the next on the list, Michael Schultz and Brent Stowers (both of New Farm parkrun), while Australia's Country Manager, Tim Oberg had attended 32 Australasian events (including East Coast Park, Singapore) plus parkruns in the UK and South Africa.

Being in the privileged position of travelling our country for twelve months, I have begun 'parkrunning Australia'. Engagement in the parkrun movement whilst travelling has enabled me to meet local people with a common interest and to gain valuable tips about how

best to explore local areas. Our country is one of diversity and con-
trast, but one thing that is constant is the spirit of parkrunners. At
each event I have felt welcomed and the spirit of courage and deter-
mination is so very evident no matter where the event is being con-
ducted. Words and gestures of encouragement help to bring out the
very best in each participant. Also indicative of the positive spirit is
the willingness of the volunteers who give up their time so that others
can enjoy the event. I am so very grateful to have been introduced
to the movement and thank those responsible for the initiative and
ongoing practice.

Annette O'Shea, Kirra parkrun

In South Africa, there are the tourists such as the Roodepoort
Raiders, members of the 50-club who regularly travel en masse for
an hour or hour and a half to other parkruns in the same province. There are those who will get up ridiculously early to drive
four or five hours into the next province for an inaugural, taking
sandwiches with them. And there is a handful who pay for flights
to various parts of the country.

Tracy Rankin first went along to Delta parkrun because it
was a chance to meet Bruce Fordyce; the beautiful park and the
fact that the event was free got her hooked immediately: 'Now
it's my passion.' Seeing a British runner wearing a 50-club T-shirt
Tracy was determined to earn one herself, and was the first South
African to reach fifty after starting parkrunning in South Africa,
although getting to the 100-club first of home-grown South African parkrunners was more of a challenge (Dieter Meyer was just
one behind her). She didn't miss one for anything – even when
she'd broken a toe just an hour before the run.

It was her visit to the UK, Tracy explained, that galvanised
her to start her parkrun tourism. She had five weeks of vacation
to use or lose and she ran at Bushy, Edinburgh, Glasgow, Cardiff
and Reading parkruns. When she returned to South Africa, more
parkruns were starting up, so she wanted to run them. One of the

things she loves is that, 'it's very familiar wherever I go and every-one's just so friendly. Wherever I go, it's the same friendly vibe. With over a million people signed up now, surely parkrun is the biggest international running club in the world.' She added, 'I've been inspired by parkrun, it's given me confidence, it's given me a dream. I communicate more with people, and I've gone from parkrun to Comrades. It's completely changed my life.'

Tracy's dedication to parkrun is such that when she ran Two Oceans, the 56 kilometre ultramarathon which is the second larg-est race in South Africa and is held on a Saturday, she seriously considered deviating from the course at 25 kilometres, running the two blocks to Fishhoek parkrun, running that parkrun, then returning to the main race. And when she ran Comrades, she mentally divided it into eighteen parkruns and visualised running her eighteen favourite parkrun courses.

Rob Green is another 'passionate about parkrun' South Af-rican presently travelling a lot, aiming to run at all the South African parkruns by the end of 2014. He notes that while Tracy Rankin is clearly ahead (and Bruce and Jill Fordyce are too), he, Peter Hawthorne, Jaco van der Walt, and Jabulani Mkhize are all heading for this goal and often meet each other as they race to complete the set of events – including the new events starting up: 'Naturally when Bruce opens a new one most of the group of five are there for the inaugural run.' He added, 'It's a fun way to travel and enjoy the parkruns at the same time.'

Carmen Goncalves and father **Carlos** have also enjoyed some parkrun South Africa tourism and are on the parkrun South Af-rica Most Events leaderboard. They ran at Summerfield parkrun when there were only two other runners there and their holiday in France was only made complete by taking the Eurostar to London to run at Bushy parkrun.

So far a handful of people have run at all the New Zealand events: Kiwis Julia and Paul Gordon, Kemp Englebretsen, Martin O'Sullivan, Andrew Capel and Christine Robertson by the end of June 2014, plus one British parkrun tourist, John Matthews, who has also parkrun in Australia, Ireland, Denmark, Poland, USA and Russia.

In Poland, the most-travelled Polish parkrunner to date is Andrzej Komisarski, having reached twelve Polish parkruns.

The Breakfast Club runners, mainly from Striders of Croydon, decide where to parkrun each Saturday on the basis of which café's breakfast they want to eat. 'Between us, we have attended Lloyd, Banstead, Roundshaw, Riddlesdown, Crystal Palace, Brockwell, Eastbourne, Dulwich, Burgess, Peckham Rye, Nonsuch, Bushy, South Bank and Kawana (both in Queensland), Bromley, Southwark, Gateshead, Whitstable, Brighton & Hove, Poole, Forest of Dean, Fulham Palace, Wimbledon and Mile End parkruns. Thanks to parkrun we have met some wonderful people, caught up with old friends, laughed almost as much as we have sweated and generally been humbled by the hospitality shown by the organisers. Some of us run every week, some of us alternate between running and supporting, but ALL of us eat and I think that the fact that the post-run breakfast is the raison d'être, *and not the run itself, has meant that those who are injured continue to be a part of parkrun and do not miss out.*
Serena Stracey (with Damian, Alan, Stephen, Kim, Karen, Sarah, Geri, Justin, Stanno, Richard, Hannah; Anna and Graham in support, and occasionally Nicola from Queensland)

Vacation destination: parkrun

In addition to the dedicated parkrun tourists aiming for or climbing up the Most Events leaderboards there are all those who are holidaying or on business trips and check whether there's a parkrun nearby so they can get their weekly parkrun 'fix' on a Saturday morning, or even design their holidays around parkruns.

In May 2014, I had a chance to do a little parkrun tourism abroad while at a conference in Poland. Arriving for Warszawa-Praga parkrun on the Saturday morning, I met a lovely lady, Ania, who made sure I found where everyone gathered (at the finish – I was vainly looking for people near the start line). I also met a couple of other tourists, Michelle Rivette and Kevin Jones from Cardiff, who were in Warszawa specifically to run the parkrun. They said that a lot of their holidays and weekend breaks are now centred on parkrun. They particularly look for new parkruns and plan the rest of the holiday around that: 'It's a fantastic thing to do, the people you meet and the places you go to, it's great.'

A British couple visiting South Africa drove 150 kilometres in a cold monsoon to get to St Francis – where there were four or five volunteers and six runners in the pouring rain – bought all the volunteers breakfast afterwards, then drove back again.

I was an occasional parkrunner, but when I calculated that by running more often I could make my fiftieth run coincide with a planned holiday in Australia that became my target. Even at 7am with an ocean breeze blowing I found it hot, but I couldn't disagree with the enthusiastic Run Director's claim that I couldn't have found a better setting for my fiftieth than this friendly Kawana run by the beach. My cousin and her two sons joined me as well. At the finish, a local who was also doing his fiftieth grabbed me for a joint photo, whilst the barcode scanner was giving out ripe mangos which I really appreciated eating on the beach watching my cousin's sons, now out enjoying the morning surf. On our holiday we experienced the wonderful Sydney Harbour and spectacular Great Ocean Road (and endured the cricket!), but for me nothing could beat my run by the beach with Aussie members of my actual and parkrun families.
David Dyer, Woodley parkrun

Joy and Donald Bell, who are members of Stragglers running club and regulars at Bushy parkrun, visited Clermont Waterfront parkrun while they were in Florida and thoroughly enjoyed it – the easy, flat, lakeside course, all on tarmac, and the welcoming atmosphere. This parkrun is only about fifty kilometres from the tourist hotspot of Disneyland Florida, and gets a *lot* of parkrun tourists – so many, in fact, that by their twelfth event they started providing a whiteboard on which visitors can write their name and origin, and including a visitors' section in their weekly run report. By the end of 2013, with fifteen overseas visitors on the last Saturday in the year, their recorded tally of touristic parkrunners was 176; there have been few weeks with only local parkrunners.

Durham parkrun, North Carolina, also gets quite a few tourists, including people travelling from Florida just for the Durham parkrun, a family vacationing in the North Carolina mountains who got up at 3 o'clock in the morning in order to drive over to Durham for the parkrun, and the occasional backpacker. 'Sometimes they email beforehand, other times they just show up,' Julie Messina, the Event Director said. 'We had one guy recently that stayed with us, because there are no backpacking hostels or anything like that around here, and there's another tourist coming soon. We'll be away but one of the regular runners is going to pick him up and get him to the parkrun.'

Lian and Noel de Charmoy at Cornwall parkrun in New Zealand have lost track of the number of Friday evening calls they have received from parkrunners saying, 'I'm at the backpacker hostel; how do I get to the parkrun?' They also often end up dropping people back at the hostel after the run.

Many Australian parkruns also get tourists; at Kawana, they commonly have ten to twenty tourists, mainly Australian but also from South Africa and the UK, and more during the main tourist season.

A group from Hull parkrun taking a trip to Poznań parkrun coincided with another group on tour from Witten in Germany.

Despite the German group not having a parkrun of their own, they all had parkrun IDs. Paul Tremere, Hull parkrun's Event Director, noted that not only were the Hull parkrunners meeting people from both Poland and Germany, but pre-parkrun, the parkrunners from Hull hadn't known each other, either.

Occasionally, when working or vacationing in locations sadly lacking in parkrun events, parkrunners have simply declared a 'pop-up parkrun' and run a 5K anyway. This has happened in locations as disparate as Central Park, New York, and Antarctica.

The Antarctica pop-up parkrun was arranged by Jodie Tersteeg, a Blackbutt and Newy parkrun Run Director. Held on the Ross Ice Shelf, it took place along a road which had been checked as being free of crevasses, and was marked by flags on the otherwise featureless snow and ice. Participants had to run in thermal and fleece layers, with gloves, balaclavas and goggles, while the marshals at the north and south extremes of the route carried two-way radios as well as first aid kits, hot drinks and spare jackets, just in case. Those without running shoes ran in large winter boots! All finished safely.

With parkrun reaching more and more countries, it's clear that wherever parkrun starts up, parkrun tourism won't be far behind.

9

Things that go beep

We just had the timer, that was all. Everyone's name and their position had to be written down by hand. Afterwards we entered all the names into the computer. It took a while, but you got to know everyone's names pretty well, writing them down every week.

Jenny Booth, early Banstead Woods parkrun volunteer

While parkruns are not races, they started off as time trials and they are very definitely still timed runs, providing an opportunity for participants of all speeds to test themselves and monitor their performance. For this to work, it is necessary for each parkrun to have a means of recording the finishing times of sometimes hundreds of participants. Given the number of events, the number of people running in them and the fact that each parkrun is managed by volunteers, most of whom have had no training as race officials, the system has to be pretty robust and simple to operate. And it is.

At the beginning, the system was simplicity itself – a program on a mobile phone captured times when the screen was tapped. Each runner was handed a numbered metal washer indicating their place number, and they wrote down those positions next to their names on the clipboard, where they had written them before the start of the run. Afterwards, Paul Sinton-Hewitt took the times and the names, typed them into a computer and sent everyone the results by email. Soon he set up a small website and started displaying the results there as well.

Finish tokens

There were fifty steel washers originally, hand stamped with numbers by Paul; another fifty were added later. The washers were kept on a metal coat hanger and taken off for each runner. Occasionally the hanger was dropped or tilted downwards accidentally and the washers went all over the place, which was a problem! After a while, the rusting steel washers were replaced, first by non-rusting, but still hand-stamped, aluminium discs and then by machine-stamped aluminium forestry tags imported from the USA. Then came the first trials of barcodes for the finish positions, using longer metal tags from the same source, with the number stamped on one side and the barcode glued onto the other, before progressing to the bright and cheerful parkrun-designed plastic numbered and barcoded tags used now.

Some people like these too much and finish tokens are always 'wandering off'. Jenny Booth was scanning at Roundshaw Downs once when she spotted a runner about to put their finish tag onto a necklace – which already held three other tags. She quickly reclaimed them, explaining to the runner that no, they were *not* finishing medals to keep, asked her where she had been running, and returned the tags to the correct parkruns.

More often, a runner or sometimes a volunteer absent-mindedly pockets a finish token and discovers it hours, days or even weeks later. Sometimes the runner appears one morning looking slightly apologetic and saying, 'You know I swore blind I didn't have that finish token, well, look what I found in my pocket.' Other times, a finish token just quietly 'appears' on the registration table while all the runners are milling around before the run. And occasionally, after a runner has been asked to please bring their tag back, an embarrassed volunteer admits they just found it in their own pocket.

At most parkruns a volunteer holds the finish tokens out to the runners and each runner takes one as they exit the finish chute; at larger parkruns there might be an assistant removing tokens from the storage pin, wire or shoelace and handing them to the finish token volunteer in groups. At Bushy parkrun, the process is organised for maximum efficiency (it needs to be). The tokens are kept on large blunt safety pins in sets of fifty – a reasonable number to hold in the hand – and the parkrunners are directed to hold out their hands so a token can be placed into each outstretched palm as it passes – faster than people reaching out to take the tokens. There are two people on duty; as one volunteer gets towards the end of their fifty tokens they count down, '3, 2, 1...' and the other person is ready for the next outstretched hand. After that, registration seems relatively relaxed, although everyone is moving quite rapidly, with each parkrunner holding up their athlete ID in one hand and finish token in the other, to be scanned in turn, before dropping the finish token into the waiting bucket. In addition to several scanning stations there is one person with a clipboard to write down the IDs that don't scan in properly.

Athlete IDs

The name recording system started with runners simply writing their own names down (in their own handwriting...) on a clipboard, then with volunteers writing down the names. Later, since about 80% of runners came back to run again, names were entered into a spreadsheet, and the sheets printed out each week. The list of previously registered runners soon grew to eight pages of double columns of names, printed out each Friday first for Bushy and then as Wimbledon Common and Banstead Woods got going, for each of the three events. The sheets were spread out on two or three tables for registration, with new runners being added in by hand.

With something like 2,000 names in the database, it became obvious that another system was needed, more easily scaled up, and less prone to errors caused by mishearing names or multiple people with the same name. In 2009, Paul made the decision to give each parkrunner their own permanent parkrun athlete ID number, with barcode, and to develop a computer system to hold and manipulate all the results. The numbers were assigned alphabetically, although numbers one to five were never used. In May 2014, parkrun ID 1,000,000 was assigned.

Once everyone had an ID number, it became possible to think about using scannable IDs, although that raised the question of how to scan them. The first scanners had to be attached to laptops in order to work, and were soon replaced by the little Opticon scanners which are still used at parkruns worldwide. With scannable finish tokens *and* athlete IDs, it became possible for these two pieces of information to be loaded onto a computer and associated with each other in a manner much less prone to error than trying to work out which 'John Smith' on the system was the one standing in front of you. Chris Cowell notes that he is in the results one week as running both in Basingstoke and South Manchester parkruns; he's always wondered which runner at Basingstoke that week was misidentified. Clearly, moving to scannable IDs has removed much of the human error.

The use of athlete ID barcodes was rolled out across the events gradually. For quite some time, the two systems were used side by side, runners having the option to queue to give in their name, or join the faster-moving line for barcode scanning. Some runners who had been involved from the very early days didn't really see the need for the barcodes. 'I reasoned, everyone knew who I was, and it wasn't as though it would ever get to the point where they didn't all know me...' Ian Callander said, wryly acknowledging his naivety regarding the growth of Bushy parkrun.

Despite encouragement, some runners just would not use their barcodes. Eventually Paul and the team took the decision to force the issue, making one event after another 'barcode only'. Paul explained, 'This didn't mean that someone who turned up without a barcode couldn't run – they could still line up with everyone else, still run with everyone else, finish and, if they had a sports watch, time themselves – it only meant that they wouldn't get an official finish time or finish position.'

A few runners were extremely unhappy with the change (one person actually walked away from parkrun altogether – 99 runs in! – in protest) and many volunteer teams were lenient with barcode-less participants for many months, adding them at the time or, if they emailed in their barcode details, during the following week. While adding in 5-10% of runners by hand at a small event was not a large chore, at an event with hundreds of runners this could take hours of work by volunteers. After a while, parkrun HQ emphasised the need for a united approach: no barcode, no result. Once this rule had been in place for a little while, runners accepted it, becoming much better at remembering their barcodes, and philosophical about losing out on an official finish time if they forgot their ID.

DFYB – don't forget your barcode! Since the parkrun system prints out six copies of the barcode at a time, most parkrunners minimise the risk of forgetting by keeping copies in multiple places such as the pocket of their running shorts, their jacket, car and wallet, or by buying plastic versions to wear on a wrist or attach to shoelaces. When they *are* forgotten, some parkrunners go to considerable lengths to be registered for their run (particularly if they think they have run a PB), leaping into their car or running off down the road, finish token in hand, to fetch their ID, saying, 'I'll be back in twenty minutes – please wait!'

There still remains the possibility of human error, such as the runner who hands in his child's barcode with his finish token and his own barcode with the child's finish token. The results then show both parents going round in forty minutes (not that surprising) and a six year old finishing (unaccompanied) in 22 minutes – rather less likely. Generally, errors such as this are sorted out after an email from the embarrassed parents, explaining the situation.

Timing

Timing at parkruns has gone through several stages. First there was Paul's mobile phone running a small program, with times recorded by tapping on the screen and later manually entered into the computer. Then Paul wrote a program which ran on a laptop, and someone pressed the space bar for each runner as they came through. This worked, but was a problem in heavy rain, as most laptops are not designed for use in the wet. Next came some fancy stopwatches from the USA, and the volunteer pressed a button on the top – much more portable than a laptop and great when they worked, but they crashed so often that even with two of them in action after a few months there came a week when neither had worked, resulting in no times recorded.

It was Duncan Gaskell who told Paul about the TAG Heuer timers; he had been talking to someone in the British Orienteering Association and asked them what they used. They told him that they used these timers from TAG Heuer, and they thought they had an old one in the garage if he wanted to try it out. So Duncan rang Paul and said they ought to try one. 'The next thing I knew, Paul had gone and got three of them' – one each for Bushy Park, Wimbledon Common and Banstead Woods. As Chris Phelan said, having been using a laptop and trying desperately to keep it dry, 'The TAG Heuer timers were large, and heavy, and expensive, but they're also very robust and reliable, and we're still using that original machine at Banstead Woods.' They are also rechargeable, have a screen which displays the number of times the button has been pressed, so you know whether or not you have recorded someone, and you can load the data straight into a computer. The second model of TAG Heuer timer used by parkruns was a bit smaller, but still very costly.

Then the parkrun team realised that the little Opticon scanners which were being used to read the barcodes recorded the time at which they scanned each barcode and could be adapted to become timers instead of barcode readers. Discussions with the distributors and the manufacturers followed and the Opticon timers were developed. These were great in several respects – rechargeable, much more portable and less expensive than the TAG Heuer machines. Unfortunately, occasionally they didn't work properly (due to machine or human error) and the lack of a display means that a malfunction might be detected only when the timer was connected to the computer to download the (non-existent or garbled) data. Some events started to use a backup stopwatch in parallel with the Opticon timer.

A model which grew in popularity with event teams was a Junsd stopwatch: inexpensive, showing the times and number of runners, and, with the right software, the data from the stopwatch could be downloaded and fed into the parkrun system for results processing. They are not perfect: they are more prone to failure than the Opticon timers (and a lot more so than the TAG Heuer machines), they use lithium cell batteries rather than being rechargeable, and they can only record just under 500 runners. However, they are also significantly more affordable than the other options, the batteries generally last for several months, and now they are being used as standard by parkrun events worldwide, with more expensive options being reserved for events regularly reaching 400 runners.

Finish funnel

Even the funnels have evolved. Originally Bushy Park Time Trial just had a designated finish line at the car park where runners were timed in and given their finish token. As the numbers increased, the first finish funnel was put into place; then that was lengthened and funnel managers were used to keep the runners moving along the funnel in the right order.

At most parkruns, a simple funnel – shorter or longer – is all that is needed. Depending on the space available this may be in a straight line, a curve, or even a zig-zag shape. At Bushy parkrun, once more than 1,000 runners started turning up, a special adaptation was needed.

On 7 January 2012, the first occasion on which 1,000 runners turned up at Bushy parkrun, it was impossible to get everyone through the funnel fast enough to prevent a pile-up of people waiting to cross the finish line. Peter Smith, a regular Bushy parkrunner, had been helping with funnel management after finishing his own run. He said, 'I just found it really frustrating and it was bugging me all weekend trying to think of a better way to queue the runners but maintain the order that they finished in. Then sometime on the Sunday it hit me.' The result was the double-funnel system.

His inspiration came from the systems used at the Eurotunnel or waiting to board a ferry, where cars are directed into lanes, A, B, C, and so on, and then released in turn to board. Peter thought, 'If we split the funnel in two, people could fill up the left side, then when that was getting full, we could block that side off and send people into the right side instead.' First he thought that would be sufficient – surely by the time the right side was full, the left side would be empty? Then he decided he had better plan for the worst case scenario. Since building an ever-increasing number of funnels, side by side, was not going to be practical, he set on a scheme of letter cards to act as 'virtual' parallel funnels.

It works like this: the first runners to finish go in the left side of the funnel. Once that's nearly full, the funnel manager sends runners down the right side instead, giving the first person a big card labelled 'A'. Reaching the end of the funnel, those people are held there for a little while – but that's okay, they can stand and chat with the runners in front and behind. Once that side gets full, people are sent into the left funnel once more – the first runner being given the card 'B'. Once 'B' reaches the front of the funnel, that runner is stopped, and the 'A' people are released – until card 'C' reaches the front of the funnel, at which point they are stopped and the 'B' runners move forward to get their tokens, until 'D' appears and they switch again.

It works amazingly well, with the efforts of everyone on funnel management to keep people moving, and an extra person who can go and take a finish token for someone if they have run too hard and have dropped out of the queue to retch or vomit!

Results processing and the Field Management System

I've lost count of the number of times that parkrunners have asked how on earth we process the results. Nowadays, due to some hard work by various members of the UKTT technical staff at parkrun HQ, it's really quite straightforward for the event teams. Stripped down to essentials, it works like this: as each runner crosses the finish line and enters the funnel, the volunteer on the timer presses a button which records a time. As the runner exits the far end of the finish funnel they are given a token with a position number on it. The runner takes their ID and finish token to the registration person who scans these using a small handheld scanner.

In the café after the run, software on the computer takes the data from the timer and scanners and converts it into text files. Next, the data are uploaded from the text files into the parkrun web-based Field Management System (FMS). This system puts the sets of numbers together: the first time was, say, 17:45, and the ID attached to finish token position number 1 belongs to Joe Bloggs – so the software reports that Joe Bloggs finished first in a time of 17:45. Further software then notes whether Joe got a PB this week, calculates his age-graded percentage and other statistics, and sends Joe an email and/or text of his result. Additionally, the system generates the results for each event and posts these on the event's website, and sends a report to the event team.

Paul started development of the parkrun FMS back in 2004. It was designed initially just for one event – Bushy Park Time Trial – and was adapted for multiple events in 2007. Amazingly, with further adaptations it continued to be used until 2012, being loaded onto the laptop of each parkrun event. Every week, each event team synchronised their local FMS data with the main parkrun database so they would have the latest runners to register on their system. In 2012 there was a changeover to a web-based system, the webFMS, removing the need for every event to synchronise their database with the central database before entering the results.

In March 2014, another major change occurred, this time in the results processing software which sat behind the scenes taking the data from the FMS and doing all the necessary manipulations to produce the age-grading percentages, notes of PBs and all the other statistics that runners appreciate. The original system, designed in 2007, had continued to work through the astounding expansion in parkrun and parkrunner numbers – with help from some very dedicated people making, when necessary, the computer equivalents of baling-twine and wire repairs to keep it going. The new system has been designed to chew through all the calculations and send the results back out to the runners within an hour of each event team sending in their results – however many events there might be.

If everything goes smoothly, with the same number of times on the timer as finish tokens handed out, everyone's barcodes scanning nicely, nobody ducking out of the funnel or refusing to take a finish token, nobody missed by the timer, and so on, then results processing doesn't take very long. However, usually there are a few athlete ID numbers to add in because their barcodes wouldn't scan, and often there are one or two other things to fix as well – a time missed on the main timer so needing to be added manually using data from the backup stopwatch, or a person to remove because they went through the finish line twice, or sorting out when someone is in the results twice because another member of the family handed over the wrong barcode.

Some of these commonplace problems took quite a bit of sorting out on the old FMS system; the new web-based system makes correcting most of the errors much easier and faster – at least after some staring at the computer screen, thinking, and consultation of the number checker's sheet to work out where the error has crept in.

Anything that can go wrong, has gone wrong...

Despite everyone's best efforts, things can and do go wrong, due to both mechanical failures and human error.

Volunteers have left one or more pieces of equipment at home and nobody has realised until it's too late to go back and get things before the run needs to start.

Timers have malfunctioned, or their batteries have run down, or distracted volunteers (me included) have failed to start an Opticon timer correctly and they haven't recorded any times. A runner has been missed, or the button has been pressed too many times when a whole group of runners arrived at once. Even when all the times have been recorded correctly, Event Directors and other experienced volunteers have occasionally accidentally cleared all the data off the timer before uploading it into the computer. Lots of people have done this over the years; Paul Sinton-Hewitt managed to erase all the data for the very first Banstead Woods Time Trial – which doesn't seem to have done that event any harm.

Stopwatches have swung around on a lanyard with the stop button hitting a solid object some time during the run; sometimes this hasn't been noticed for some unknown length of time after it's happened and it has been impossible to sort it out. Volunteers have become confused and pressed the stopwatch's start/stop button for each runner instead of the lap button. Stopwatch batteries have run out in the middle of a run.

Finish tokens have been given out in reverse order, or dropped on the floor all over the place. Tokens have stuck together, or those which have gone missing haven't been replaced before the following week's run. Runners have gone through the finish line then ducked out of the funnel before taking a finish token.

Things that go beep

Barcode scanners have got condensation inside the scanner screen or raindrops on the outside, preventing them from reading the barcodes. Scanners have accidentally been set to silent mode, leaving the poor volunteers thinking that they are refusing to read anything at all. A volunteer has become confused and accidentally scanned the finish tokens first and then the athletes' IDs, or has been pressing the button to clear data each time rather than the scan button. A team of two volunteers have scanned all the IDs with one scanner and all the finish tokens with another one. All the data has been deleted before being loaded into the computer (as Carla Potter of Norwich parkrun said, it's important to ensure that volunteers know *not* to press the small button on the scanner). The scanner has stopped working due to cold: each winter, as the colder weather starts, all parkrun teams are advised to 'love your scanners' and keep them warm inside clothing until they are being used.

Most errors can be corrected when the results are being processed on the computer. The present web version of the FMS can manage an amazing variety of amendments. You can, for example, add any number of minutes or seconds to each time – so if you realised that the timer hadn't started properly, rather than trying to call all the runners back (no chance!) you simply start it at say one, five or ten minutes after the start and make the correction on the computer later. It's also easy to add in or remove a single time, to correct for the missed runner or the extra beep. If a group of finish tokens have been dropped, so that runner 25 is followed by runner 42, with tokens 26 to 41 not used, that too can be sorted out on the computer.

One of the more confusing errors, the first time it happens, is when you look at the results and there are two runners in each position (helpfully flagged up in pink on the laptop screen). This happens when the scanner has not been cleared of the previous week's results before being used. Happily it is simplicity itself to correct this by opening the file containing the scanned in data and removing all the results with the previous week's date on them.

The pen is mightier...

In 2009, when featured as 'parkrunner of the week' in the parkrun newsletter, Euan Bowman, Basingstoke parkrun's Event Director, gave some advice to other organisers: 'The first thing on my checklist on a Saturday morning is a pen and paper. If I forget something or there's a glitch with anything, then pen and paper always saves the day so I can correct things later!' His advice is very sound, as many event teams have discovered. Electronic timers, barcodes and scanners make it easy to quickly load the results into the computer and squirt them off to the servers. However, if anything goes wrong with any of the systems – a scanner not working, or the number tokens not making it to the parkrun on a Saturday morning, not to mention if the person on the timer thinks they have missed a runner, or someone has dodged out of the finish chute, then good old-fashioned pen and paper enable notes to be written or even, in extreme circumstances, every runner's finish position to be written down.

And of course, with pencil and paper the batteries never run out!

10

The family that parkruns together...

parkrun is not just about the running (or walking or jogging). The people here have opened their hearts to my husband and me, but most of all my boys, eldest just three years and youngest ten months old. It has become our Saturday mornings.

Christina Edwards, Leeds parkrun

Many people complain that families never share activities any more, that children, particularly teenagers, would rather play video games or chat to their friends online than spend time with their parents, siblings or grandparents. parkrun is bucking the trend, providing a venue where children – even teenagers – participate alongside other members of their family and enjoy it. Additionally, it's becoming a venue where extended families can meet, and it provides an opportunity for far-flung families to share in a common activity despite miles, even oceans, separating family members.

Phyllis and Declan Flynn are long-time club runners and heard about parkrun from their friend Jim Desmond back when there was only Bushy Park Time Trial. They got involved with Banstead Woods when that event started, with Declan helping to design the course, Phyllis marshalling and both encouraging friends from their, and other, running clubs, to turn up and run.

Nowadays they and their daughters, Hannah-Mai, Mary-Kate, Li-Norah, and Anna-Li, are found most Saturdays either at Banstead Woods, another of the local parkruns, or, during vacations, further afield as parkrun tourists. Their oldest daughter, Hannah-Mai, is a very good runner and the Flynns possibly hold the distinction of a family clean sweep at a parkrun: one week at Riddlesdown, Declan was first male finisher, Hannah-Mai first female, while Phyllis achieved the highest age grade. Their youngest daughter, Anna-Li, decided that she would make her parkrun debut once she was seven, and ran her first parkrun at Nonsuch in April 2014. The following week the whole family ran together at Banstead Woods to celebrate Mary-Kate reaching the 50-club, finishing all in a group.

Meanwhile, at Amager Fælled, the Müller family dominated the points tables for both 2012-2013 and 2013-2014. Henrik, Helene Sofia and their daughter Sinaq are all in the 100-club – and Henrik has done more parkruns than any other Danish runner. For the Müllers, parkrun 'is our Saturday ritual. It's the best way to start the weekend', said Henrik, adding, 'I think it's a combination of the competition, meeting good friends, the fresh air, and that we do it as a family. But most important – the first cup of coffee after parkrun is the best cup you can get!'

The family that parkruns together...

For James Russell, one of the original thirteen parkrunners, parkrun is 'a family thing'. Mostly, James runs with his sons, who are keen to reach the 100-club. Additionally, they meet up with James's sister, brother and sister-in-law, who are all in the 100-club, and with their children. 'It's very much a family day,' he said, 'the kids call it parkrunday; it's the way we kick-start the weekend.' James recognises that without parkrun it's probable that he and his siblings and their families wouldn't see each other nearly so frequently, and the cousins wouldn't see each other anything like as often – and then there are all the friends he's made at parkrun and sees regularly on a Saturday. It's not just his family, he adds. 'I see it more and more, kids running the parkrun with their parents. It's so much more than just a run and it's an easy introduction for the kids to running, not with regimented training but just as a fun family event. I'm sure we're going to get some young Olympians out of this. And I love the inclusivity, with everyone running from Olympians to people running this distance for the first time.'

My first parkrun was out of desperation on a wintry morning when I needed some inspiration (and perspiration) to get me going! My second parkrun was a way of getting my twelve-year-old twin grandsons out of the house and away from the computer games for a while. They loved it – but were nervous. Could they keep up with Granny or would they have to hang about waiting for her? We had such fun! The Huddersfield folk were welcoming and friendly. It was a large group with kids in buggies and tiny tots running with their parents. I ran the hilly bits well and the boys zoomed past me on the downhills. We finished together. We have made a pact to try all the parkruns within easy reach of Leeds (where they live) or Halifax (where I live) and to make it a regular date throughout the year. A fantastic way to bond with my teenage grandsons and granddaughter. Who knew?! Such a super way to engage them in physical activity and share memories over a cup of hot chocolate at the end.
Manghanita Kempadoo, Leeds parkrun

The four members of the Moore family are regular participants at Lloyd parkrun. James Moore started first, in August 2011, with daughter Jessica starting in October 2012 and her younger sister Leanne in March 2013. Leanne got hooked very quickly and wanted to run more often, which led to her mother, Foong Cheek, starting parkrunning in May 2013 to accompany Leanne. I recall words along the lines of 'only for my daughter' as Foong finished, exhausted, the first time – but she has obviously grown to enjoy it, since she now runs even on days when Leanne is volunteering.

We hear so much about sibling rivalry, but acts of generosity between siblings don't get the same press. In June 2013, I saw a true act of sibling love: Leanne had just completed her first ten runs, was understandably very proud of this and was eagerly awaiting her 10-club T-shirt. The following week she turned up – and Jessica had let her borrow her own 10-club T-shirt. Leanne was grinning from ear to ear.

Faldiela Mallick makes sure she schedules every Saturday morning at Greenpoint parkrun, South Africa, and hasn't missed a single run since this event started. Fellow Greenpoint parkrunners have come to know Faldiela and most of her ten children as regular participants, because every week she takes along the younger ones who still live at home and encourages the older ones to meet and participate. Greenpoint parkrun, situated in scenic Cape Town, gets international visitors participating every week and Faldiela uses this opportunity to welcome these visitors to the beautiful and friendly city. She counts herself lucky to spend this time with her family in this healthy pursuit. 'We meet like-minded people and engage in friendly banter.'

Christina Edwards, who runs at Leeds parkrun, is 'a married mum of two young boys who always said I *cannot* run!' She adds, 'However with parkrun you don't need to run! With the encouragement and support of so many friendly faces you cannot help but try your best and feel proud when you get that PB... even if you're generally last person home.' As an additional benefit, 'My three year old now says he wants to be a runner when he grows up just like daddy, who has progressed from parkrun to his first Great North Run in 2013 in just under a year and a half! What a fabulous way to best ensure a healthy lifestyle for him.'

I've been a runner for many years and loved it; there was nothing I wanted more than for my sons and husband Woody to share this love. When Woody saw a notice about parkrun, he registered along with my son Pete. Pete moved away to Manchester and parkrun became not only a passion for him but also a saving grace. Due to the element of competition between my sons, they soon all became involved, my oldest son Harry being equally as passionate as Pete. My youngest sons Mike and Joe are very occasional parkrunners; we're working on them! In 2012 I found out that I have an incurable degenerative eye disorder, but thanks to parkrun and the element of competition, I have people who act as a guide for me when I run. Hopefully this year I will manage my long-term goal of a parkrun in under 32 minutes. I'm certain that without parkrun my running career would have finished and my longed-for hope of my family sharing the love and joy of running would not have been possible.
Lisa Medcalf-Woodward, Forest of Dean parkrun

At Eastleigh parkrun, Jess Lott and her daughter Lara run, together with Lara's friend Millie-Mae, who, like Lara, is eleven. 'It keeps you fit and healthy,' said Millie-Mae. 'I really love it,' said Jess. 'For a family, it's really bonding. I love coming here together; it's something we can have in common. And I lost two stone coming to parkrun, so it's been really good for me.'

Not only am I exercising, I am doing it with my husband. We look forward to Saturday mornings together and then wait for our results.
Robyn, Cleveland parkrun

The Harvey family at Eastleigh parkrun also find that a combination of running and volunteering helps the whole family to get involved. Brenda said: 'I like it that we can all do it as a family, all at our different paces, so we can all be together.' The day I visited, Brenda and son Harry were running, and for Harry the best thing was that, 'I get to run about,' while for Brenda, 'What I like about parkrun is that it's so inclusive. It's all shapes, all sizes, all ages.' For Amber, the youngest, volunteering (on that occasion, marshalling with her father) is good because it means she can take part without running!

For the Johnstone family at Roundhay, it was mother Vicki and oldest son Daniel who started parkrunning first, with the teenager going from running with hands in pockets in thirty-something minutes to finishing in under twenty minutes, running his first 10K days after his sixteenth birthday, and joining the 100-club. Meanwhile, father Pete decided he really had to lose weight and get in shape. So he did his first in 33 minutes, his brother-in-law accompanying him, walked and jogged and thought he was going to die. But he PB'd the next several weeks and got the bug! Then the younger children started to come as well – Billy age ten, Lucas age thirteen. Pete is delighted that the youngest, five-year-old Marcus, simply assumes that this is what you do at weekends: on a Sunday you get up and run 2K (at Roundhay juniors) and on a Saturday you volunteer at the parkrun and when you're old enough you run the 5K.

I started running at parkrun for my own fitness but since then I have been joined by more than twenty friends and family and regularly run at Huddersfield parkrun. Since parkrun my life has changed considerably; my training runs have become more fun and more about improving so that I can improve my parkrun PBs and achieve something for myself. I have also gained friends, rekindled

The family that parkruns together...

friendships from high school and even brought my friends and family closer, all through parkrun and the joy of running, and running for personal goals.
Matthew Pattison, Huddersfield parkrun

At Tilgate, Stacey, Faye and Ellie Buche take part, with Faye normally running with nine-year-old Ellie, while Stacey generally uses the run for speed training while preparing for marathons. Ellie, who has already earned her 10-club shirt, just enjoys running. Faye said: 'It's nice that we all come together. And it's like-minded people; you can talk to anyone here.' Ellie's younger sister takes part in one mile events with the Saints & Sinners Fun Runners, so will no doubt graduate to parkrun in the future.

For Isobel Longley-Cook, running was something other people did, and she had to cope with her partner, who ran and was addicted to this ritual which took him away from her every Saturday morning. However, she got curious, went along and was encouraged by the volunteers to join in with cheering the runners. She was also beginning to realise that she needed to start exercising as a stress-reliever to improve her mental health. But running?

One day, inspired by the autobiography of ultramarathon runner Sharon Gayter, in which Sharon admits to barely being able to run a few hundred metres when she started running, Izzy bought some jogging bottoms and went out one evening to do her first jog, secretly building up her runs until the day when she stood on the start line at Albert Park, Middlesbrough. It was snowing and only about seventy people had made it to the park, but for Izzy, 'It was one of my top ten life experiences – beautiful.' Properly hooked, she loved the community feel and started going every week. After a while her younger daughter, sixteen at the time, thought she might start running to help her lose a little weight... and was soon not only running but a regular volunteer. Then her older daughter started. Now, running is something they do as a family, parkrunning together when her daughters are at home, as well as running together on the North Yorkshire Moors and on holiday in France.

Sometimes parents introduce their children to parkrun, and sometimes children get their parents started. Valerie Hamilton's daughter discovered parkrun while at Manchester University, and thought it would be good for her thirteen-year-old brother to take part at home, in the Forest of Dean parkrun. Valerie watched him running there and not only enjoyed seeing him running near the front of the pack but loved the friendly atmosphere. Soon, both she and her eighteen-year-old daughter were hooked on parkrun and on running: 'We look forward to our Saturday run and it's great to think of my daughter in Manchester running at the same time.' Valerie has joined a running club and begun planning to run a half marathon.

For a young runner from Gdańsk, it started when his father talked him into coming to parkrun, saying he would not regret it. 'During the run I promised myself never to come again – it was not for me.' However, after reaching the finish line he changed his mind. 'I surprised myself because previously I didn't like running. Now, I've already done nineteen parkruns and earned my club shirt with "10" on the back. I run with my younger brother, aged seven and my dad and my uncle.'

Scott Northey started running following medical advice, to help to control his blood pressure and blood sugar. Having been told about parkrun by a neighbour he started attending Newy parkrun in New South Wales. 'It's something you get addicted to very quickly, not so much the run as the people, the parkrun community mentality,' he said. Now he mostly goes to Blackbutt parkrun, with his young sons, aged four and three; his wife often cannot be there due to work but joins them sometimes when her commitments allow. While Oliver and William still mostly ride in the buggy while he pushes it, they are starting to get out and run some sections and he is delighted that they are growing up running, swapping high-fives with parkrunners coming in the opposite direction on out-and-back routes, and seeing running as a fun, social activity, rather than as something that has to be competitive – that it's great to be outside, exercising, on a Saturday morning.

At Cleveland parkrun, Queensland, the event team is absolutely full of parkrunning families and they all help look after each other's kids. Olivia Coop attends with daughter Ella aged seven – who acts as assistant Run Director: 'She even says the ready, set, go and starts the run!' – son Jye, aged five, who has just started participating, and husband Chris who has also just started attending. Jacqui Rhodes and her husband Dave take it in turns to run with the kids – Lola (age four) and Elliott (two) are pushed in a double pram, while Abbey (seven) runs. Amy Strong, her husband Garth, and their kids Hayden (seven) and Tia (five) all participate – with Tia usually in a pram. Natalie Fulton comes with husband Gary and their son Beau (seven), who has started running. Ian Donald and his wife Monique run while their children Emily (seventeen) and Brooke (fifteen) are both 10-clubbers – they all did their first parkrun together and haven't stopped. Blair Habberjam's son Finn (nine) has run a couple of times and was timekeeper at their Christmas-themed parkrun which was managed entirely by junior parkrunners. And Jules Coleman runs with her dog, Basil.

Extended families

Porirua parkrun in New Zealand attracts a lot of families, Event Director Astrid van Meeuwen-Dijkgraaf said. 'There's the Riddle family, who started at Lower Hutt but then moved to the Porirua parkrun once we got started, there's the Hunter family, where a couple bring their thirteen- and eight-year-old nephews every week, and the boys just love it, while in the Campbell family there are three generations involved – there's Dad and daughter and grandchild, and sometimes Grandma pushing the child.' Astrid is always amazed by the people who run with buggies, particularly the ones pushing two children: 'That's a lot of weight to push around the course.'

Ian Riddle's family was introduced to parkrun by his brother Andrew, who still runs at Lower Hutt, as does his daughter Alexandra and sometimes his wife Jeanette and other daughter Amber. In Ian's family, initially Stanley, aged ten at the time, and Suzanne ran while Ian and daughter Phoebe watched, but soon they were all involved; now they rarely miss a Porirua parkrun and have encouraged Ian's brother David and his son, Tim, to start parkrunning. Stanley, who really loves the long runs, was the first of the family to reach the 50-club, with his father not far behind. Suzanne has fewer runs to her name, having had time off running with a foot problem; she volunteered during this time, which kept her involved and really helped to motivate her to get through her injury and back to running.

For Phoebe Riddle, a keen swimmer, parkrun is all about the volunteering. She's run a couple of times but is most commonly seen timing or scanning barcodes, and (at age nine) took on the role of Run Director on the day that the whole event was managed by juniors in January 2014. Astrid explained. 'At Porirua we had a juniors day with all the volunteer posts, including Run Director, carried out by juniors – aged eight to thirteen. That really showed people that volunteering, doing these jobs, is not that hard. Knowing that juniors can do it really gives the adults that confidence.'

One of the great benefits of the proliferation of parkruns is that members of a family can run 'together' even if they are actually hundreds of miles apart, can see one another's times and age-graded percentages on the respective parkrun websites, and whether they got a PB, and discuss their results. For example, David Parsons and his son run at Southwick parkrun, while David's two brothers do different UK parkruns. They all look up each other's results, communicate about it later on the Saturday and the ten year old thinks that it's great because he's faster than his father and uncles.

Similarly, Matthew Browning, running at Banstead Woods, likes parkrun partly because it is something he can do with his two sons, 'Even if I only see them at the start and finish!' Additionally, he has cousins who parkrun elsewhere in the UK, and a half-brother, Scott Browning, parkrunning in Brisbane, Australia. 'It's something we can chat about, slightly competitively,' he said. 'It's something you can have in common, albeit you might be thousands of miles apart.'

> *My parents, sister, cousin, cousin's kids and husband, aunty and uncle, plus many friends and their families have all joined parkrun simply from my husband initially trying it and convincing me to give it a go. I love turning up on a Saturday morning to see so many people close to me getting active and enjoying it. I'm hoping our kids will grow up thinking going to parkrun is the norm. They will feel linked to their local community as I do and they will have a free, weekly activity that they can enjoy, while helping them balance a healthy lifestyle.*
>
> *Kirsty Moore, Cleveland parkrun*

Three generations of the Day family participate at Cleveland parkrun. John Day grew up in a small Essex village during the Second World War, emigrated to Australia in 1948 when eighteen and enlisted in the RAAF, serving as a navigator. In 1980 he and his three sons, inspired by the Commonwealth Games in Brisbane, started running and worked up to half marathons, but later John gave up due to knee pain. Fast forward to the start of Cleveland parkrun and John decided to give it a try. After 45 parkruns, his time has reduced from just under forty minutes to about 33 minutes, and both his son Jonathan and his grandson Chris, age fifteen, are also enjoying the parkrun: 'And of course leave me far behind but like all parkrunners understand that we compete only with ourselves.'

Similarly at Banstead Woods, Liz Mason, her two daughters Annelise and Kelly, her son Mike and even a five-year-old grandson run, finding it great to have something they can do as a family. Annelise, having to travel up from Dorking, doesn't get to the woods every week, 'But I'm really happy when I do get here because it's like you're just one big family, it's so friendly here.'

Carmen Goncalves, who was the first South African junior to run fifty parkruns, said that she sees a lot more of her cousins due to parkrun. Often, the family will decide on a South African parkrun to visit and not only Carmen and her father Carlos will go but assorted cousins, aunts and uncles – even grandparents. 'Sometimes we have as many as sixteen members of the extended family at a parkrun,' said Carlos. Usually they all go for breakfast together after the run, sometimes with other parkrunners as well.

I stepped up to be Event Director when the previous Event Director was unable to continue here at North Shore parkrun and I'm so glad I did. parkrun has not only helped transform my life in getting and keeping active, it has enhanced the life of my family. My husband has started to get more active again after illness and finally now has participated in a few parkruns; he volunteers a lot also. My children get involved and can be right there with us, out on the track or volunteering.

Leonie Norris, North Shore parkrun, Queensland

Love is in the (parkrun) air

parkrun has also become a place where romances blossom, engagements take place and pre-nuptial celebrations are held.

The family that parkruns together...

parkrun changed my life. I met my fiancée there, I run with my labradoodle Coco there. Both my mum and dad often run there. My fiancée's mum and dad run there. Due to parkrun I have got fit, become a regular runner, joined a running club, lost weight and now I run almost every day and have run five marathons. I have met so many friends, visited many away parkruns with friends and family. Saturday morning is now parkrun day. Love parkrun for ever.
Mark Gadie, Hull parkrun

Stephen and Jenny Cooney might never have got together if it hadn't been for parkrun. They ran for rival clubs – Sutton Runners and Collingwood AC – but they both started running Banstead Woods parkrun in 2007 when it was still a Time Trial. They later discovered, as they got talking, that they had started parkrunning on the same day. Fast forward, and they are now both running for Collingwood, still running at Banstead Woods parkrun, with Stephen sometimes pushing a buggy containing their young son, Josh, around the course. As well as having met each other, they have made lots of friends at the parkrun and several members of their family on both sides have started parkrunning: Jenny's mother, sister and brothers, Stephen's brother and sister – with many approaching their hundred parkruns or heading towards 250 (Stephen having passed that landmark a while back).

Jenny's mother said, 'Jenny made me do it, starting three years ago. The first time running here I thought I was going to die, the pain in my chest was so bad, but I kept at it and now I'm doing triathlons. And it's all thanks to her making me get off the couch and come to parkrun, and it's due to parkrun.' The family involvement reaches even further, with Stephen telling me that his father-in-law volunteers regularly. 'He can't run due to health problems, but he can enjoy the volunteering side.' Apart from the friendliness, Jenny thinks that the most important thing about parkrun is that 'it gives everyone the opportunity to exercise, whatever their ability. Everyone is made to feel welcome, nobody is made to feel silly if they can't run.' Her mother agrees that the friendliness is key, that and the fact that your time and placing don't matter: 'you get encouraged, whatever you do.'

Mick Turner also met his wife, Lorraine, through parkrun, in their case at Roundshaw Downs. Like Stephen and Jenny, they ran for different clubs and if it had not been for parkrun, probably they would never have got to know each other. Many of the wedding guests ran at Eastbourne parkrun on the morning of the wedding.

It took Michael Escolme two years to persuade his fiancée, Mary, to try her first parkrun at Congleton, but now it's an embedded part of their lives together. He said, 'parkrun has allowed me to share running, which has been both my hobby and a significant part of my life, with my fiancée. We both benefit from the many emotional and physical benefits from a regular run and that we do it together has helped bring us closer together.'

More and more, runners are bringing their hen or stag parties to parkrun, wearing various interesting costumes up to and including fluffy antlers and bunny onesies, and there have even been parkrun wedding proposals. Finish-line proposals have taken place at several parkrun locations, including Stewart parkrun in Middlesbrough and Falkirk parkrun in Scotland, while there was a pre-run, all-singing, all-dancing flash mob proposal at Bushy parkrun in February 2013.

With all these parkrunner weddings, it's not surprising that more and more parkrunning couples are bringing their babies to be pushed around the course in buggies – and no doubt many of these 'parkrun babies' will graduate to running their first junior parkrun events as soon as they are old enough.

Left & Below: Bushy: Paul Sinton-Hewitt

It all began at Bushy in October 2004...
The original runners (top) and three of the volunteers – Alan, Robin and Jo (right). Fifth anniversary celebrations in 2009 (below).

Left: Bushy, John Norman

Right: Sheringham, George Carman
Below: East Coast Park, Agnieszka Banas

Every weekend, runners line up at over 500 different parkruns – here at Sheringham (top), East Coast Park, Singapore (left, with tourist Nneka Okonta in red) and Porirua, New Zealand (below).

Right: Porirua, Conor Daniel

Left: Nahoon Point, Peter King
Below: Portrush, Mike Johnson

Some of the best running locations in the world – from the beaches of Nahoon Point (above) and Portrush (right)...

...to the historic surroundings at the National Trust's Fountains Abbey (below) and extreme conditions in Antarctica (left).

Above: Xenia Brundin
Right: Fountains Abbey, National Trust/Brian Kay

parkrun is for everyone, from veteran London Marathoner John Hanscomb (above) and international athlete Sonia O'Sullivan (left), to wheelchair athletes and blind runners such as Ari Seirlis (right) and Susanne Laustsen (below).

Left: Bushy, David Rowe
Below: North Beach, Angela Bax

Above: Albert, Melbourne, Kon Iatrou, IKON images
Right: Amager Fælled, Jonathan Sydenham

Right: Hamilton Lake, Josh McCosh
Below: Poole, Martin Yelling

Whether you're running with a buggy (Liz Yelling at Poole, left), a dog, or a buggy and dog (Graeme Hawthorne at Hamilton Lake, above)...

...for your health (Richard Tanner before and after 50 parkruns, right) or with the family (the Flynns at Banstead Woods, below).

Above: Rachel Tanner & Roundshaw Downs, Martin Lloyd
Left: Banstead Woods, Richard Carter

Right: Crane Park, David Rowe
Below: Bushy, David Rowe

The parkrun clubs reward persistence in runners of all ages and speeds. Darren Wood (left) was the first to join the 250-club, parkrun pioneer James Russell (above, with his sons) joined in 2013.

Many people help make parkrun happen every weekend – from parkrun Country Managers (right) to volunteer marshals who cheer you on (Jim Beisty high-fiving at Newy, below).

Above: Richmond, Tim Oberg
Left: Newy, Penny Redhead

Left: Livonia, Spencer Greve
Below: Wynnum, Hennie Coetzer

parkrun continues whether with cold and snow in Livonia's winter, a waterspout at Wynnum, skirting the ostrich at Naval Hill or running backwards at Gdańsk!

Above: Naval Hill, Karien Potgieter
Right: Gdańsk, Bartosz Cicharski

Left: Blackhill, Lee Nixon
Below: Severno Tushino, Moscow, Semyon Lazarev

Christmas offers parkruns a chance to do something special as demonstrated here at Blackhill (above) and Severno Tushino, Moscow (right)...

...and celebrations can be held for anniversaries (Augustine Heights, left), for reaching ten junior runs (Stirling juniors, below) or for other special occasions – any excuse for a party!

Above: Augustine Heights, Alison Angier
Right: Stirling juniors, Brian Smith

Right: Woodley juniors, Peter Cook
Below: Bushy juniors, Paul Graham

Small beginnings for small runners – the first Bushy junior parkrun (left) and starting with a warm-up at Woodley (above).

...now junior parkruns are proving just as popular as their 5K equivalents and children enjoy earning their wristbands!

Above: Paul Graham
Left: Bushy juniors, Debra Bourne

Left: Gdynia, Michał Lewczuk
Below: Bradford, Jo Smith-Eccles

Becky Thurtell didn't let a broken leg stop her while touring to Gdynia (above). Finishers are cheered on by volunteers at Ardgillan (left), Bradford (right) and Aberystwyth (below).

YOU`RE AWESOME

FINISH

Above: Ardgillan, Agnes Małsa
Right: Aberystwyth, Jodi Bennett

Right: Severnoe Tushino, Moscow, Vitaly Kobylkin
Below: Ardgillan, Agnes Malesa

And after the run is over, a chance to socialise with fellow parkrunners...

...while the results are processed by events teams (above) and the numbers are crunched at parkrun HQ (right).

Above: Tim Oberg
Left: Lloyd, Debra Bourne

Left & Below: Bushy, Debra Bourne

Celebrating ten years of parkrun in October 2014 – the thirteen original parkrunners back at Bushy (above) and pioneer Karen Weir with her golden barcode (right).

parkrun founder Paul Sinton-Hewitt CBE volunteered as a barcode scanner (left) for some of the 1,705 runners (below)!

Above: Bushy, Debra Bourne
Right: Bushy, Sarah Finney

11

junior parkrun: it's for the kids!

We have a special problem at the juniors; they eat the finish numbers. Well, chew them, anyway. Many of the finish tags now have tooth marks.

Nicki Clark, Run Director, Bushy junior parkrun

It's just like the main parkrun events, but with more children. There are very few people about while the finish funnel, start line and registration tables are being set up, then suddenly there are people everywhere – children of all ages (including tots too young to participate), their parents, and the occasional spectating dog. Questions are asked by anxious parents of anyone wearing an official-looking fluorescent vest: is this the right place? ('yes'); where do they need to register before the run? ('you don't need to register before the run'); where is the start? ('there, where the line of markers has been placed'); where is the finish? ('there' – pointing to the finish funnel with bright orange cones marking its entrance).

The children congregate behind the start line and are led through a series of dynamic warm-up exercises, moving their arms and then their legs vigorously, then are encouraged to shuffle back to the start line (having usually moved forwards somewhat during this time). The Run Director delivers the briefing, including suggesting that smaller, slower runners should start further back, not on the front line, before issuing the final most important message – that the event is for fun!

A check that the timers are ready – then they are off, a colourful mass of children, legs and arms pumping, the youngest, accompanied by a parent, at the back of the group. Some are wearing white 10-club T-shirts and a few even have red 50-club shirts, indicating that they are veterans of the main Saturday 5K parkruns in addition to this shorter event.

There are a few minutes of relative quiet at the finish, then suddenly there's a massive hive of activity as the children arrive, first in ones and twos, then a trickle, becoming a flood. How the timers manage, with three runners a second finishing at some time points, is a mystery, but they do manage, doing a great job. The young runners line up and eagerly present their parkrun IDs and finish tokens to be scanned, while their parents hover nearby.

Bushy juniors leads the way

The first Bushy junior parkrun was held on 1 April 2010, with nine runners; brother and sister Luke and Ruby Penney were the first male and female finishers. These monthly 2K runs, for children aged four to fourteen only, soon took off and a year later numbers were pushing the 100 mark. On 6 October 2013, the day after parkrun's ninth anniversary, there were 432 runners; a few months later, weekly junior events were starting. In this age when children are spending more and more time sitting and playing with electronic devices, and less and less time outside and running around, it's an amazing achievement.

Bushy juniors was the brainchild of Paul Graham, runner, coach and occupational therapist. He had been helping a friend, Helen, a registered physiotherapist, who had started taking her son and a few other kids to run and play in Richmond Park on a Sunday morning – just trying to get them to run and have fun, get physical exercise, improve their sensory and physical integration, tire themselves out – all the things children should be doing. From this a Thursday evening training session developed for junior runners at Stragglers, which grew and became almost too popular, particularly in summer. Additionally, it quickly started attracting far younger children than had been expected and it became obvious that there was a lack of opportunity for younger children to take part in running.

Generally, Paul noticed, clubs didn't want to include children under twelve years of age, parents didn't know how to go about getting their children running, and often there was a real fear, even amongst trained adults, of including children in the six to eight age group. There was even a feeling that children under the age of twelve shouldn't be encouraged to run – which is in huge contrast with cultures such as the Tarahumara in Mexico, with their running game, as portrayed in Chris McDonald's book *Born to Run*, and even with British children from a few decades back, for whom walking a mile or two to school and running back home afterwards was totally normal.

Paul Graham was very keen to fill that gap and provide the opportunity for children to run: not in the structured environment of a club, rather something that everyone could access. He considered linking with childrens' events which were already happening but these tended to be orientated towards children already in running clubs, and to be either winter cross-country or spring and summer trail events.

He analysed what makes people do and continue doing something. 'It's really important to keep children running in some sort of structured format all year, so that it becomes a habit, just like brushing their teeth. That's what helps them to keep going with it,' Paul said. He wanted a low key, encouraging event, not competitive (except for self-competitive) – rather a similar ethos to parkrun, but making it easier for children to develop their skills and self confidence in an event less difficult than the full 5K parkruns. And he wanted something that was year round, like parkrun...

At the end of 2009, he approached Paul Sinton-Hewitt and asked if he would let him have a go at providing an event for children, calling it junior parkrun. And Paul said yes.

Paul Graham's choice of the two-kilometre distance for the junior parkrun was based both on his experience as a coach and on the available evidence regarding growth in children, including skeletal development and growth spurts. 'It's a good speed session for the older developing athletes, without getting too tired at the end, and for the younger ones, 2K is a distance that's achievable, while 5K is bit daunting. Also, the younger children can complete it in 26 or 27 minutes, while they're still engaged and remembering what they're doing, not wandering off to start picking up sticks or something.'

The 11 o'clock start time was chosen to make it as convenient as possible for parents and children. The monthly timing was due to several factors: Bushy Park wasn't prepared to have another weekly event, with associated congestion; it was asking less of volunteers than a weekly event; and it required less support in general.

junior parkrun: it's for the kids!

The very first Bushy juniors event was supposed to be in March, on a lovely sunny day. However, on the day, there was a big race going on in the park 'and nobody could find us. We must have looked very sad, standing there.' Paul accepted this as a good learning experience and they moved the start to near Teddington Gate so people could find it easily. At the end of 2013 it moved back again, at the request of the Royal Parks, but it's very different, now there are so many people coming, and they know where they're going.

Paul Graham is the first to admit that he couldn't have started up Bushy juniors by himself; volunteers such as Simon Brazil were essential. He's also very grateful to a regular runner in those early runs, Zac McChesney: 'Those first few events with little publicity and no IT set up, we had very few runners. Without Zac we would have been struggling, but he turned up to every one.' Zac had already started running in the normal Saturday parkruns. As soon as he heard about the juniors event he went to that as well, enjoying having the two different distances to run.

Like all parkrun events, Bushy juniors had a few teething problems. At the second event, the timer hadn't been started at the beginning of the run; thankfully there was a backup timer. 'We did everything wrong that anyone could do on a parkrun, I think. We learned the hard way. Then Nicki Clark, Event Director of Riddlesdown parkrun, came on board, which was lucky because she knows what she's doing. Everyone needs a Nicki!' He smiles and recalls a Sunday during the 2012 Olympics. 'I got a text from Nicki saying she'd forgotten the finish tokens. I tried everything possible to enable her to get a set from my house. In the end they ripped a cardboard box into bits, wrote the finish positions on those and people's barcodes on the back, and went back to the coffee shop after and had these bits of cardboard everywhere and had to process them all manually.'

Some problems have developed simply because the event has become so successful. 'When we started, I told the parks that we wouldn't ever have more than fifty runners. I remember getting to one hundred people at Bushy juniors and thinking, "We can't take any more than that!" And look at it now: we had over 400 people in October [2013]. You just don't know where parkrun is going to go, how big it's going to be. We've had to evolve, find ways of ensuring that as it has got bigger it's still safe for the children.'

Paul thinks that in some ways the 300 to 400 runners over the 2K is even more hectic than 1,000 runners coming through the finish for the main Bushy parkrun. With the shorter distance, there's a much narrower time period during which the bulk of runners finish, with three or more a second at the peak. It gets very congested at seventeen to eighteen minutes but then it's all over very quickly compared to the 5K parkruns.

All goes well so long as everyone keeps moving, but… 'we had one kid come through who had obviously been drinking a blue sports drink and vomited it all over the finish line and everyone else had to run though it. And when it hit its peak and we were really having problems getting them through the funnel, one of the children decided to stop and pull his socks up! While this was hilarious, it meant that a bottleneck formed really quickly and they were all piling into the back of each other… So you assess all the safeguarding aspects, but you can't allow in the risk assessment for a kid pulling his socks up. And it was a moment of great stress for the volunteers, but of course the child was completely unaware of what was going on behind him.'

And then there's the decidedly unglamorous side of junior parkrun, such as washing the sticky finish tokens!

We want one too!

Once the word got out about Bushy juniors, other people wanted these events for their own communities.

Forest of Dean juniors started in January 2011 and generally attracts forty or fifty runners. Dave Lucas, the Event Director at Forest of Dean parkrun, saw online that Bushy juniors was happening and thought that it would be good to have such an event for his local juniors, fitting in with their cross-country training. Because the format for the junior parkruns had not been set, except for distance, Dave chose the last Saturday of the month at 10 o'clock. 'We get sixty to eighty people for the main parkrun and quite a few are parents who are ready to stay and marshal, or run with their younger children, and we only have to move two signs to convert the 5K main parkrun course to the 2K juniors course, so it works very well for us. On Sundays, we would have to bring people in again, and many of the parents are off doing their longer run – ten or twelve miles or whatever.' About half of the junior runners each week come from the Forest of Dean AC, but Dave also encourages participation by other children, for example by giving talks to schools telling them about the event and encouraging them to let their pupils know about it.

Savill Garden junior parkrun in Windsor Great Park, Surrey, started in October 2012 with 43 runners at the inaugural event. Like Bushy juniors, it takes place on the first Sunday in each month, but at 9.30 am.

The driving force was John Ricketts. He had taken his daughters to run Bushy juniors, but then they moved and naturally he wanted a junior parkrun near his new home. He contacted parkrun HQ and was told that they would back him if he could get the necessary permissions from Windsor Great Park. Through his daughters' school, he managed to organise a meeting with the Superintendent of Parks, Tom Jarvis, and he got Paul Sinton-Hewitt to come with him to the meeting. John had already worked out his preferred route, at the Savill Garden. He went to the meeting armed with all the reasons why it should be there rather than tucked away at the back of the park: there was a café, and parking; he pointed out the potential revenue to the park from people going into the shop after the run. He explained that if they started at 9.30, they would be finished by 10 o'clock when the garden opened, and Tom Jarvis agreed to allow a trial of three months, with an initial test in September.

Very different from Bushy juniors, this is multi-terrain, including road, trail and grass, with an uphill finish to the lawns. The toddler area there is a definite bonus. John said, 'The park superintendent was supportive, but also somewhat anxious initially. After six months he said to me, "I suppose I should be bringing my children to do this," and he embraced it. He's told me that it has been really useful for him, giving him the chance to see the park through the eyes of a park user, a perspective he wouldn't otherwise have had.'

The event has grown solely by word of mouth, with children telling their friends about the run and encouraging them to try it. Paul Graham, who advised his old training partner on the practical and safety aspects, and helped to risk assess the course, commented, 'He was disappointed with the numbers in the first year but it took us two years to get to that size – the expectations have obviously moved.' In May 2014, 134 children ran.

Most of the volunteers are people who have children running in the event. For John, managing this event has been a fantastic chance for him to give something back to running. 'It gives young people a chance to run and enjoy running and get a feel for what cross-country running is about, but it's all in the sight of their parents, so there's not a lot of harm can come to them. That's really rewarding; the children and their parents really appreciate it.' John also notes that there are not many opportunities for children under eleven to participate in running competitively. He thinks that the junior parkruns provide a fantastic stepping stone at which they can push themselves if they want to do so, and can hopefully get the running bug and go on to enjoy running for the rest of their lives.

Woodley junior parkrun, the fourth of the original monthly juniors events, started in April 2013, also on the first Sunday in the month at 11 o'clock, initially with 44 runners. Anthony Collins started the push for this event, and asked Jenny Oakley if she would come with him to meetings with two local councils, Reading and Wokingham, to see if either was interested in the idea of a junior parkrun and would help to fund it. As it turned out, Wokingham Council, which had recently provided funding to start up Woodley parkrun, had set aside money which could be used to set up a junior parkrun. The leisure director was delighted with how successful the main parkrun event was and wanted to have the juniors in the same park, which made the choice of venue very easy. Inevitably there were one or two glitches, with a lot of safety and child safeguarding aspects to be worked out. They have also had to designate an alternative course for very wet weather when the normal course can get flooded.

After only a few months, a change of job took Anthony Collins out of the area, and Jenny's husband Nick became her co-Event Director. They divide the tasks, Nick carrying out the pre-run briefings and starting off the runs, while Jenny is in charge of the social media side. 'We're very grateful for the help we get from the main Woodley and Reading Event Directors, who have children and bring them to the juniors,' Jenny said. 'They're very helpful with the results processing – it's easy to forget something when you're only doing the processing once a month, although we think we've got it now.'

'It's great to see a hundred or more children, who have all chosen to be there, with beaming faces – the enthusiasm rubs off on everybody,' Jenny said. 'Seeing them all warming up simultaneously and putting their all into it always makes me smile. One of the volunteers who leads the warm up, who is also a teacher, said that if the children she taught were this enthusiastic, her job would be totally different.'

Jenny and Nick's own children like the juniors event because it's shorter than the main parkruns, and because they can run it on their own, rather than having to stay with a parent, as well as the camaraderie of being in a group of other children, rather than mainly adults. Since adults do accompany some of the younger children, Nick always reminds the children, during the briefing, that they must stay with their grown-ups so the grown-ups don't get lost! He loves that they also get children who, part way round the course, tell their parents to leave them, saying, 'I'm okay now.'

juniors goes weekly

Early in 2013, Chrissie Wellington, four-times Ironman Triathlon World Champion, was appointed as head of the juniors parkrun series.

In 2004, Chrissie Wellington was working in international development policy with Defra when she found triathlon, or triathlon found her, and (on the back of a lot of hard work, including altitude training as part of her daily life while working in Nepal) she rocketed to the top, turning professional in 2007 and winning the Ironman World Championships four times in five years: 2007 to 2009 and 2011 (missing 2010 due to illness). Each Ironman triathlon involves a 2.4 mile (3.86K) swim, then a cycle ride of 112 miles (180.25K) and finally a 26.2 mile (42.2K) run, i.e. a marathon. When she decided to retire from international competition, Chrissie realised that as a high-calibre professional athlete she had a platform on which she could combine sport and development, her two passions, and

junior parkrun: it's for the kids!

she vowed to use this as an opportunity to effect positive change, to provide a sporting legacy that would be about 'so much more than victories and times'.

Chrissie Wellington met Paul Sinton-Hewitt at an event and they quickly connected due to their shared belief in the power of sport to make a change: to increase not only physical activity but also wider social participation. She told Paul of her desire to get involved in something that would overcome the barriers that children face in getting involved in physical activity, and they started wondering if they could work together to make something happen. Initially they considered a school-based running event, but given the success of the four existing monthly junior parkruns, their focus shifted to further developing the junior parkrun series.

Paul, with Tom Williams, soon invited Chrissie to lead the development of this new series of junior parkrun events. Paul Graham, pioneer of the junior parkruns, thinks she's a great choice to get the juniors series moving. He noted, 'parkrun works because it's community-based and people want to be involved in it. If you tried to force people, it wouldn't work. Running is a cool thing to do; we need to get that message across, that it's fun, and it can open up opportunities. It also develops transferable skills that they're going to need later on in life.' He thought that Chrissie would significantly assist in communicating that message.

After considerable research and extensive internal and external consultation with a wide variety of individuals and organisations, Chrissie drafted and finalised the junior parkrun policy. The rationale of both Chrissie and parkrun HQ was to encourage young people to get involved in regular, habitual physical activity and a key shift was to make the events weekly. Building on Paul Graham's research before he choose the 2K distance for Bushy juniors, further research and additional consultation with child development experts confirmed that this was a safe distance for the weekly format. Allowing parents to accompany their children during the run (although adults don't get a time or finish position) encourages family participation and engagement in physical activity.

As part of her role, Chrissie developed a parkrun-specific child safeguarding policy. 'I sought advice from a variety of organisations, including the Amateur Swimming Association and UK Athletics, as well as from a number of parkrun Ambassadors and other parkrunners with DBS [Disclosure and Barring Service] experience,' said Chrissie. 'It was vital for us to follow not only legislative requirements but also best practice, therefore the Event Directors and Run Directors for each event have to undergo checks. UK Athletics is carrying out those checks for us in England and Wales, NI Athletics in Northern Ireland, and Children 1st/Scottish Athletics in Scotland.' As she points out, child safeguarding is so much more than just a security check on a few individuals, and they have put in place the policies, processes and procedures that she and the rest of the parkrun team feel will best safeguard children at all parkrun events.

The pioneering junior parkruns remained monthly, at least initially (Woodley juniors changed to weekly in August 2014), but all new junior parkruns starting up are weekly. So far these are only found in the UK.

Southampton junior parkrun was one of the first two weekly events to start. James Saunders had previously got two 5K parkruns up and running and had wanted to get a juniors event going in the area for a couple of years. 'For the younger children, the main parkrun events may be okay occasionally but they are too long really. I wanted a parkrun which both my sons, including seven-year-old Daniel, could really run and enjoy.' In 2013 he started serious discussions with Chrissie Wellington and others at parkrun HQ about the proposed weekly junior parkruns, saying he would really like to start one. Major preparatory work included, in parallel, applying for funding, looking at and fulfilling the required child safeguarding procedures, and looking for suitable 2K courses, with initial searching using online mapping tools followed by trips to the potential venues. The venue and course in Riverside Park was finalised with a long lap of 1.3 kilometres followed by a shorter lap of 0.7 kilometres and was measured accurately to determine the proper start and finish locations.

In addition to all the usual requirements for starting up a parkrun, including filling in the risk assessment and checking the electronic and other equipment, the child safeguarding policy had to be printed out in full and summary versions prepared, as well as course maps, inventory lists to make sure everything got to each event and came back home afterwards, writing notes for the pre-run briefing to marshals and the one to runners, starting to develop the volunteers' roster…

James started to publicise the event via a dedicated Facebook page set up by Danny Norman, and via Twitter, also using phone calls, emails and a local newspaper to spread the word and ask for volunteers. The first run was held on 24 November 2013, with 68 runners. The first finishers that day were Sam Costley in 6:44 (still the record after 28 events) and Isla Allan in 8:07 (which she bettered on the 28th run). It continues to attract more than sixty runners on average, passing one hundred for the first time in March 2014 and repeatedly in May 2014.

Roundhay junior parkrun in Leeds also started on 24 November 2013, with 66 runners, and in May 2014 passed the one hundred runner mark twice. Graham Pawley, the Event Director, is a keen parkrunner, having started off at Hyde Park (the original Leeds parkrun) before moving over to Roundhay parkrun where he is now Event Director.

Graham became aware of the junior parkruns in spring 2013 when four-year-old Daniel Goldsmith featured in the parkrun UK newsletter as 'parkrunner of the week', with Bushy juniors as his home parkrun. Thinking that this was a great idea, he contacted Paul Sinton-Hewitt to find out about setting one up, and Paul explained about the forthcoming development of parkrun juniors as weekly events.

Finding the venue – Roundhay – and getting permissions was not a problem, although raising the necessary £3,000 to get the run started was more of a challenge. 'We got £1,500 from Leeds City Council from their Area Well-being Fund for this section of Leeds, which was useful, and some from the Olympic legacy fund Sportsmakers and raised the rest by whatever means necessary, including selling cakes and rattling buckets at the local supermarket.' It took a further six weeks to get all the necessary elements in place, including a team of volunteers.

Designing the course involved a few false starts. Graham's original choice had to be abandoned because it had a downhill start – there is too much risk in a junior parkrun of children tripping or falling if the start or finish are downhill. No sooner had the course been chosen then they realised it would be icy in winter and had to rapidly design an alternative winter course on grass – with a soft landing if anyone did fall. The course is also designed with child safeguarding in mind: for the winter out-and-back course, each of the five marshals can see at least two others, one on either side. The summer course is two laps and the runners are in sight of the start and finish practically the whole time, but there are still six marshals around the route.

The volunteer team is almost entirely different from the core team active in the Saturday Roundhay parkrun; mainly, the volunteers are parents who would be hanging around anyway and are very happy to help instead of just standing waiting for their children to finish the run.

Graham Pawley has noticed that most of the runners at the moment are in the eight to ten years age group, probably because – as Paul Graham had noted previously – there are very few opportunities for children of this age to take part in any sort of structured sporting activity. 'For the boys, there is rugby and so on as they get a bit older, but for the girls there is not even that, as we are very aware, having three daughters. There's not a girl's football or rugby culture and there are no netball courts, for example.' He thinks it will be interesting to see whether the children running the junior parkrun regularly will stick with it as they reach their teens, or will go off to do other sports.

Wimbledon Park junior parkrun was the first junior parkrun to begin in 2014, with a trial event on 5 January and the first proper run on 19 January, with 68 runners and a starting course record of 7:32 by Alice Harray. Paul Graham left Bushy juniors in the capable hands of Nicki Clark on 5 January to go and help make sure the test event went smoothly, and was there for the next couple of events.

Expansion and encouragement

Expansion of the junior parkrun series has been quite rapid, with twenty weekly and four monthly events in place by the end of June 2014 (more than 1,000 children participating weekly) and eleven more in the pipeline. With more than thirty further enquiries having been received from communities across the UK, there is obviously a demand for these events.

In keeping with parkrun's ethos of encouraging habitual participation, in May 2014 coloured wristbands were introduced to be awarded to children running in the juniors events. Based on the lengths of long-distance running events, the blue wristband is for a cumulative half marathon so is awarded after eleven junior parkruns (which actually adds up to 22 kilometres, so slightly over the half-marathon distance of 21 kilometres (13.1 miles). The green Marathon band is awarded for 42 cumulative kilometres (26.2 miles), i.e. 21 junior runs, and the orange Ultra Marathon band is awarded for children who have clocked up 100 kilometres, i.e. fifty junior parkruns. When these were launched they were also awarded retrospectively to the children who had previously reached these milestones.

Chrissie realises that it is important that the events develop organically, in response to demand from the local communities. At the same time, she sees the possibility that some of the areas which could most benefit from a junior parkrun – areas where there are few athletics or other physical activity outlets for young people – might also be less likely to recognise the benefits that such an event could bring to their community and, therefore, less likely to ask for one. Paul Graham agrees that providing junior parkruns in areas where safe outlets for running are otherwise lacking, such as inner city areas, is particularly important.

Chrissie understands that encouraging such communities will be a major challenge and an important part of her role. It might involve ambassadors providing outreach into these communities, helping them to have the information they need to decide whether they want a junior parkrun for their young people, to stimulate demand and build capacity to manage the events.

She acknowledges that there are barriers to young people participating in sports, and she is considering how those obstacles can best be overcome. parkrun provides a hugely valuable means of overcoming some of these barriers: it's free, regular, open to all, welcoming; there's no need for specialised clothing or other equipment. However, there's still more work to be done to break down the barriers for all children.

'We need to work with the schools, with the local community centres and with outreach centres in those communities,' Chrissie said. 'We need to make physical activity, running, appealing to young people, trendy even. They need to realise that these events are free, they can wear what they like and nobody is going to look at them and tell them they're not dressed appropriately. They can come with their friends, as often or as rarely as they want to, they don't have to commit to it in advance, they don't even have to register if they don't want to – they can just turn up when they want to.' She added, 'junior parkrun is an amazing way of getting children – and their families – active. The snowball has only just begun to roll and I am so excited about what the future holds for the series and for parkrun generally!'

12

Behind the scenes at parkrun HQ

It's a really, really good bunch of people and it works really well, this distributed thing with two in London and two in Glasgow and one in Sunderland.

Alan Dempster, UKTT systems support and development

parkrun HQ isn't really a place, it's a group of people, working together from different physical locations. The closest there is to a physical HQ is the converted shed at the bottom of Paul Sinton-Hewitt's garden. The rest of the team members are based all over the country and beyond, with Anita Afonso in France and the Country Managers each in their own parkrunning country.

Modern technology, providing not just email but private messaging spaces and multi-person conference call facilities, makes it much easier for people at disparate locations to keep in touch with each other throughout the working day. Using a group messaging system 'helps us to all feel more connected,' Chris Wright says.

When I visited parkrun HQ, the little office was housing not only Paul, his wife Jo, and Chris Wright, but three large boxes of stopwatches waiting to be sent out to new parkruns. This wouldn't have been too much of a problem except for the fact that some of them had arrived from the manufacturer with a daily alarm set. Not all the watches were set to the same time, so they were beeping for thirty seconds or so at random intervals through the day, sometimes alone and sometimes in chorus. After a particularly noisy ten minutes Chris announced that he'd had enough: the boxes would be banished to the storeroom.

Who's who at HQ...

For historical reasons, the UK is home not only to parkrun UK staff but also people working for UKTT: the technical people who develop and maintain not only the visible websites but also all the essential background technical infrastructure powering those websites and crunching all the results.

Nearly everyone working for parkrun UK or UKTT started off as ordinary, enthusiastic parkrunners. They had generally been giving their time as regular volunteers, on management teams, or offering computer or other expertise, well before they were employed by parkrun. The whole team is steeped in the ethos of parkrun and is working for the organisation because they believe in it.

UKTT staff include Paul Sinton-Hewitt, Chris Wright, Alan Dempster, Jane Niven and Richard Leyton.

Paul Sinton-Hewitt

Paul was born in Rhodesia (now Zimbabwe) in 1960 and moved to South Africa when he was six months old. His father grew up in Scotland while his mother was a second generation Dutch South African. Finding himself in boarding school in South Africa from the age of five, it was a foregone conclusion that Paul would be involved in some way with sport. Not very good at ball sports, Paul found himself focussing on running and swimming and represented his school in the 800 metres, 1500 metres and cross-country, and butterfly in the pool. In his final years at school he represented his province, Western Transvaal, in the aquathon.

In the early eighties, while Paul attended university in Durban, a family friend asked if he would second him at the Comrades Marathon. Not understanding the enormity of the task, Paul joined his friend, Bruce Sandilands, fifteen kilometres outside the Pietermaritzburg start line and ran with him to the gates of Kingsmead Stadium in Durban [about 75 kilometres]. Paul had never done any distance running before that. It goes without saying that he didn't run again for a very long time.

Paul joined the Rocky Road Runners running club in Parkview, Johannesburg when he was 23. He started doing local road races covering most of the popular distances. He ran at work most days where he met and befriended Noel de Charmoy – a Comrades silver medallist – and Brian Chamberlain – the winner of the Two Oceans Marathon in 1977 and 1978. These two individuals were most influential in directing Paul's running and in 1984 he entered and completed his first marathon, the Johannesburg Marathon, in 3:15. Paul went on to run his fastest marathon at Stellenbosch in 1988 in a time of 2:36.

Paul's initial inspiration for starting parkrun was to offer a class of event that did not exist locally, namely a weekly, 5K time trial, and to ensure that he stayed in touch with his friends as he had suffered a long-term injury keeping him away from the running club.

Paul, the founder of UKTT and of parkrun, only started working for parkrun/UKTT as his full-time job in 2010. Previously, while working full time in the corporate world, Paul handled all his work for parkrun in his spare time. In 2012 he passed on the role of UK Country Manager to Tom Williams. Paul is still the driving force behind the global development of parkrun.

Chris Wright

A member of Ranelagh Harriers, Chris heard people talking about the Bushy Park Time Trial, finally went along one Saturday morning – and got shouted at for going the wrong way, so nearly didn't go back! However, he was there for the first anniversary and he started to get caught up in the atmosphere and the social aspect, as well as chasing PBs to confirm his own improvement. His first contribution other than as a runner was when he produced a new version of the Bushy course, with photographs and a turn-by-turn guide; this was put up on the BPTT website. He eventually became the Bushy parkrun Event Director, meanwhile acquiring the nickname 'Crispy' – his middle initial being 'P'.

When the idea of starting up other events beside Bushy Park was emerging, Paul asked Chris if he would consider working for the fledgling organisation, to help with the day-to-day management – which was how Chris came to be the first paid employee of parkrun, while Paul continued in his day job in project management and worked on parkrun in his free time.

In the early days, Chris's job involved developing the policies for what was, and was not, appropriate for the organisation. Paul, Chris and other key people worked out the core principles that we now take for granted: parkrun is free; the length of the course is 5K and is measured as accurately as possible; children are permitted to join in, since this is a timed run, not a race. On Saturdays, Chris and Paul manually uploaded the data sent by email from the events, and processed the times, producing the information about PBs and so on. 'We would be there until 6 or 6.30 pm, back when there were six to ten events,' Chris said. 'If we still did it like that we wouldn't have all the results processed in a week.' This led to the other part of his job: looking at the basic computer systems which Paul had started off and Stuart Lodge had developed further, then developing a proper database to hold all the results. This facilitated the later change to Alan Dempster's web-based system for results processing. He was also in charge of setting up the websites for the new parkrun events as they started up, and for a website redesign in 2009.

Alan Dempster

Alan, a very keen runner favouring 5K and 10K distances, discovered parkrun in December 2008 while scouring the race listings for races. He couldn't believe that the listed Glasgow parkrun was really on every week but he turned up and it was real! This was only the third running of the Glasgow event, with just 22 runners, Alan coming in eleventh with a time of 21:29. He started volunteering the very next week, continued both running and volunteering during 2009 and by the middle of 2009 he was run directing as part of the core team. For Alan, this was an event and community which was dependable, where he could socialise as little or as much as he wanted, and where he found himself making new friends.

During 2009, between contracts as a software developer and studying towards some professional exams, Alan wrote a web application covering the results submission functions of the Field Management System (FMS, used by the web teams to process results) in a more user-friendly way. In 2010 he showed it to Richard Leyton, who was already helping with parkrun IT. Richard liked it and showed it to Paul, who also liked it. Early in 2011 Alan travelled to London to spend a few weeks integrating his new system – basically the webFMS which we now all use, with the parkrun database. parkrun happened to be looking for another IT expert and Alan was offered the job, which he took, working from home back in Glasgow. It was only after Richard also started officially working for UKTT that they got a little office.

Next, Alan worked on adding user authentication to the new system, and took over from Crispy the job of creating the websites for the new events. This was also when parkrun started offering texting of results in the UK, so he was involved in setting that up. 'There was a lot of maintenance of existing systems as well such as web pages written by Chris in PHP [a programming language] which needed occasional tweaking to cope with the increasing and changing demands of the growing number of events.' In 2012 he started working to replace the Volunteer Management System, at that time an Access application, with a web application which is now integrated into the webFMS. Since then he has worked on other aspects of the results processing system, and, together with Richard, moved the event websites from the old system to the new Wordpress platform.

Jane Niven

Jane started parkrunning at Sunderland parkrun on its second run and got instantly hooked. When the Event Director was going on holiday for several weeks, she volunteered to stand in – and she's been the ED ever since.

Jane ended up working for UKTT after Paul tweeted that they were looking for someone on the development side. Reading the job spec, she decided it was too technical, but after several conversations with Paul, Jane found herself leaving her job of seventeen years to work for UKTT. A major part of her job is answering queries from parkrunners worldwide, which come in mainly via the runner support form online but sometimes as direct emails. Most she answers herself; when necessary she passes the query on to someone else in UKTT, or to the relevant parkrun Country Manager.

The other side of Jane's job is setting up the websites for the new events and making updates to websites of ongoing events. The standardised format of the websites makes this relatively straightforward once the information has been provided by the event teams, but she does need the correct data, in the standard format, in order for it to work. For example, the template includes the set text: 'Every week we grab a post parkrun coffee at...', so it is important for the event team to provide an actual location to finish the sentence. 'I have to be very strict about keeping to the template,' Jane explained, 'because once I change it for one event, other teams will expect that and we just wouldn't be able to keep on top of it – not with 400 plus events.' She added, 'The parkrun Ambassadors help the new teams with the information, because they understand what's needed.'

Each course map has to be created in Google Maps – that too is now being delegated to event teams, but final polishing is Jane's job – and the event's Flickr page needs to be set up for the photographs. Jane also helps event teams when they have queries about the FMS, but as much as possible she explains to the event teams how they can manage things for themselves, so that they can do it on another occasion without needing her input, rather than (as would be quicker, if it was just once) sorting out the problem herself.

Richard Leyton
Richard first became involved with parkrun when he started up Glasgow parkrun (now Pollok parkrun) in 2008. In the first years he mostly volunteered, but he's since managed to run often enough to join the 100-club and has run at twenty-two other parkrun venues besides Pollok Park, mainly in Scotland but as far afield as Gorky Park in Russia in 2014.

As a freelance computer expert, Richard had some free time, so in early 2010, when Paul was having problems trying to send out the weekly newsletter to thousands of people, due to the email-hosting company putting in new limits, Richard offered to help. He solved the problem by setting up a mail server to send the emails directly, using a spare laptop of Paul's and some software to set up a virtual machine running the computer operating system UNIX. The rest of the system, the website and so on, was also starting to creak. It had originally been designed for the single Bushy Park Time Trial; by 2010 it could no longer cope with the number of events, particularly with the number of photos people were uploading in addition to everything else. So Richard started to help with short-term fixes initially, and later a move to a new machine just for the website – as well as two for the emails.

It was only early in 2012 that Richard started to get paid at all for what he was doing for parkrun, and he became a UKTT employee during 2013. One of the big areas he worked on from 2012 to 2013 was capturing all the information from the old event websites and moving it over to the new platform. The main thing, he explained, was that while the new system looks very like the old system for the visitor, it can cope with the much higher demands as more and more events start up.

parkrun UK employees include Country Manager Tom Williams, Anita Afonso, Joanne Sinton-Hewitt, Danny Norman and Helen Hood.

Anita Afonso

Anita was an experienced events organiser in Europe, involved in organising a variety of events including the Rugby World Cup in France in 2007, when she moved from France to the UK in 2008 to improve her English. She was working for Nike when her boss mentioned to her that there was this small company starting up and he thought she might be interested in working for them. After taking part in a parkrun and chatting with Paul and Chris, hearing about their vision for the future, to grow parkrun throughout the UK, she found she was definitely interested.

Anita joined parkrun as the second paid employee on 1 April 2009, taking on the role of Event Activator, helping any community which was interested in starting a new parkrun. 'It's been an amazing journey,' Anita said. 'Arriving in a new country and less than a year later finding myself travelling round the whole country, meeting all these people. I never expected that when I moved to England, but I loved it. People have been so welcoming everywhere – Scotland, Wales, Manchester, Newcastle – people have been great.'

'Every time starting up a new parkrun,' said Anita, 'is like having a new baby. You're as nervous as the local team when they hold their first event – and then you have to leave.' One of the benefits of the job (apart from learning to understand varied accents) was that Anita knew all the parkrun events and got to know all the Event Directors. With the increasing expansion of parkrun, some of that job had to be taken up by other people and now the volunteer Ambassadors play a large part in helping new events.

Tom Williams

Tom became involved with parkrun when he set up Leeds parkrun while working as a lecturer at the university. In September 2010, when Tom's contract with the university came to an end, he let Paul know that he was available to help, as he would love to be involved with parkrun.

By late 2010 the number of potential and actual events in development was becoming too many for Anita to manage. Early in 2011, therefore, Tom started working for parkrun as the

Event Activator for North England, helping event teams with all aspects from measuring the course to training, helping teams get their volunteers started and so on. Towards the end of 2011, Paul Sinton-Hewitt was becoming swamped with trying to cover so much for both parkrun UK and the global organisation, so he asked Tom if he would become the UK's Country Manager. 'I was the Operations Manager really, at that point,' said Tom, 'while Paul was still in charge of the commercial and strategy sides for parkrun UK.' Near the end of 2012, Tom became the Country Manager for the UK in full, with Paul moving totally to working for UKTT.

Tom's role includes responsibility for the day-to-day operation of parkrun UK, including training, sorting out any conflicts, providing support, and dealing with the relationships with the commercial sponsors and other partners. He also writes the leader column for the weekly parkrun newsletter.

Danny Norman

Danny started running at Bushy Park Time Trial in August 2005. He became quite heavily involved at Bushy parkrun, doing all the volunteer roles at some time or another, writing a lot of the run reports, and then presenting the parkrun show *podcasts with Tom Williams and Martin Yelling. He also developed the original Time Trials tree logo.*

Danny left his artwork job in 2011. In spring 2012, Paul offered him a job to not only produce *the parkrun show* podcast but also work on a variety of other aspects such as editing the newsletter; driving forward the social media, brand and communications elements; and designing bespoke posters. So Danny became parkrun's Social Media and Communications Manager. 'Doing the podcasts,' he says, 'is brilliant. The interaction, the engagement you get from people. It's amazing. You go to different parkrun events and people are delighted to see you, to have you there, and it gives a personal side helping to engage the parkrunners.'

Joanne Sinton-Hewitt

Initially Joanne, as Paul's wife, just supported Paul in his time-consuming hobby of putting on a 5K timed run in Bushy Park every week: running sometimes, volunteering more than she ran – and putting up with the fact that this little timed run was taking over the house and all of Paul's time outside work. Once he converted the summerhouse at the bottom of the garden into a home office at least the computer was no longer in the corner annex of their bedroom – but parkrun still dominated the household.

Joanne's involvement in the administration side of parkrun came gradually, first helping to answer emails from runners – most of which were along the lines of, 'How do I get a barcode?' and, 'I didn't have my barcode, can you add me into the results?' When Anita went on maternity leave Joanne became involved in new event activation, and her responsibilities in that area later expanded. In 2013, as much of that work became shared with the parkrun Ambassadors, Joanne became Operations Manager. In this role she worked more with the teams that were already established, helping them with any equipment needs, making sure all the risk assessments were kept up to date and logged into the parkrun system, assisting teams to deal with and log any incidents, and helping with any complaints. In September 2013, with the new weekly junior parkrun series starting up, she also became the activator for those events.

Helen Hood

Helen had been running at Colwick parkrun since their third event in 2011, volunteering by the following week. She became Event Director about six months later, as well as becoming a parkrun Ambas-

sador, helping new events as they were set up in the Nottinghamshire area.

Helen started working for parkrun officially in 2014. She works in operations and has a very varied work life, including helping to develop the junior parkruns, writing parts of the UK newsletter for the main parkrun events and answering queries. 'I never know exactly what I'm going to do each day,' said Helen – and she likes it like that.

… and what they do

Over the past ten years, parkrun has grown from one event to more than 500, with the number of events almost doubling each year. The number of people working at HQ to keep everything running has not grown nearly as fast.

It's fair to say that parkrun bears some resemblance to the old saying about a swan – the average parkrunner most of the time just sees the serene surface, with the events taking place each Saturday followed by the results, run reports, photos and newsletters appearing. Meanwhile, the HQ team are working hard under the surface to keep everything working and looking good.

Paul wants to keep the HQ team as small as practical, minimising costs. Therefore part of the UKTT team's work involves designing the systems to enable parkrun event teams and individual parkrunners to manage most of their own data.

Event activation

Event activation in the UK involves both parkrun UK and UKTT personnel. For example, Joanne (parkrun UK) sends the new event team a list of possible equipment (hi-vis jackets, marker arrows, finish funnel supplies etc.), helps them work out what they need, orders it all and makes sure they get it. Meanwhile Paul

(UKTT) sets up a laptop with the software the new event will need to accept the data from the scanners and timers. And Jane (UKTT) takes the information about the new event and adds it to their website pages.

Event support

Every Saturday, hundreds of parkrun events take place. In the next few hours, tens of thousands of parkrunners are notified of their results by email or text, with many going onto their parkrun's website to look at the complete day's results. A major part of the job of the UKTT team is making sure that all the software is up and running to allow all this to happen, and helping when there are problems.

While the runners settle down to their post-run coffee and chat, hundreds of event teams start to process the results. Inevitably, some teams encounter problems, so each week one member of the UKTT team – Paul, Chris, Alan, Jane or Richard – is on duty to help those volunteers. The number of telephone calls each Saturday can vary from just one or two to a dozen or more. 'Richard somehow always gets the weeks when there are lots of problems,' Alan said (and Richard agrees). 'Although this, too has been helped by the development of the parkrun Ambassadors. Often, people are unwilling to contact us for what they think is a trivial problem, but is one that they can't sort out themselves. Now, the new event teams have their local Ambassador they can call in the first instance, which they prefer.'

Once in a while, there are larger-scale problems. On rare occasions, something goes wrong with the parkrun servers on a Saturday morning and chaos results – or at least, delays in results getting through to the hundreds of event websites and the tens of thousands of individual parkrunners.

For the volunteer teams it can sometimes be hard to determine whether it's a laptop problem, an internet connection problem or a server-side problem. Initially it can be quite scary if something goes wrong, but experience brings a more relaxed attitude. If the connection fails repeatedly, then it is time to sit back, chat, have a tea or coffee and try again in ten minutes. Usually by then everything is fine. Just occasionally it still doesn't work.

My own solution at that point is to wait until I get home from the park then try again. If it still doesn't work then I put up a holding message on the Lloyd parkrun website and on Twitter, and wait. I also check Twitter and the global parkrun website for any information about a generalised problem. I try not to call if there appears to be a server-side problem: if whoever is on duty is busy getting the server sorted out then the last thing they need is dozens of event teams ringing up to ask if they have noticed the problem!

Non-urgent queries from event teams come into Event Support by email, are looked at by Paul or Chris initially through the week, then passed on to the most appropriate member of the team to solve.

Runner support

Queries from parkrunners nowadays come in via the contact form on the website. This can be reached from the global parkrun website, from each country's website, and from each individual event's website.

Before reaching the contact form, the parkrunner will have been directed to pages of FAQs designed to answer most of their questions and, when possible, help them to solve the problem themselves. For example, parkrunners can correct mistakes in their profiles, change their names (for example, to a nickname, or following marriage) and even change their email address, so long as they still have access to a link to their profile. The support page also provides a link by which parkrunners can contact their event team – the more appropriate step if there appears to be a results problem.

Runner queries reaching the HQ team are rapidly assessed and sent to the most appropriate person for reply. Additionally, queries can be tagged as to type, allowing later statistical analysis, and can be marked as pending (to be answered), on hold (waiting for the parkrunner to reply), and solved (solved!). This minimises the risk of a query getting lost in the system.

Donations

Once a week, Paul, not as part of his UKTT job but on a voluntary basis for parkrun UK, manages the donations made through the main and individual event websites.

Paul makes sure that each donation is credited to the correct event and thanks the person making the donation. Sometimes donations are made electronically by an Event Director after they have been given cash by a parkrunner, and the publicly available list of donations makes this clear. If donations come in without any accompanying note regarding which parkrun they are intended for, Paul does his best to work out which is the donor's home run and initially credits the money there. If it's not possible to work this out then the money is assigned to the general new event fund at this stage. The email sent to each donor offers them the opportunity to inform Paul if he's allocated the donation to the wrong event, and to tell him to which event it should be given.

All the emails from the donation processing site go into a folder where the whole parkrun HQ team and the accountant can see them and the system is set up so there is a permanent record of all the movements of monies. As the donations are processed they are automatically listed online within minutes, so everyone can see all the donations: who they are from, which event they are made to, and for each event, how much money has been donated, how much has been spent and how much remains in that event's 'pot'. This money is for the individual events to spend (with 15% of each donation to an individual event going to the overall new events fund) and is managed separately from central parkrun funds. Individual event teams are encouraged to use their money for things the event needs, not to save large amounts of money in their fund.

The kit pixies

No 'behind the scenes' description would be complete without mention of those unsung heroes of parkrun UK, the volunteer 'kit pixies' Ray and Ann Coward. In the UK, all the parkrun T-shirts for the 50-club, 100-club, 250-club and (for under-18s only) 10-club, are handled by Ray and Ann. This is a huge undertaking, which can involve picking out, packaging and posting more than 1,000 T-shirts a month. Once a month, Ray prints out pages showing, for each parkrun, the names of the people who have earned their T-shirts and their requested sizes, plus stickers listing the runner's name, size and parkrun. Then he, Ann and an assistant spend a day to a day and a half in the parkrun walk-in storage compartment, picking out all the T-shirts, sticking the labels on, and packaging them up for each event. After that, they take them home (in two cars!), arrange for couriers to collect the largest packages and spend another several hours at their friendly local post office, sending the rest of the packages.

Ray says it's fairly straightforward, except when they run out of stock, at which point there can be long delays. That's not surprising when you realise that the shirts have to be ordered, manufactured, shipped to the UK, sent for printing and returned to parkrun HQ before they can be sent out. It takes two months for a small order to be filled and three months or longer for a large order.

'I can understand people getting frustrated when their T-shirt takes months to arrive,' Ray said. 'Particularly for the younger children for whom ten runs is a big milestone. But there's nothing I can do to speed up the process.' In a way, this is an area in which parkrun is a victim of its own success. When the first black jackets were given to the first few people reaching one hundred parkruns, the present numbers of parkrunners could never have been dreamed about.

As parkrun continues to grow and expand globally, the small team at parkrun HQ works diligently to ensure that tens of thousands of runners can enjoy their Saturday parkrun (and their results) both now and in the future.

13

And now
for the news

And we get photos on the internet as well, thanks to
eager supporters.

Manghanita Kempadoo, Leeds parkrun

After the first Bushy Park Time Trial, Paul Sinton-Hewitt sent an
email to all the Ranelagh Harriers giving the results: reporting
back was an important part of the event right from the start. In
addition to providing the results, the local event teams, country managers and HQ team between them keep parkrunners informed about people, milestones and special events at their own
parkrun and more widely in the parkrun world.

parkrun newsletters

For many years a weekly newsletter has been provided on the parkrun website and emailed to parkrunners who have opted to receive it.

The newsletter covers a wide variety of subjects and areas of interest. Sometimes an issue concentrates on one important theme, while other newsletters cover several topics. For instance, in the newsletter of 25 March 2009, Paul Sinton-Hewitt highlighted the achievements of a group of novices from Winchester & District AC, who had graduated from their beginners running programme by completing the Basingstoke parkrun. He mentioned other milestones: the highest ever turnout across all the events (1,996, across eleven parkruns); the 265 runners at Bramhall parkrun, which set a record for number of runners at any event other than Bushy Park; three new course records and 27 age-category records – a section that was dropped from the newsletter later that year, with this information being provided elsewhere on the parkrun website.

Also in this issue was a request for volunteers to help at the London Marathon, and a sad notice of the death of Dave Davies, a regular Banstead Woods parkrunner. The 'feedback from the field' section included a note from someone for whom parkrun 'has got me back into competitive running after a 10 year lay-off' and one from a runner living in Canada, expressing how much they had enjoyed running Bushy parkrun while visiting family in the UK. The 'parkrunner of the week', Alyson Hoggarth from Albert Park, Middlesbrough parkrun, wrote, 'Where else can a bunch of people aged between about ten and over seventy get together, have fun and get exercise and all for free?'

And rounding it out was the regular 'Crispy Corner' from Chris Wright, which included a request for donations of laptops for new events and another for parkrunners who might be interested in working for parkrun on the IT side.

From very early on, Paul included messages from parkrunners. Reading the 'feedback from the field' is especially heartwarming as it always reveals the wide variety of parkrunners and the many ways in which parkrun has been beneficial and has positively changed their lives. There are also special thank you messages from parkrunners to particular volunteer teams or communities and sometimes notes about parkrunners' charity challenges.

Occasionally the newsletter carries tributes to parkrunners who have died. In the issue for 16 April 2009, Chris Phelan and Don Esslemont, co-directors of Banstead Woods parkrun, wrote of Ted Baker, Chairman of Reigate Priory AC and 'a stalwart of the local running community'. Chris expressed his condolences to Ted's family and friends, noting that he would be missed 'at Banstead Woods and beyond', and both men described the moving tribute from Reigate Priory runners.

Don Esslemont said that in his thirty years of running, 'I can't recall another occasion when I have felt so overwhelmed and emotional by the scenes experienced on Saturday.' He went on to describe how the club members, all wearing their red running club T-shirts, ran round the course as a block, then as they approached the finish, 'with fifty yards to go they stopped, parted to each side of the track, and applauded all of the slower runners through to the finish, before reforming into an orderly single file and walked one by one through the finish line.'

The tradition of the newsletters has continued as parkrun has grown and expanded into other countries. Each country's newsletter has its own character and its own publication schedule. As in the example above, there is always a section of general news, highlighting recent events or an important aspect of parkrun. There are useful listings of forthcoming event cancellations and of anniversaries. There's 'feedback from the field' and a 'parkrunner of the week' or a 'volunteer profile'. Other sections vary – the UK has the 'parkrun corner' written by a different UK parkrun Ambassador in each issue (continuing from the old Crispy Corner); Australia includes 'Professor Alan's Essential Stats'; South Africa provides news from several of the individual events in each issue and New Zealand has a section from each of their events.

The newsletters also provide regular reminders about aspects such as barcodes, volunteering, the need for children under eleven years old to be accompanied and the support site where parkrun FAQs can be found. Additionally, there are various messages from parkrun's sponsors including information about giveaways, competitions or which events sponsors will be visiting.

In the UK, there's also a junior newsletter containing news specific to the junior events. This is emailed to junior parkrunners and is, like the main newsletters, available in the news section of the parkrun UK website.

Between newsletters, the website news pages sometimes carry press releases and additional announcements about special events. The news section on the global website is used particularly for welcoming new parkrun events, but also for other news of global parkrun significance, including, for example, the publication of the SparkLE research paper about the beneficial effects of parkrun (see chapter 16). Occasionally there's information about upgrades and new features on the technical side powering the results, for any interested techies. Very occasionally, it's been used to explain a technical problem leading to delays in results.

In June 2014, all the newsletters contained a very special story. In the Queen's Birthday Honours list, 4 June 2014, Peter Paul Sinton-Hewitt, founder of parkrun, was awarded a CBE for services to grassroots sports participation. Every Country Manager, as well as Chrissie Wellington for the juniors, was delighted to report this. Paul responded on the global news page, thanking everyone who has been involved with parkrun.

Run reports

Each parkrun's website includes a news section, covering local races, notices of cancellations or special events, and particularly the weekly run report. At its most basic, this can simply be a list of the computer-generated statistics, such as fastest finishers, highest age-graded runners and numbers of personal bests, which are automatically sent to each parkrun event.

However, most run reports are far more than that. A good report tells a story of that week's parkrun and parkrunners. It may highlight outstanding runs and amazing finishes; thank volunteers; publicise good deeds such as pacing a slower runner to a PB, or stopping to help someone who was having problems; celebrate important events in the lives of regular parkrunners, including milestones such as reaching the 50-club. Additionally it might record birthdays, wedding dates, wedding anniversaries, births of children of parkrunners, and parkrunner deaths and funerals.

For many people, writing the run report – perhaps initially with some trepidation – has been their first experience of this kind of writing and has led them to discover an ability they didn't know they had. For example, Jo Quantrill, a long-time Banstead Woods parkrunner said, 'I got a lot more self-confident through writing the report and other volunteering roles and know others who have too.' Run reports are very variable and individual. If written by someone who was helping at the finish funnel, they might provide descriptions of an amazing race down the back stretch for 156th and 157th place, or a mother and daughter coming in together. Alternatively, written from the point of view of someone running that day, they might comment on the depth of the mud round the far corner, dodging (or failing to dodge) the puddles, the effort up the hill or the push into the wind. Each run report is different, with different aspects emphasised – and that's a good thing.

Occasionally reports are written in unusual formats, including poems, plays and a 'David Hatinburrow's' *Life on Earth*-style narration: 'We're here on the left bank of the Hutt River to observe an unusual ritual. Early every Saturday a diverse assortment of creatures gather; they come in all shapes, sizes, colours, and levels of fitness. You can see some of them starting to gather now behind me, as the rising sun paints the clouds tangerine. Some partake of pre-event exercise; stretching limbs, running for short distances, but most stand looking sleepy and cold in loose huddles.' (Script by Astrid van Meeuwen-Dijkgraaf, Porirua parkrun.)

Many run reports also include photographs, taken during the parkrun by a volunteer photographer or photographers. The pictures are also available on the dedicated photo section of each event's website, linked to a group pool on Flickr. Thus, anyone who has taken pictures and wants to share them can simply join the pool and upload their photos. Depending on the number of photographers and their enthusiasm, there might be dozens to hundreds of pictures associated with a given parkrun on any particular Saturday.

It's great to see yourself in the pictures, and it can help you to note a problem in your running form which needs correcting. On occasion the photographs prove invaluable to event teams trying to work out a results problem. They also capture some of the social side of parkrun, from pre-run banter and shedding of outer clothing while runners warm up, to groups of people standing near the registration area after their run, chatting and cheering in later finishers.

The equipment used to take these photographs varies hugely, from smartphones and point-and-click cameras to high-end SLRs. The dedication of regular photographers is amazing, since they not only take the photographs but also sort them out: discarding bad shots, cropping, and sometimes adding text (such as the date of the run), then upload them onto the web. Chris Phelan, Event Director at Banstead Woods, noted, 'The photographs as well as the weekly run report really help to keep people involved with the parkrun during the week, until the next event. Photographs are not a requirement of parkrun, but they do help to bring the community together.'

Chris also developed an excellent relationship with the local paper. He started providing basic information about the run – number of runners, first three male and female finishers, and other details, with pictures of the first male and female runners, and other pictures which seemed appropriate. Their sports editor introduced a weekly third-of-a-page article on the event, with at least one photograph and headlines based on the names of the first finishers. This extended knowledge about the run through not only the running community but also the local community in general, and the paper always provided a web link to the parkrun website for people wanting to know more.

Social media

In addition to the official parkrun websites, many parkruns are making good use of Facebook and/or Twitter. Not everyone uses these and Paul Sinton-Hewitt is very clear that they should be additions to, not substitutes for, the official parkrun websites – which are visited by many more people than use either Twitter or Facebook. In addition, not everyone chooses to be on Facebook or to use Twitter, so dedicated parkrun sites are essential. Some parkrun events and their associated communities do share information and photos predominantly on the event's Facebook page rather than the core event website. There's no doubt that Facebook is a great place for the community to hold a conversation, and it is evident that active parkrun event Facebook sites can be great for the community.

Personally, I love being able to see all the information about a parkrun – present and historical results, course details, news and photographs – all on the same website. However, the social media sites have provided a useful additional way by which parkruns can contact their parkrunners, whether to let them know the run report is up on the website, call for volunteers, or warn of problems or even a late cancellation, for example due to bad weather. Also, they provide an easy way for parkrunners to swap stories, photographs and information, and have, particularly via Facebook photo tagging, helped to spread the word about parkrun and contributed to its growth.

Then there are the group and individual blogs written by parkrunners, from runner's blogs occasionally mentioning parkrun, to dedicated parkrun fan sites.

the parkrun show

the parkrun show developed as an offshoot of *Marathon Talk* – podcasts about running, specifically marathon running, by runners, for runners (the other offshoot is *TalkUltra*, about distances longer than marathons).

Tom Williams proposed *the parkrun show* in 2011. By that time he and Martin Yelling had been creating the *Marathon Talk* podcasts for about eighteen months. Tom had been reading Danny Norman's run reports for Bushy parkrun, so he immediately thought of Danny to do *the parkrun show* podcasts with them, aiming to recreate the entertaining element from those reports. Danny remembers that on the very first occasion he was really nervous, wondering whether he would stumble over his words. Since then he's got very used to it!

And now for the news

Tom, Martin and Danny were co-hosts initially, then it was hosted by Danny and Tom, with Nicola Forwood joining them in March 2012. Later Tom dropped out as he got too busy, leaving Danny and Nicola, with various guest presenters when one or other is absent.

Nicola was originally a fan of *the parkrun show*, listening weekly and responding to polls and questions posed on the show, including coming up with a relevant film title for each parkrun (Danny particularly remembers *The Incredible Hull*). One week when Danny couldn't reach a parkrun, Nicola was requested to report on Conkers parkrun, and subsequently she was asked to become part of the team. Nicola brought a different view of parkrun: that of a slower runner, sometimes walking round with someone, later pushing her baby, Poppy, in a buggy – quite a contrast to the fast runners Danny, Tom and Martin. She provides an outlook to which many slower participants can relate.

The aim of *the parkrun show* is to provide a weekly light-hearted round-up of 'the goings on in parkrun world'. 'It's like catching up with your family,' said Nicola. It generally starts (after a bit of banter, of course) with a quick round-up of the statistics for that week, before the presenters talk about their most recent parkrunning experiences. Some time ago, Danny started running at a different parkrun every Saturday as often as possible, to provide something unique to the listeners each week. An unexpected spin-off from this, he found, was that, 'it's become an information resource for people, they go back and listen to an episode to find out about a particular event before they go there.' More recently, they've included sections from 'roving reporters'.

Then there are the parkrun highlights, including welcoming runners to the 250-club: at the time of the first podcast, Neil Sunderland was congratulated as only the fourth member of that club, after Darren Wood, John Hanscomb and Richard Fletcher.

Additional elements have included tweets of the week, mention of forthcoming inaugural parkruns, and interviews with Event Directors and a wide variety of interesting parkrunners. The show has evolved over time, expanding from thirty minutes to more than an hour and then back to thirty minutes.

Nicola has enjoyed being on the show for many reasons: it's given her an excuse to tour, she's loved bringing in the elements of parkrunning while pregnant and with a buggy, and she's got to know lots more people. Also, 'It's loads of fun. Danny has a great sense of humour.' She adds, more seriously, 'And he cares so much about parkrun.'

In 2013, Dave 'Robbo' Robertson and Ross Jeffries, who had been listening to *the parkrun show*, decided that Australia needed its own version. In the Australian show, after the presenters described where they had been, there were sections from the previous Saturday's launches and anniversaries, and a set of brief 'parkrun postcards' highlighting interesting bits and pieces from parkruns around the country. The show finished by letting listeners know what would be happening in the near future in parkrunland, particularly the following Saturday. 'We've enjoyed doing this,' Robbo said, 'and it's helped parkrunners to get a sense of what other events are like.' There was also a section where parkrunners asked numerical questions which they would like 'The Prof' (aka Alan Burrell, Event Director at Wynnum parkrun) to answer. This ran for fifty episodes, with the conversation then continuing on Facebook and Twitter.

All the websites, newsletters and run reports, supplemented by *the parkrun shows*, Facebook pages and Twitter, help to keep parkrunners entertained between their Saturday morning parkrun 'fixes'. As Bushy parkrunner Nick Rowe noted, 'Now each parkrun day my Facebook page is full with tales of various parkrun escapades – fast, slow, but all with a smile.'

14

Celebrations!

When I want to celebrate, parkrun is a great way to
get my running friends together without them having
to find money for a night out.

Gemma Rathbone, Leeds parkrun

There's a lot to celebrate at parkrun. Anniversaries in particular, but also achievements of individual runners, Christmas, New Year, and other annual or one-off events. At Bushy there are so many runners that it's rare for a week to go by without someone bringing cakes and champagne to celebrate their birthday, reaching the 100-club or another significant milestone. Other parkruns might not quite match that, but they're certainly equally enthusiastic.

parkrun: much more than just a run in the park

Anniversaries

At the end of the first year of Bushy Park Time Trial, Paul Sinton-Hewitt arranged an anniversary celebration. Food and drink was provided and the runners' achievements were celebrated with prizes, including the very first points prizes. Chris Wright was there. 'There was a big turn out,' he said, 'and the party – it changed the whole feel. There were T-shirts being handed out, and the kids were latching onto the event as something to be involved in.'

Andrew Lane, who had been at the inaugural run, agrees: 'The first anniversary was where it really took off – the photos, the food and drink, the prizes. The number of runners shot up amazingly – from the thirties to fifties right up to 155. That was the first time that there were more than one hundred runners.'

Anniversary runs are special. For a start, they're a great excuse for a bring-and-share picnic, with lots of cake, biscuits and other goodies – or in Australia, a barbecue. Many parkruns mark their anniversary in special ways. Most tack their anniversary celebrations on at the end of the run, but some have a separate event or an evening celebration.

For parkruns with an anniversary at the end of October, the proximity to Halloween provides a good excuse for a fancy dress (costume) parkrun with ghosts, skeletons, zombies, gorillas, witches and other monsters running round the park. Hillsborough, North Lakes (Queensland), Sheffield Hallam and Lloyd are among the events which run in the reverse direction to usual; some people think their course is harder the 'wrong' way round, while others prefer it.

At the first anniversary of Claisebrook Cove in 2013, the first occasion when any parkrun in Western Australia passed 200 participants, there was a pyjama party theme. Lots of people wore animal onesies, while the first person to finish was wearing a traditional long nightshirt and hat and carrying a night lantern. Canning River's first anniversary used a Disney theme; while many people carried Disney plush toys or wore Disney-themed T-shirts, others wore Mickey Mouse ears or even onesies!

Some of the anniversary cakes are quite elaborate. Many have the parkrun logo iced onto them and a candle for each year the event has been running. Others have intricate designs illustrating the individual course, with accurate contours, paths, trees... even volunteers in fluorescent bibs.

> *For the fifth anniversary of Bushy parkrun, in October 2009, there were special celebrations. As part of these, Danny Norman had prepared an amazing picture. Starting with the photograph of the first thirteen runners toeing the line at Bushy Park, and working with 4,000 image squares created from 991 archived images from Bushy Park parkruns (supplied by David Rowe), Danny built up a picture which, when viewed from a little distance, recreated that first line-up – a real labour of love. Danny also worked hard to bring together a book of photos of every member, to that date, of parkrun's 100-club, each wearing their black parkrun T-shirt, and gave this to Paul.*

At the anniversary, parkruns award the yearly points prizes. Individual parkruns vary in what other prizes or awards they give out, whether small tokens of appreciation to everyone who has volunteered during the year, or a trophy for the Volunteer of the Year, prizes for most PBs, greatest percentage improvement in running time, or others. At Banstead Woods, the David Davies Memorial Trophy for the Volunteer of the Year is given. At their second anniversary, where this prize was first presented, the recipient was Jenny Booth who, as Jo Quantrill wrote in her Report: 'is always in the Woods, quietly fulfilling the volunteer roles required of her, supporting her husband and dispensing smiles and friendly comments to everyone.'

Points prizes

The points prizes, like many things in parkrun, are simple in concept but require a computer for the calculations. Every parkrun participant is awarded points: the first male and first female to cross the finish line each get 100 points, the next get 99 and so on down the line with every participant getting at least one point. At larger parkruns, points may start at 200 or higher, otherwise most people would only get a single point. The computers keep track of all the points and total them for each person at a given location. Volunteers receive maximum points each of the first three times they volunteer in a given parkrun's year; this avoids discouraging runners from volunteering because they have their eye on the points competition. Trophies or certificates for the top scorers are awarded at the anniversary celebrations, generally to the first three people on each of the male and female points tables, sometimes with extras for the top-scoring juniors.

Although the fastest runners get the most points in any individual week, it's notable that commonly it is *not* the fastest runners who win the points prizes. Rather, they tend to be won by people who consistently run at the same parkrun, virtually every week – and who volunteer at their parkrun on the weeks that they are not running. Faster runners who stick to a given parkrun and run it very regularly do have an advantage, but it's fantastic to see the variety of people winning the points prizes, sometimes that person's first ever experience of winning anything for running – as it was for Alison Mears at Eastleigh parkrun. Towards the end of the first year of Eastleigh parkrun another runner commented to Alison that she was well ahead in the points table. Alison told me, 'I didn't even know there was a points table. I take 33 minutes to run it and I won! I've never won anything in my life before and it was a great achievement. Now I'm one of the Run Directors.'

Celebrations!

At some parkruns, perpetual trophies have been named for, or in memory of, special parkrunners. For Bushy parkrun, the women's points prize winner gets the Sonia O'Sullivan Salver while the men's winner gets the John Hanscomb Trophy. At Banstead Woods, the trophies are named after GB international marathon runner Anne Roden, who has been a regular volunteer at the event from the beginning, while at Richmond parkrun, the men's winner is presented with the Stephen Instone Trophy and the women's point winner is given the Hugh Brasher Salver.

'parkrunner of the month' prize

In the UK, each parkrun awards a 'parkrunner of the month' prize. This prize is sponsored by the Sweatshop chain of running stores, and each winner gets a certificate entitling them to a free pair of running shoes from their local Sweatshop store. The prize is awarded for 'consistency, persistence and improvement'. The management team at each parkrun nominates its Sweatshop prize winner each month, based on those basic requirements. Although the management teams receive some handy statistical information on their runners each month, such as number of runs, number of PBs, improvement and number of times volunteered that month, there is, quite deliberately, no mathematical formula for who wins the prize.

parkrunners may be nominated for their event's prize for different aspects of their participation: notable improvements in their running speed; turning up each week with a smile on their face even in the foulest weather; unofficially pacing or encouraging other runners; lending a hand in sorting out equipment after the run... The exact reasons for winning this prize vary with each recipient, but one thing definitely stands out: recipients of this prize are those who, when they don't turn up one week, are missed by the other regular attendees.

Merry Christmas and a Happy New Year

Christmas Day and New Year's Day runs have become a special feature at many parkruns worldwide, whether or not those days fall on a Saturday. Some parkruns put on Santa Runs, either on Christmas Day or the Saturday before, with lots of red-and-white costumes and false beards flowing across the parks. Some events, such as Barrow parkrun in the English Lake District, celebrate New Year's Day by running the course in the reverse direction to normal.

For some families, Christmas Day parkrun has become an integral part of their family tradition. Rachel Stanhope, one of the original Bushy thirteen, recalls that the first time she and her husband took their sons to Bushy Park to run on Christmas Day 2004, her younger son, Oliver, was not entirely willing, but now it's a traditional part of the day for the whole family. They have a minor family competition at the Christmas Day run and Rachel said that Oliver had been really keen to beat his older brother, James. On Christmas Day 2013, James was unable to run due to a nasty bug, so was not there to see Oliver take four minutes off his PB to come in at 22:44.

The best Christmas run at Waterworks parkrun, Belfast, Matt Shields said, was in the cold weather at the end of 2011. The old reservoirs, making up about three quarters of the area of the park, froze over so hard that after the run the parkrunners stood on the ice, drinking their mulled wine. 'If you ask regular Waterworks parkrunners which was the best parkrun, the one they enjoyed the most, they'll still hark back to that event.'

For New Year's Day 2012, parkruns in the UK were given the freedom to start at any time from 9 o'clock to 11 o'clock ('never again!' says Tom Williams). A number of parkrunners who had previously run a Bushy Park and Banstead Woods New Year's Day parkrun double saw the possibility of fitting in three parkruns ('a trifecta of parkruns' as Danny Norman put it) and planned how to do this, with many choosing the triad of Bushy Park, Nonsuch and Riddlesdown. Additionally, some runners ('truly hardy and/or insane individuals' as Riddlesdown's Event Director Nicki Clark described them) decided that for additional fun and exercise, they would cycle between the events.

Nicki was at Riddlesdown from 8 o'clock, organising the course markers, the registration gazebo (sheltering the registration area and three special cakes) and the 28 volunteers, and worrying about how many people would turn up. It could be almost nobody, if they felt too tired after the earlier events, or hundreds converging from Bushy Park and the local events Banstead Woods, Roundshaw, Lloyd and Nonsuch. Towards 11 o'clock, a sizeable field gathered, including some well-known and fast runners, with a chaotically festive atmosphere developing despite the wet and muddy conditions.

Aware that cars and cyclists were still arriving, Nicki delayed the start for as long as she dared, calling the runners to order at 11.07, spinning out the announcements and warnings about mud and safety – then sent them off. For some cyclists the hat-trick had turned out to be a bit more of a challenge than they had intended; they pedalled furiously to Riddlesdown, dumped their bikes and chased after the disappearing runners. Despite the filthy conditions, Clare Elms set a new women's course record (18:20), coming in fifth overall – having run nineteen minutes to set a new women's course record at Roundshaw an hour earlier. Paul Sinton-Hewitt completed his hundredth parkrun, Riddlesdown regular Ange Norris ran her fiftieth; Anthony Jackson, having finished first at Bushy Park and Banstead Woods, managed second at Riddlesdown, with a fresh-legged Patrick Caravan first.

Freedom runs

Apart from providing the organised parkrun events at a set time every Saturday morning, the presence of parkrun courses, whether permanently marked or not, provides local runners with a known 5K route, and they make good use of this.

Chris Wright had noted that this was happening: 'Quite often I have gone over to one of my local parks during the week only to see folks walk up to the official parkrun start line and press their stopwatches. I've watched these folks run the course and as they approach the finish line they press the stop button on their watches again. They're running a parkrun!' This got him thinking that it ought to be possible for people to record such runs. This facility was first piloted at Leeds parkrun, and a small survey was carried out to see the impact it had on the local parkrun community. In March 2010, parkrun started providing the option for runners to record 'freedom parkruns' – times when they have run an official parkrun course, but not as part of an official parkrun.

These runs do not count towards any parkrun club T-shirt or event points prize. Nevertheless, dozens of freedom runs are recorded on the parkrun website each week, and it's probable that for each freedom run recorded, there are many more which are run but never entered into the database.

The longest parkrun

'The longest parkrun' was really an extension of the freedom run. The idea for this came initially from Chris Wright and in 2010, a number of parkrunners decided to spend the Sunday after the longest day in the year running several parkruns, variously driving or cycling between locations. Beginning at Bushy Park at 9 o'clock, 28 runners started at the original start line and ran the course in the original (anticlockwise) direction. Next came Bedfont Lakes, Old Deer Park, Richmond Park, Wimbledon and

Kingston before the by-now depleted group finished off back at Bushy Park once more at 6 o'clock, this time in the current clockwise direction.

This was repeated in 2011 and so became a tradition. By 2012 the longest parkrun was being replicated in other areas of the UK boasting several parkrun courses within a reasonable distance of one another. Even more areas adopted this extended event for 2013: East London, north-east London, North London, Cheshire and Manchester, Lancashire, Yorkshire, East Midlands and North Kent Coast. In the south-east London/Kent area, there were enough events and people wanting to take part that several alternative routes were plotted, starting at two locations, coming together in the middle of the day and then diverging again towards the evening. By this time also the idea had been exported to Western Australia and the Brisbane area of Queensland.

Chris Wright posted several tips in 2013 covering the practicalities. He reminded people that the combined distance is closer to a marathon than to a normal Saturday morning parkrun, but that runners could reduce this and still take part, by not running all the laps at multi-lap courses. He suggested thinking about transport and parking in advance, and making sure that food, drink and sunscreen or a waterproof jacket (as appropriate) were available. He finished with the reminder to, 'Please look out for your fellow runners, and make sure someone is looking out for you.'

'Longest parkrun' events were discontinued for 2014 due to concerns over possible insurance risks. However, parkrunners still get together on that Sunday or other dates to have fun running multiple courses. In June 2014, a group of Strathclyde parkrunners decided to run all eighteen parkruns in Northern Ireland (90 kilometres or 55.8 miles) over a period of three days, and a group from a Belfast running club decided to surpass this by taking on the same challenge in two days – no mean feat by either group, considering not only the running distance but also the amount of travel required in between. And in the Newcastle area of Australia, they hold a rolling run of parkruns on New Year's Day, starting at Belmont, followed by Lake Mac, Blackbutt, Fingal Bay and Newy.

Other celebrations

There are really too many parkrun celebrations to describe all of them! Just to give a flavour:

At Southwick Country Park parkrun, there's a tradition of running the course backwards when the clocks go back in October. Leamington parkrunners have also reversed direction, in their case on 16 March 2013 for their hundredth parkrun, combined with St Patrick's Day themed fancy dress.

Bunyaville in Queensland holds a lot of theme days, such as Valentine's Day, St Patrick's Day and the Queen's birthday – when the Run Directors dress up as kings and queens.

At Easter 2014, several parkruns in Australia tried for a world record for running with an egg and spoon. At Kawana parkrun in Queensland, all went well for the first couple of kilometres; unfortunately, near the lighthouse turn-around point, while checking there were no problematic dogs around, the key runner lost concentration on his egg and spoon and the egg went flying. Young parkrunners tried their own egg and spoon racing with less breakable plastic eggs, each containing a small chocolate egg for eating afterwards.

When the Giro D'Italia cycled through Northern Ireland on 10 May 2014, many parkruns, particularly those close to the race's route, made this an excuse for a celebration. Nat Glenn said that it was a very special occasion at Larne parkrun: it was their six-month anniversary, most people turned up in pink and anyone not wearing pink was provided with a pink hat or bib to wear.

Celebrations!

The sun shone, they presented their first 10-club T-shirt, there was a thirteen-year-old running his first 5K, on his birthday, buns were baked and it was a really nice day – even if Portrush's Mr Blobby photo just beat Larne's pink people photo in the parkrun Facebook photo competition.

Also on 10 May 2014, a very special parkrun was held at Modderfontein Reserve in South Africa. It was highly promoted by parkrun South Africa's sponsors for World Move for Health Day and during the preceding week, Wayde Morsink, the Event Director, watched as the number of new parkrun registrations kept on growing. He spent the whole of Friday night producing finish tokens up to number 2,000 and on Saturday morning he watched car after car arriving. In the end, 1,803 people crossed the finish line. Wayde said, 'The success of the whole day wasn't the number finishing but the smiles on faces. Wow, that was marvellous.' The volunteers also had fun and runners kept offering to help once they had finished. Thirty-six people volunteered, including Bruce, Gill and Cara Fordyce. The final people to cross the finish line, ninety minutes after the event started, were Wayde and eleven other volunteers, belatedly running the course to finish off their fantastic day!

15

parkrun and the wider running community

I recently completed the London Marathon. At five kilometres from the end, there was a sign that said, 'Keep going, only a parkrun to go.' It was just what I needed.

Sarah Aldington, Porirua parkrun

Some running clubs took enthusiastically to parkrun right from the start while others took longer to be convinced. By now most running clubs in areas where parkruns have become established have probably realised that parkrun is increasing rather than decreasing membership of running clubs, by encouraging grassroots running.

Early adopters

Some well known and highly respected club runners were very important in the early years of parkrun. John Hanscomb was a member of Ranelagh Harriers and one of the 'Ever Present' London Marathon runners from 1981 (aged 45 and finishing in 2:54:29) to 2008. John started running Bushy Park Time Trial in January 2005 and found that it fitted in well with his running at that time, as he was getting older and finding cross-country races harder. parkrun was recreational, as opposed to a hard race; he saw the same people every week; and it was enjoyable. As he had already amply demonstrated by his 28 London Marathons and 45 Finchley 20-mile road races, 'If I find something I enjoy I keep doing it.' Which he has.

In October 2010, John was the second parkrunner, after Darren Wood, to reach the acclaimed 250-club and early in 2014 he passed 400 parkruns. As a club runner for many years, he thinks that one of the best things about parkrun is that, 'you don't have to pay a damn thing – it's free. It's lovely.'

Similarly, long-time runner and Ranelagh Harriers member Wally Garrod started parkrunning at the sixth Bushy Park Time Trial back in November 2004. Now 78 years old, he commented that while he used to run marathons, he's gradually dropped distances so the 5K is just about right – and he's run more than 250 so far. He notes that while some members of clubs still think that parkrun is taking people away from club runs at weekends, in his opinion that's ridiculous; rather, with the increase in people running due to parkrun, some will naturally graduate to clubs. Wally has visited events in Poland twice, Iceland once, and is now considering Russia. 'Even though Bushy parkrun is now so large, it's still very friendly, people taking an interest in one another,' he said. 'When I returned to the parkrun after having had heart surgery, people were following my progress in the newsletter, even.'

He also likes the family aspect, having run with his daughter, his grandson and his partner.

In 2006, a team of Bushy Park Time Trial regulars entered the Green Belt Relay, a 200 mile, two-day relay race around London organised by the Stragglers running club, as 'BPTT.com' in order to promote the existence of BPTT in the running community. It worked – particularly because the BPTT.com team put together by Jim Desmond won the race! The race nicely highlighted the connection between BPTT and running clubs: Paul Sinton-Hewitt ran stages eleven and twenty for the Ranelagh Harriers' 'Old Dogs' veterans team (which came in first veterans) in addition to acting as team manager for BPTT.com.

From parkrun to running club

For many runners who are not particularly fast, going to a running club can be a daunting prospect. They think that running clubs are elitist, that everyone there will be a much faster runner than they are; they worry unnecessarily that they will be unwanted or will get left behind on club runs. At parkruns, new runners have a chance to improve their running in a supportive atmosphere, and to meet members of running clubs, discovering that not all are so very fast, and that many clubs cater to runners of a wide range of speeds.

Right from the start, when parkruns were still Time Trials, the organisers encouraged new runners to join running clubs. Chris Phelan, interviewed on Episode 21 of the running podcast *Marathon Talk* in 2010, noted that he would often get new runners asking him for advice about how they could improve their running. He would always ask where they lived and then recommend their nearest running club.

A university coursemate dragged me along to my very first parkrun at Black Park in my final year when I took up running after my weight got out of control, and I carried on after graduating and moving to Milton Keynes. It has inspired me to move up to half-marathon level (what better way to improve your 5K time?) and to join a local running club, not to mention the positive impact on both my physical and mental health.

Donna Law, Milton Keynes parkrun

In general, membership of running clubs *increases* due to participation in parkruns, as do entries to local races. As Gavin Oosthuizen, a regular runner at Ebotse parkrun and also a member of a running club said, 'For anyone who's starting off, 5K seems incredibly long, but they go there and they do it. Before long they start thinking, "Well if I can do 5K, I can do a 10K race," and when they start getting involved in that, they start getting caught up in the whole community of the running spirit.'

When Waterworks parkrun began in Belfast in November 2010, North Belfast Harriers had about fifty members; three years later, membership had increased to about 250 adults and fifty children. Now, whenever Matt Shields (currently Country Manager for parkrun Ireland) is starting up a new parkrun event, whether in the Republic of Ireland or in Northern Ireland, he always seeks out the local running clubs and tries to get them involved. 'Nearly always they're nervous about having this on their doorstep, but they're very comfortable once it has been explained – in fact some clubs would try to nearly own the event!'

Synergy

Ideally, parkruns and running clubs have a synergistic relationship. Many parkruns rely heavily on a local running club, at least initially, not only for runners but also for volunteers, until the numbers build and the parkrun organically develops its own broader volunteer base.

In its turn, parkrun provides publicity for the running clubs. Each parkrun event's website provides a list of local clubs, hyperlinked to the relevant websites, and wherever a club is listed in the results tables, there is also a link to that club's own website. Each runner's club is listed in the results every week, and commonly indicated in the weekly run reports. The event websites have a clubs list showing all the clubs which have been represented at that event, and the country and global websites even give information on the most-represented clubs.

Many running clubs, including my club, Striders of Croydon, have a really great relationship with parkruns. Striders was involved in the start of Roundshaw Downs parkrun and Mick Turner, a member, has been co-Event Director there since 2009. Roundshaw Downs now has a closer relationship with Collingwood, which is geographically closer, while Striders has a greater involvement in Lloyd parkrun. Both courses were designed by members of Striders, and the club has assisted Lloyd parkrun in many ways over the past few years, such as donating some extra course marker arrows. Additionally, my clubmates have supported Lloyd parkrun by volunteering as well as by parkrunning. In turn, Lloyd parkrun has encouraged quite a number of beginning runners who have gone on to become members of the club, and has provided unofficial assistance at water stations during Striders' Croydon Half Marathon. As a bonus, runners who have volunteered at finish line positions at parkruns are much less nervous about taking on similar roles at club-organised races such as the Switchback 5-mile cross-country.

Matt Shields has found that if Waterworks parkrun ever have a shortage of volunteers, they can always ask at North Belfast Harriers and two or three people will offer straight away. The club also helps with special events, or assists if the parkrun needs a special skill. Matt notes that local clubs can easily advertise their existence and capabilities at their local parkrun, for example by turning up and conducting pre-event warm-ups, inviting runners to join in. This happens, 'Particularly at the Dublin events,' Matt said, 'that can really help the relationship to gel.'

Linda Bussey, Event Director of Bradford parkrun, has also found the local running clubs to be very supportive. She said, 'I think most of the local running clubs in Bradford have built up a special link with the parkrun. Eccleshill was in right from the start because, being my club, I asked them to recce the route and do the trial runs when we were setting up.' The relationship between Bradford parkrun and the local clubs is very much reciprocal: 'I always make sure I promote any club-organised races and events, most of the clubs include parkrun in their club championship and we have an arrangement where they "adopt" the event every so often: providing all the volunteers, having lots of their members run in their club vests to show the range of abilities that the club caters for and they usually have a stand at the finish providing information as well as water and often bananas, buns or biscuits.'

Mike Fleet has spent fifty years coaching youngsters in running and other athletic disciplines at Croydon Harriers. When parkrun first came to the Croydon area: 'I wasn't worried at all, I thought it would be quite interesting, wanted to see how it evolved.' He did admit to some concerns when there was a club fixture which involved travelling, if people wouldn't want to go away when there was an easy option of parkrun on their doorstep. However, Mike has found that although this has happened occasionally, it has not been a major problem – rather, parkrun has provided an option when people could not travel due to conflicting responsibilities such as a family wedding, which he can only see as a good thing. Additionally, 'You see parents coming out with their kiddies, so you start to see mums and dads starting to do a bit.' As a further benefit, he's noticed that some officials have become far more confident after volunteering regularly at parkrun, it's helped the confidence of a variety of runners, and it's encouraged youngsters who are mostly concentrating on other athletics disciplines to run as well.

I am a member of my local running club and have been running since 1984. I have run lots of races; marathons and half marathons, 10Ks and 10 miles. I love running! I was never the fastest runner in the club (faster than some – slower than most) but enjoyed competition. Well, time passes and here I am looking at my 63rd birthday. Some of my running partners have given up while some still run a few times a week to keep fit. Then I discovered parkrun. I can turn up any Saturday that suits and run 5K with another 200 or 300 runners. I can check my times against others in my age group (not many but growing) and I love it. 5K is a perfect distance; everyone can do it. It is good to see families running together; mothers with buggies; dads with their kids; new runners struggling to the line; and seniors returning from illness or injury. Participation is free, there are no charges and even better no one is making a profit from it. How brilliant is that?

Patricia Goodwin, Whitley Bay parkrun

Phil and Claire Anderson, who manage the challenging Bunyaville parkrun in Queensland, have found Bunyaville Trail Runners supportive of the parkrun. Many parkrunners go to local running groups and many local running groups come to parkrun – which is as it should be. They have also had a local group volunteering. 'We get a lot of good cross-collaboration, help each other out.'

Mob rule

parkruns have proved to be a useful venue for local running club challenge events and mob matches. Club challenge events are competitions within a club to see who can finish first – sometimes with separation into the various veterans age categories as well as males and females. While these commonly take place within local races, sometimes a parkrun is chosen as a venue.

Mob matches are competitions between clubs using a very simple format: each club encourages as many of their club members as possible to take part, and every club member running gains points for their club, with more points for those placing higher up in the finish order. While scoring systems vary, the winning club is often the one which persuades the most runners to turn up! Mob matches are generally held between two or sometimes three neighbouring clubs, and if each running club has strong links to a different parkrun they are often reciprocal, with one mob match held at each of the relevant parkruns.

Additionally, parkruns provide a great opportunity for runners from different clubs to meet each other properly. Although the members of different running clubs do meet at league matches, at those events runners mostly stay with their clubmates; parkruns provide a venue, every week, at which runners tend to mingle. This has, as noted previously, provided the opportunity for inter-club romances – and has even enabled members of bitter rival running clubs to start talking to each other, leave the hostilities behind and begin working with instead of against each other.

parkruns and local races

It is fair to say that many organisers of local races, particularly the shorter events, were initially very concerned that parkrun, by providing free, timed events, would lead to decreased attendance at races where competitors had to pay. However, where parkruns have been present for a while, attendance at races of all distances greater than 5K has generally increased. There are several reasons for this.

First, simply by providing an encouraging running venue, parkrun is increasing the number of people taking up running, thereby increasing the potential numbers of people running races. Second, while not races, there is inevitably an element of competitive running at parkruns: very few people can prevent themselves from responding with at least an attempt at running faster when the runner next to them sprints for the line! Having found they enjoy this, they start to think that they could tackle an actual race. Third, parkruns provide a venue where the existence of local races can be publicised. Finally, because beginners get to know other, more established runners at parkruns, they discover that not everyone running local races is fast and they find the prospect of going to a race less daunting, knowing that there will be other people there whom they will recognise.

> *If you'd have told me five years ago that I'd be addicted to running I wouldn't have believed you, but I've now completed five half marathons, countless 10K races and many more. I even joined a running club last year and am proud to now consider myself an 'athlete'. I'm the fittest I've ever been and parkrun has been a major factor in all of this.*
>
> *Paul Chapman, Cardiff parkrun*

In June 2013, in the parkrun South Africa newsletter just after the annual Comrades Marathon, Bruce Fordyce highlighted the encouragement which parkrun people gives to reach longer distances. In particular, he mentioned two parkrunners, Andrew Wainwright and Tracy Rankin. Tracy, from Delta parkrun, is well known in parkrun South Africa because she was the first South Africa-based parkrunner to reach the 50-club. Andrew started running at Modderfontein Reserve parkrun in January 2013 and by the beginning of June – just five months later – had run Comrades.

Additionally, North Beach parkrun started in Durban in November 2012, so beginning in 2013, a new tradition was born: visiting Comrades runners from all over South Africa, UK, Australia and elsewhere parkrun there on the Saturday morning before running Comrades the following day, resulting in noticeable peaks in numbers at the parkrun. After running Comrades in 2014, UK parkrunner Alison Gay said, 'If you're running a notoriously hot and hilly 56 mile race on the Sunday, perhaps a parkrun isn't the obvious way to start your Saturday morning.' Despite this, and her very slow parkrun time (she had a gentle jog around, chatting with a friend), she was glad she did it. 'Taking it slow meant it was a good leg stretch, it helped to settle my nerves, and I think it also helped me to acclimatise to the heat.'

I started parkrunning to maintain my fitness out of hockey season but became addicted. I began entering every race ESPECIALLY the trail runs and have graduated from my 5-kilometre parkrun to 36-kilometre trail runs.

Tracy Mackay, Nahoon Point parkrun

Mixed feelings

Inevitably there have been some running club runners who were unsure about parkrun and a minority who flatly disliked parkrun, claiming that the very existence of these free, weekly, 5K timed runs discouraged runners from entering local races and joining running clubs.

Alan Hedger, Chief Race Official for Ranelagh Harriers when Bushy Park Time Trial first started, thought then that it was 'a damned good idea', which is why he volunteered at the very first run. He still thinks that it's doing a great job encouraging people to run first thing on a Saturday morning, and even getting runners to bring their family out with them. But he admits that he has had, and continues to have, mixed feelings. On the one hand, 'there's no doubt that it's got thousands of people running, at various stages of their running.' On the other, as he says, 'I was a racer, and people aren't *racing* parkrun.' He also worries that people will run parkrun and then not run the cross-country races for their clubs on a Saturday afternoon.

Martin Shute, one of my own clubmates, admitted to me that, when he first heard about parkrun he thought that it wouldn't last. However, 'now you can see it's not just a whim. Everyone enjoys it for their own reasons – good club runners doing it for a good time, others just looking to beat their own PBs, which is fantastic – and hats off to the volunteers.'

Pete Mulholland, member of Hercules Wimbledon AC and a regular Wimbledon Common parkrun volunteer, thinks that parkrun is great for getting people running, particularly children, and for giving the youngsters a stamina session to add to track training sessions. He's not very happy when he sees people running the parkrun on a Saturday morning rather than a club cross-country race in the afternoon, 'but I can see their point, particularly the younger ones – there's no pressure at parkrun.' He thinks clubs could do more than they do to recruit runners from parkruns, just by talking to them, letting them know the clubs are there.

Unfortunately a few long-time running club officials have been rather forthright in their opposition. One such official expressed his objection in a letter to UK Athletics. In addition, he sent an email (full of erroneous 'facts') to other running clubs, suggesting that they should lodge similar complaints and encouraging them to boycott the parkruns. This found its way to a local newspaper and the response was overwhelmingly in support of parkrun. Some people wrote to Paul Sinton-Hewitt expressing their support, while many people replied directly to the newspaper article to give their own experiences, as parkrunners, of being encouraged to join clubs and run races, or (if already established running club members) of seeing people coming into their clubs and gaining the confidence to enter races, via their parkrunning.

Paul wrote a very dignified letter to the paper, also published on the parkrun website, in which he encouraged readers *not* to boycott the running club at the centre of the furore, nor their races (as some had suggested).

Even now there are still those who think that parkrun is 'ruining athletics', but thankfully there are many more who see it as quite the opposite. Olympic athlete Liz Yelling thinks that parkrun has the potential to contribute to the regrowth of European running: at elite level by bringing children through from the grass roots, but also improving general health and fitness at a national level. 'It's about giving children access to a sport that's not necessarily competitive – you can make it competitive but you can also just run for the fun of it. I think that's missing in kids' sport. Even cross-country at school is about winning, there's no emphasis on running for fitness and health. parkrun has a role to play in battling obesity and in taking part in sport for the pure joy of doing it as opposed to winning it.' She added, 'and it's about making sport accessible. parkrun's free, it's consistent, it's there every week at the same time, you know what you're getting and that's what's needed for people to engage; it gets people – including kids – up and off the sofa.'

Liz has noticed that in her area, where there are a lot of small running clubs, parkrun has also brought the running community together, which she thinks is great. 'Running's a great sport and we should all be in it together. It's good having people supporting each other.'

parkrun: much more than just a run in the park

Sadly, there are still a few people who look at the fact that more people run parkruns than are members of their local running clubs and grumble that without parkrun those people would join the clubs. This ignores the fact that most parkrun participants who are not running club members would never have considered joining a running club, perhaps never have started running, if not for parkrun. Tony Flowers, a run leader at Striders of Croydon noted, 'I might complain sometimes that not many people come to the Friday evening run because they're all resting for parkrun on Saturday morning – but if it wasn't for parkrun, I would never have found Striders in the first place!'

Thankfully, and much more commonly, in each new geographical area club runners and officials who initially greet parkrun with a degree of scepticism and concern, gradually change their minds once they have seen parkrun in action and experienced its positive effects on the local running community. Quite simply, more people running translates into increased club memberships and more people participating at most local races. Those of us who know the names and faces of people who started off running at our local parkruns can watch with a great deal of pleasure as we begin seeing the same runners, some of whom could not run the whole 5K of a parkrun when they started, now looking determined as they battle through the mud in a county league cross-country match, proudly wearing their club vest, or grin triumphantly as they come over the finish line in five mile, 10K or half-marathon races, and set their sights on their first marathon.

As Linda Bussey noted in Bradford, 'When we first started, some of the running clubs were quite cautious and even suspicious of the event, seeing it as a possible threat to the clubs and local races. But over time we've worked really hard to build relationships with them, encourage unattached runners to join local clubs and really promote club-organised events. Now we've been going for nearly four years, the relationship is excellent and all the local clubs have seen membership and entries for races boosted significantly which is fantastic!'

Additionally, she said, 'I know that some events are wary of runners who come to parkrun in their club vests and whether it gives the impression of it being an elite or race event but personally I love to see lots of running club vests at Bradford. The runners are the ultimate advocates for their clubs and unattached runners often see club runners coming into the finish long after they have – which gives them the confidence to look into joining a club knowing that it's not just all elites! Club-vested runners will strike up conversations with unattached runners and build a social relationship which leads to increased membership.'

James Saunders, who has been involved in the development of several parkruns in the Winchester-Southampton area, has also seen great synergy between parkrun and local running clubs. parkrunning has led to James joining a running club and becoming event director for some local races, in addition to starting up parkruns, acting as a parkrun Ambassador, continuing to direct Southampton junior parkrun and working his way up in running to half-Ironman length triathlon.

More generally, clubs have supported parkruns, including providing volunteers, while parkruns have supported clubs, encouraging people to join, and publicising local races, both via the parkrun websites and social media, and by providing a weekly opportunity for local races to hand out leaflets. James has seen the Lords Hill Road Runners increase in membership from eighty to nearly 300 over the four year period since the local parkruns started up, while local races, such as the Eastleigh 10K, are packed with parkrunners, as are the local leagues. 'I've seen a lot of people who have started parkrunning and said they would never go further, but while many never join clubs, others do, and start competing in local races and the local leagues. There certainly has not been any drop off in entrants to local races because the parkruns are available.'

In January 2013 I was encouraged to go to Carlisle parkrun's inaugural event by a friend who is a keen runner and triathlete. I hadn't run since school cross-country and I spent most of those hiding at a friend's house listening to punk music. Couldn't make it round one lap, never mind all three! I have osteoarthritis in my spine and I'm in a lot of pain so I struggled but I finished and I came back. People gave up their time to organise it so I had to come back. Week by week I ran a bit further and a bit faster. When I made it all the way round the feeling was amazing. People knew my name and said hello and cheered me on. I made friends and joined a local running group. I tried training at the local athletics track. I've entered 10K races and enjoyed them. Never fast but enjoying every minute. I've made new friends, gained enough confidence to volunteer and parkrun is now part of my life. I'm fitter, happier and getting more from life since that first parkrun.

Rachel Lee, Carlisle parkrun

Beginners' running groups

parkrun also has a two-way relationship with beginners' running groups. Some people start out walking a parkrun then decide to join a local beginners' group and work up to actually running the parkrun. For many beginners' running groups or personal trainers getting people going in running, parkrun is a fantastic goal which their beginners can aim towards. For example in Belfast, participants in the Jog Belfast Couch to 5K programme organised by North Belfast Harriers graduate by running at Waterworks parkrun. Similarly in Larne the local clubs bring their Couch to 5K beginners out to train on the challenging Larne parkrun course and then they progress to running the parkrun, while Seapark AC has a beginners' jog group which graduates by running Carrickfergus parkrun.

Tony Barclay has noted that more people are joining Seapark's jog groups now there's the parkrun to graduate to, and many have continued parkrunning, because it's free, supportive and timed. One lady was a bit nervous of trying the parkrun for the first time, not sure she would be able to finish, so he told her that she could be his guide for the parkrun (he's registered blind) and they would do it together – and they did.

New running clubs

parkrun has also led directly to the development of new running clubs. On quite a large scale, this has included the development of five30runners. This running club started at Newy parkrun and was founded in September 2012 by Garry 'Guru' Wells, who is now the Event Director at Blackbutt. It originated to enable runners in the Newcastle, New South Wales area, who were completing parkrun in about thirty minutes, to engage with each other between Saturday mornings. Garry had the idea while pacing a friend to a 32 minute finish, particularly when he realised, looking at the statistics, that about 25-33% of runners were finishing the 5K in over thirty minutes and many, it appeared, were aiming to get under that time. By May 2014, five30runners had members all over Australia and one in the USA. It is also welcoming to runners of all speeds, whether around the thirty minutes mark for the 5K or faster or slower. The five30running Facebook page is very active, with everyone supporting one another, meeting up at races and getting together for parkrun tourism trips to various venues.

Another sort of running club to emerge from parkrun has been church-based running groups. To the best of my knowledge the first of these was Chiltern Church in Sutton, Surrey. Here, Tim Grey and a few others knew that each other were runners, and had some friends who were runners and were considering starting a running club – but they wanted it to be simple and free. In 2011, Tim said, 'We saw the light, and realised the answer had been under our noses all along – parkrun!' After getting some T-shirts printed at a local shop, and emailing parkrun to let them know that there was a Chiltern Church Runners club, they started running 'officially', mostly at Roundshaw Downs parkrun, which Tim considers to be 'a hidden gem of a parkrun', although with some of their members sticking with Banstead Woods parkrun down the road.

Then, Tim remembers, 'One day a couple of blokes sidled up to us at Roundshaw and asked, "How come you get your church's name in the results?"' After he explained, Andy Crossley and Micky Wheeler went on to set up the Selsdon Baptist Church Runners, with Lloyd parkrun as their home event, supported on their first official outing by Chiltern Church Runners. This was followed by the Good Shepherd club based around Nonsuch parkrun, Molesey Church Running Club based at Bushy parkrun and Christ Church Runners of New Malden parkrun.

These groups are easily spotted because of their distinctive T-shirts with the church running group name on the front and a variety of slogans on the back: 'Blessed are the Pacemakers', 'Feed the 5K', 'The last will be first' and many others. All of them, while having a core of running enthusiasts who train regularly and run races, also contain many people who have only come into running through these clubs and parkrun. For variety, the groups sometimes visit each other's home parkruns either on a purely friendly basis or for a mob match.

'We know at least two other church clubs (Cornerstone iFIT and St Mark's Runners) are out there,' Tim said. 'We're hoping to make contact with them soon, and there may be more we don't know about.'

Not instead, but extra

For many people who were already club runners, parkrun has provided something extra. 'If you had told me ten years ago that the UK running scene was missing something, and what it really needed was a weekly 5K timed run for people of all abilities, I would have laughed,' Andrew Lane admitted, 'but it works.'

16

parkrunning for health and happiness

parkrun has played an important part in improving both my physical and mental health, I've made some friends, been encouraged to run and cheered home every week, as all our runners are.

Sam Standerwich, Bryn Bach parkrun

Hundreds, perhaps thousands of parkrunners have stories to tell about how parkrun has improved not just their running and their fitness but also their general health.

When Richard Tanner, a regular runner at Lloyd parkrun, reached the 50-club and got his red T-shirt, he brought 'before' and 'after' photos to the park for us to see. I looked at the 'before' photo in disbelief and Richard shared his story with me. He had always struggled with his weight, reaching 18¾ stone (119 kilograms), becoming out of breath walking upstairs, with high blood pressure and high cholesterol. His doctor put him on medication for these, telling him he would be taking tablets for the rest of his life. Soon after, his father had a heart attack – and Richard decided he had to change his lifestyle.

He started to lose some weight and his wife, Rachel, suggested running. Initially it took him an age to recover from a mile and a half at the local park. Then someone recommended Roundshaw parkrun and they started there in January 2011, later trying Lloyd parkrun and finding both events very friendly and welcoming. 'Now,' Richard said, 'I'm 12 stone 10 [81 kilograms], off all the medication, don't have high blood pressure or high cholesterol.' He added, 'And we're all parkrunning now – it's a real family activity.' He looked at his younger son, Charlie and asked him, 'Do you remember when Daddy couldn't run?' Charlie shook his head and Richard all but glowed at this confirmation that Charlie knows him as a fit, active father.

Garry Wells, who is now the Event Director at Blackbutt parkrun, New South Wales, and founder of the five30runners running club, also started running to address high blood pressure. His fitness has improved, he's no longer on the medication and, as he says, 'It's amazing how much better you feel after a hard day if you get out there and have even a 5K run.' From his own experience and from observing other people, he's seen that 'parkrun changes lives'.

Sam Standerwich decided early in 2013 that she had 'had enough of being fat and forty', so joined a gym, began a diet, started the Couch to 5K (C25K) programme and partway through discovered a love of running. She said, 'I went along to parkrun in November 2013 not knowing what to expect and with some trepidation about my size and the time it would take me to complete the 5K. The regulars at Bryn Bach parkrun couldn't have been more welcoming and supportive.' By March 2014, 100 pounds lighter than a year earlier, Sam had completed fourteen parkruns, taken six minutes off her PB, started running 10K races and was in training for her first half marathon.

> *The decision to start running was prompted by my husband's giving up smoking fourteen months ago. That was the beginning of what has become, certainly for my husband, a passion and a lifesaver, any time he feels like a ciggie, he puts on his running shoes and takes off. We wake up eagerly on Saturday mornings, come rain or snow, and 90% of the time get on our bikes to cycle the seven kilometres to parkrun, yes, even in the snow, and then we run. I don't think I'll be saying anything new when I say that the fact parkrun is free means that you'll get a large cross section of people taking part. No one cares if you are a lawyer or a bricklayer, what counts is your passion and the good spirit which flourishes during these morning meet-ups. Even people who hate having to get up so early on a Saturday morning leave the parkrun site with a smile on their faces. It has certainly added another dimension to our lives.*
>
> *Pia Regan-Jasinski, Gdańsk parkrun*

For Chris Aldred, the spur to start exercising was the shock of being told that he was diabetic: 'I had always considered myself reasonably healthy, despite being a little overweight, something I told myself that I could easily lose if I wanted to.' Looking for a challenge to help improve his fitness, he decided to enter the Great North Run; he also discovered there was a weekly event called parkrun, which he thought might help with his training. Initially he couldn't even run the three-quarters of a mile from his house to the start line of the Harrogate parkrun. Nevertheless he persevered, completing first one, then two and finally all three laps of the course, finishing in around 34 minutes.

Nearly two years and 84 parkruns later, his time was down to under 25 minutes, his age grading up to 60%. Chris said, 'parkrun has changed my life in so many ways. All the diabetic indicators are under control; I weigh 2½ stone [16 kilograms] less and I've made some great friends who I go out running with during the week. I've also run two Great North Runs, raising over £5,000 for charities, including Diabetes UK.'

I'm a regular at Poole and Bournemouth parkruns, where my 5K time has improved from 27ish to 22:56 – my current PB. I'm outspokenly proud of having gone from a 24½ stone [156 kilograms] morbidly obese couch potato to a 12½ stone [79 kilograms] marathon runner – accomplished through careful healthy dieting and an introduction to running. Poole parkrun has helped me stick to my goals of doing a regular weekend workout and it's where I get to burn calories, meet friends, aim for a better PB and welcome in my weekend. I truly felt part of the community once I'd started volunteering, giving something back to the event that has helped me stick to my goals on my twelve-stone weight loss journey. Now I'm considering how I can help inspire others in my old position to stick at it, as living proof that with the right frame of mind, and a great network of support and encouragement that parkrun helps to provide, dreams can become an incredible reality.

Dan Meineck, Poole parkrun

For Claire Ellis and her partner, Telford parkrun has helped them lose over four stone between them and they have now completed several 10K races and are targeting their first half marathon. Additionally, parkrun has become a family affair, 'involving my older step children, son-in-law, my daughter aged seven and our son aged two (in the buggy).'

Reading the parkrun weekly newsletter, there are many similar stories from individuals who have started running and are losing weight, reducing their blood pressure, feeling fitter.

parkrun: much more than just a run in the park

One of the reasons why parkrun is so successful in encouraging regular exercise in those who are overweight or have a variety of health problems limiting their physical abilities is that participants of all speeds are not judged but encouraged – by marshals around the course, by volunteers at the finish and by other parkrunners. Added to this are the community spirit, the development of friendships and the sense of achievement each time you've completed the course.

Mental health

Most people who run know about the 'high' that running can bring, and how getting out and going for a run can help you to de-stress, step away from the pressures of work or family and mentally relax. Going to parkrun is no exception, and might bring additional benefits.

> *In the very darkest of times, through two lengthy periods of unemployment, parkrun has been what has got me up in the morning. I cannot overstate the importance of parkrun to me and my family. Over a very challenging few years it has been the stable rock, the community I am proud to be a member of and a group of friends who, somewhat unknowingly, have kept me from being a sad and lonely failure. I remain in awe of the effort put in by our run directors and volunteers, I constantly aspire to be as good as them.*
>
> *Anonymous parkrunner*

John Mallon knows what it's like to suffer with mental health problems. Several years ago he came close to ending his life and considers that he was very lucky that he turned the other way and found someone to talk to. He's also lost members of his family to suicide. Part of his recovery involved photography and getting out walking and running. Now, he sees people who are battling with depression coming to parkrun, and sees the difference that it makes to them. 'I've seen people in the depths of despair, locked away in their house, but they hear about parkrun and they manage to get out and give it a go. And Matt [Event Director of Waterworks parkrun] and the team help them, mentor them and make it easy for beginners to get running. And then they're not locked away, they're out in the park, running, and they feel that they're part of a group, and that's very important.' John Mallon strongly believes that parkrun is not about just running or walking: 'parkruns are vital for our communities, they're a coming together of community. You're getting outside, you're breathing in fresh air and you're meeting people.'

In 2012 I was diagnosed with a mental illness, one that I'd been living with for years and had avoided successfully for such a long time, then one day my body had enough and gave up; I was forced to seek treatment and admit I had a problem. How did I deal with it? I thought about the things my mind was telling me to avoid and did them, step outside of my comfort zone. I entered a half marathon and I signed up for parkrun volunteering. I was already an active parkrunner but had never explored volunteering – I couldn't do that, it was intimidating and meant coming into contact with people I didn't know. Becoming a volunteer was the best thing I could possibly have done; I interacted with new people and made LOTS of new friends, all outside in the fresh air FOR FREE. Even hubby signed up, at first only to support me but now he's inspired too! I did have to squeeze a few parkruns in between volunteering – I had a half marathon to train for which I completed (with sixteen-plus other friends) in May 2013 in 2 hours 44 minutes. I'm now expecting my first child, a child that has already been 'adopted' by Stewart parkrun. I'd love to sign off by saying 'parkrun saved me' – it didn't, I saved myself, but parkrun has made me happy, healthy and proud, priceless emotions when you're in a rut.

Michelle Shaw, Stewart parkrun

The mental health benefits of parkrun might be related to the exercise, the green space, and the whole parkrun atmosphere. Matt Shields, Country Manager for Ireland, said, 'There are a number of women running at parkruns who have told me that they're handling a lot of stress during the week, with work and family. When they get down here on a Saturday morning and run, it puts the week away for them.' Even without the exercise component, volunteering at parkrun appears to bring its own benefits, judging by the number of non-running people volunteering regularly. 'They get hooked on the social aspect,' Matt said.

Serious illness and injury

parkrun has also been useful in helping people return to running after injury – sometimes massive injury – or illness, or in discovering that they have an illness.

Mike Dearing, in his early seventies, started parkrunning at Hull in June 2012 after becoming hooked just by watching the parkrun once: 'I hadn't been able to get my head around the fact that you could just turn up, run and get your time.' Once he'd started, he kept going back regularly, running or volunteering. In February 2014 he felt a bit of pain in his chest after the run and then again during a cycle ride, so he went for a check up. Just days later he had been diagnosed with a severely blocked cardiac artery and was having a stent fitted to open it up. The doctor jokingly said: 'We'll have you up and running in a few weeks...' Although Mike missed the next parkrun because he was not allowed to drive, the following week he was back, walking, and he's now dipped under 32 minutes and is determined to get his time nearer to 28 minutes. 'My doctor said that my fitness due to running helped me through the problem, and parkrun has certainly helped me getting over it faster.' (Sadly, Mike died of cancer in September

2014 after a short illness; his last parkrun was 16 August and he volunteered just a couple of weeks before he died.)

Keith Conkerton, aged 49, diagnosed with multiple sclerosis, as well as having arthritic knees, thought that he would be unable to do any serious exercise. However his wife encouraged him to join her in entering a 10K race and he finally agreed. Wanting to train for this, he went along to Hull parkrun, close to where he lived. He said, 'This proved to be one of the best decisions in my life. I've always been quite gregarious, but I was staggered at how quickly I got to know my fellow parkrunners. I found more and more of these strangers becoming friends and I now have, through the power of parkrun, some of the best friends that I've had in my life.' Additionally, seeing in the results that people in their sixties, seventies and eighties were still running shattered his conception that he was too old to run. 'This has inspired me greatly and has changed my life from a gradual descent into an armchair sports enthusiast, accepting the MS hand that fate had dealt me, into a living, breathing sports participator.'

> *When I was first invited to participate it was called Time Trials and when I went to Banstead Woods, there were all these strapping young people and I thought no, this is not for me. Then I heard that the name had been changed to parkrun and that that it was not a race but a run. So I joined in. I usually come first in my age group, basically because at 79 I am the only one! I have had stomach cancer, skin cancer and at the moment I am getting over prostate cancer. Over the last three years I have had five operations for this and all the time I have kept doing parkruns. I am probably the only parkrunner who has run with a catheter and a leg bag (in tracksuit trousers of course). parkrun has given me the motivation to keep going, to get 100, 200 and now 250 runs. Then it will be 300 runs for my eightieth birthday. Every Saturday morning come sun, rain, mud, snow or ice, parkrun kicks me out of bed. I have never regretted doing a parkrun – I might have half way round, but never ever afterwards.*
> *George Frogley, Banstead Woods parkrun*

parkrun: much more than just a run in the park

John Robson had always been very active as a PE teacher and a fire officer. He completed challenges such as mountain climbs and marathons, raising over £93,000 for local charities. In March 2013, he had a knee operation. 'Within three weeks I'd lost two stone, upper body muscle, and didn't have the strength to use a light switch... I was confined to a wheelchair!' Five weeks and many tests later he was told that he had developed polymyalgia rheumatica, placed on high dosage steroids and told to forget about running and climbing. John refused to accept this. Soon parkrun became his focus. Over five months he learned to walk again and by September 2013 he managed to run for five minutes: 'it was fantastic, out of this world, a magical experience – I was running with a smile.' He ran Riverside parkrun, where he had friends, in October 2013, finishing more than five minutes slower than his PB of 20:15 but 'it didn't matter because I was running again'. He's since also run at Durham, Cheltenham, Carlisle, Sedgefield and Whitley Bay parkruns.

In summer 2012, Cathy Wiser fractured the top vertebrae in her neck 'and I should have died'. While she returned to most normal activities remarkably soon, she found she couldn't run. Following specialist help, she was told to run on soft, flat ground. She said, 'enter parkrun invitation (let no runner forget the power of invitation). What a blessing; Colwick parkrun is flat, soft and *so* friendly. Just didn't matter how fast, how slow, or whether one had children or dogs in tow. Everybody was chatty before and afterwards and I had numerous chats whilst running. I love how there's no specific gear you have to wear or speed you have to be. I love the diligence and friendliness of the volunteers without whom I would have got very lost. I've only volunteered once so far but that's fun too so will again. Thank you parkrun for assisting my recovery.'

Another parkrunner, who had always found running the hardest part of triathlons, came, through parkrun, to actually look forward to the run. Then he was knocked off his bicycle and broke his pelvis. parkrun, he said, gave him 'a terrific incentive to keep up my physiotherapy so I can get running again as soon as possible.'

My boyfriend Lee and I began parkrunning in December 2012 at Cambridge parkrun and it's enabled us to enjoy doing something 'together' even when we're at opposite ends of the country. We were both quite new to running (it was my first 5K) but nevertheless decided to sign up to the 2013 Loch Ness Marathon. Measuring our progress each Saturday really kept the motivation up, and the parkrun community is especially useful when all your friends and family think you've gone mad. I was diagnosed with an autoimmune disorder two weeks before the marathon, which explained some of my training struggles. I don't think it's an exaggeration to say that without parkrun I would never have considered the marathon (that's how good my first finish felt!) and without testing myself during marathon training I would never have bothered getting these things checked out. They are now under control and I can't wait to improve my running – better health is my 'secret PB weapon' this year and I can't wait to share it with the parkrun community!
Katie Godfrey, Cambridge & Wimpole Estate parkruns

Jenny Fairclough used outdoor walking and then running as a way to maintain and improve her fitness during and after treatment for breast cancer. Once she had her five-year 'all clear' she wanted to continue running but without the 'Jenny: breast cancer survivor' label. Turning up at Cuerdon Valley parkrun for the first event, 'immediately I felt welcomed by the event team and encouraged by the amazing community feel of the run.' Starting to go with other parkrunners for the post-run cuppa, getting to know the other runners, being supported in her efforts to improve her own speed, watching other runners progressing, taking part in special events... 'All these things mean that Cuerdon Valley parkrun has truly marked the beginning of my return to normality.'

Julie Oldfield suffered a brain haemorrhage in 2009, affecting her ability to speak and to write, such that she had to give up her job, and leading to seizures, which meant she could no longer drive. She said: 'I started to walk/run as a way to keep fit. A friend was heavily involved in parkrun and suggested I should try it. Fortunately Roundhay parkrun is nearby so I could walk there independently which means a lot to me. After three runs I was hooked; the encouragement from the fellow runners was great.' She has since run a 10K race in Leeds (mindful that a hospital was close by in case of a seizure), then in 2013 a half marathon, as well as reaching the parkrun 50-club; in 2014, her aim is an autumn marathon. Julie said, 'parkrun has improved my health both mental and physical and provided me with a new community of lovely friendly people. I run most weeks, I have had a number of volunteering roles and currently write the weekly report.'

Good habits

parkrun also encourages people to *keep* exercising. One of the greatest problems with exercise programmes in general is that people do not want to keep doing them in the longer term. Many people, for example, join a gym all fired up with enthusiasm in January, with every intention of going three times a week – but by February or March, they are going only a few times a month, and by July, not at all. parkrun is different: it's habit-forming (some say addictive) and it's a good habit to have. When parkrunners start talking about parkrun, their enthusiasm shines through.

Something about parkrun – the near-instant feedback, the camaraderie, the multitude of different goals you can set for yourself, all of these in combination – encourages people not only to return to parkrun week after week, but also to start exercising more during the rest of the week. Repeatedly, Event Directors and other volunteers have novice parkrunners, after a few weeks or a few months asking them, 'do you think I could improve more if I did some running during the week?' Or, 'I'd like to get faster. Do you think it would be worth my joining a running club?'

The science of running and health

Personal stories are one thing but proving the benefits of parkrun needs more than just anecdotes.

A large number of scientific studies over the years have shown conclusively that exercise is good for you, being associated with changes in blood pressure, lipid and lipoprotein profiles, insulin sensitivity, markers of inflammation and so on which are linked to reductions in various chronic diseases. There have been a variety of studies showing that regular running can be beneficial in improving bone strength, improving cardiovascular health and helping people to control their weight. It might even, as indicated by some studies, increase cartilage thickness and help to protect joints.

Running also can improve mental health – for example, being as good as doctor-prescribed medication in helping to control mild to moderate depression. A review published in the *American Journal of Preventive Medicine* in 2013 found that moderate levels of exercise can help in the prevention of development of depression: that is, people who exercise are less likely to become clinically depressed.

Additionally, there are studies indicating that exposure to natural, green spaces can help both physical and mental health. Many studies have shown that, for a given population, people with a low income have higher rates of mortality both overall and due to heart disease. However, one study found that exposure to green spaces reduced the difference between higher-income and deprived individuals in both total mortality and heart-related deaths. And a review published in *Environmental Science and Technology* in 2011 found that exercising in natural surroundings was 'associated with greater feelings of revitalization and positive engagement, decreases in tension, confusion, anger, and depression, and increased energy'. The same paper found that people exercising in natural environments, rather than indoors, 'reported greater enjoyment and satisfaction with outdoor activity and declared a greater intent to repeat the activity at a later date.'

parkrun and SparkLE

parkrun is, literally, a run in the park. It combines both exercise and exposure to green spaces. Is it possible to show scientifically that parkrun is really having a positive impact on people?

Clare Stevinson, a Lecturer in Physical Activity and Health at Loughborough University, and Mary Hickson, Honorary Senior Lecturer and Adjunct Professor in Nutrition and Dietetics at Imperial College London, both thought not only that it was highly possible that parkrun was bringing benefits, but that this should be investigated. Clare was one of the founders of Bramhall parkrun, back in 2008, while Mary, married to Chris Wright, was a great example of the power of parkrun to convert a non-runner not only to running regularly but to actively enjoying the experience. They noted that while the benefits of parkrun are blindingly obvious to anyone who has experienced a few of them, local councils, other potential partners and sponsors, and policy makers want hard evidence of why they should support parkrun.

In 2011, Mary and Clare put together a pilot project, Study of parkrun on Lifestyle and Exercise (SparkLE), to start exploring whether parkrun did indeed have the potential to improve health not just as reported by anecdotes from a growing number of individuals but shown by scientific data on a community scale.

The SparkLE study asked parkrunners to complete a question-naire providing basic personal information such as date of birth for age calculation, height and weight, plus data on their present level of exercise and their level of exercise when they had started parkrun. Finally, they were asked to rate their fitness, health prob-lems, weight control, mental wellbeing, confidence for running, and sense of community on a five-point scale. The subjectively-reported data were combined with the information held in the parkrun database on each runner's initial times and their fastest times, which could be used to indicate fitness, and the change in their age-grade percentage between their first run and their most recent run. The parkrun database also enabled the researchers to look at how often and how regularly any individual participated in a parkrun.

With information from more than 7,300 individuals from 130 parkrun events, there was a good amount of data and Mary and Clare were able to crunch the numbers to give some interesting findings. Their paper, indicating that parkrun might represent a cost-effective community-based intervention for improving pub-lic health, was published in the *Journal of Public Health*.

The study showed that parkrunners improved their fitness (as indicated by their speed for the parkrun) on average by 10.2%. Not surprisingly, parkrunners who were non-runners before they started parkrunning showed the greatest improvement, 15.8%.

Reported physical (fitness, weight control, general health) and psychological (mental wellbeing, confidence for running) benefits were shown to be greatest for the parkrunners who had not been regular runners when they started parkrunning. A massive 96.4% of people who had been non-runners or occasional runners before they started with parkrun felt that their fitness had improved, with nearly two-thirds feeling they had improved weight control due to parkrun. Additionally, more than 85% of people who had not been regular runners before they started with parkrun also felt that their mental wellbeing had improved, that they had improved confidence for running and that they had an increased sense of community, while a majority also felt that it had helped with general health problems: not bad for a run in the park! Similar but more modest improvements were shown for those who had already been regular runners before they found parkrun.

The initial SparkLE study found that on average, people who had been non-runners before they started parkrunning were now completing two hours of vigorous exercise a week. Almost half of them had reached the level of physical activity at which it is considered that real health benefits do occur.

Additionally, and not surprisingly, the study showed that the people who attended parkruns regularly rather than occasionally had the higher perceived benefits.

For Clare and Mary, one of the important aspects of parkrun, as shown by their study, was that it was encouraging regular exercise – and the associated physical and mental health benefits – to sections of the population who are often less likely to get involved in physical activity: middle-aged and older people, and women. Women make up 49% of parkrunners, while for people in general involved in any form of running, jogging or athletics, they make up only 40%.

Following on from the initial study, SparkLE 2 recruited nearly 900 people who were just starting out parkrunning for a longitudinal study, gathering information on their physical activity, fitness and wellbeing at the time they registered with parkrun and then again at six and twelve months after registration. This is being analysed to see if there have been any changes in these aspects now that the participants have started parkrunning.

The parkrun Research Board

Research involving parkrun does not stop with the end of SparkLE 2. parkrun holds a fantastic resource of information on hundreds of thousands of runners, and it is possible to extract anonymised data based on age, sex, number of runs and so on, with data being available from people running weekly over periods of months to years. Additionally, parkrunners meet at known locations on a weekly basis, where it is relatively easy for researchers to meet them and try to recruit people to take part in running-related research. These facts make parkrun highly attractive to many researchers and could lead to some good research which would help inform parkrun and parkrunners. High quality research can be used to demonstrate to local councils and other parties the benefits of parkrun and why it should be supported, and has the potential to provide some answers to questions about, for example, children and running and women running during pregnancy.

One such study has been carried out by the Green Exercise Research Team at the University of Essex. This study, focused on four parkruns in the east of England (Colchester, Chelmsford, Bury St Edmunds and Gorleston), aims to understand whether participating in parkrun improves the psychological wellbeing of participants (reducing stress levels, improving mood), which other elements (such as age, weather conditions, speed of the participant) might influence the improvement in psychological well-being, and to see whether the health benefits associated with parkrunning vary depending on the environmental scenery at the parkrun, e.g. the presence or absence of water features. As with SparkLE 2, the data is presently being analysed.

parkrun is keen to encourage and support high quality research, but needs to avoid spending excessive amounts of time extracting data (parkrun having only a very few paid members of staff) and to prevent any individual parkrun event's volunteers and runners from being overrun with researchers. Therefore the parkrun Research Board (pRB) has been set up, with Mary as the Chair. The Board is made up of seven academics – all parkrun enthusiasts, serving on the pRB voluntarily – and four people from parkrun: founder Paul Sinton-Hewitt, Tom Williams, Chris Wright and Chrissie Wellington. Mainly they work by email, assessing research proposals and asking for clarification and amendments if necessary. Ethical principles must be adhered to in the research and all research approved by the pRB also has to either be approved by the ethics committee of the researcher's institution or have written agreement that due to the nature of the research such approval is not needed.

Anecdotal evidence of the benefits parkrun has brought to many people is available in every parkrun newsletter, numerous tweets and Facebook posts, blog posts and every queue of smiling, happily chatting parkrunners waiting for barcode scanning after their run. Hopefully, the work carried out in the SparkLE studies and other research overseen by the pRB will soon provide robust scientific evidence to back this up.

17

Bounding dogs and bouncing buggies

I've become pretty passionate about parkrun: you can bring your family, family dog – the little ones in the prams don't miss out either.

Leonie Norris, North Shore parkrun

In keeping with parkrun's aim to encourage everyone to run, and unlike most races, parkrun allows people to run with a dog or pushing their children in a buggy (also known as a pushchair, pram or stroller, depending on location).

Bounding dogs

The inclusion of dogs wasn't planned, it just happened. The first parkrunning dog was Tim, Paul Sinton-Hewitt's English

Springer Spaniel. Others saw Paul and Tim running in the Bushy Park Time Trial and realised that they could do the same – so they did, with a wide variety of dogs. Paul likes the fact that people run with their dogs – it helps to keep both the dog and the dog's owner exercised, and as a side benefit it is another sign that parkrun is a timed run, not a race.

So long as the dog is friendly and the owner is sensible, generally all goes well. parkrun policy on running with dogs states: 'we ask that dogs are under firm control, kept on a short lead or harness, and extreme care taken to avoid tripping other runners.' And, of course, it's expected that all runners with dogs will bring their poop-bags and if necessary will stop during the run, pick up their dog's 'offering' and carry it until they can deposit it in an appropriate dog waste receptacle.

A few parkruns are held in locations such as nature reserves or conservation areas which do not allow dogs. Additionally, some courses are not really comfortable for dogs in the middle of crowds of runners and each event organiser has the responsibility to consider this. For example at Nahoon Point in South Africa, Bob Norris decided that it was not suitable because dogs were becoming anxious in the narrow sections, surrounded by large numbers of unfamiliar, fast-moving people.

Everyone who has anything to do with dogs and walking them will have seen, heard about or been involved in situations where a dog on a lead goes around one side of an obstacle, and the owner goes around the other side, with the inevitable confusion that results. And when running, the obstacle in question might be another runner, which leads to the potential for more confusion. The chance for problems to arise gets even larger when there are two or more dogs involved. Over the years, inevitably, the inclusion of dogs has led to occasional problems, with dogs veering across the path, tripping other runners, leads getting tangled around legs and so forth.

Although most of the time owners are sensible and dogs are quite well behaved, the occasional incidents led, in 2012, to an amendment of the official parkrun policy on dogs, resulting in a one-runner, one-dog policy. This is, most definitely, not aimed at preventing people from running with dogs. Quite the reverse! It is intended to make sure that people can keep running with dogs while minimising associated risks. If you have two dogs – well, there's nothing that says you cannot lend one to a friend so that each dog can run with a different person.

Chris Wright set out the new policy in the weekly newsletter to all parkrunners, in which he also said, 'My deepest wish is that this change will help to ensure that dogs are welcome at our runs for many years. I would therefore ask everybody to please help implement this small change in policy.'

Despite the care taken in formulating the policy, it (perhaps inevitably) caused some bad feeling at first, particularly when the message was misunderstood. parkrun tourist John Cassells remembers being at Braunston parkrun soon after the new policy had been announced; a very heated discussion was going on among some runners who were indignant that they would no longer be allowed to run with their dogs. 'Thankfully I was able to explain to them that it wasn't a total ban, just a one-dog limit.'

An aspect which had not been thought about when runners first started bringing their pet dogs to run with them, was the Cani-X (pronounced 'cani-cross') movement. Cani-X involves running attached to your dog or dogs by a wide belt, a two-metre length of bungee line and a special padded harness. It began as a form of off-season training for dog sledding, but any dog breed or mongrel can be involved. So far so good. Problems arose when Cani-X runners, particularly those using two dogs (while this was still allowed), started coming in as the fastest runners at some parkruns, producing times much faster than the times which the same runners could produce without the canine assistance. This resulted in some runners feeling that the Cani-X runners were 'cheating'.

One of the basic principles of parkrun is that each runner is running against the clock, not racing other runners. So it's obvious that if Cani-X runners set a dog-assisted PB then they were only cheating themselves, if they were cheating anyone. However, the Cani-X running times did produce some confusion: it is difficult to compare fastest finishing times to determine the relative challenge of different courses, for example, if you do not know whether the times were run with or without canine assistance. Not wanting to stop people from running Cani-X style, a solution was added to the parkrun software: parkrun volunteer teams now have the ability to mark in the results when runs are dog assisted, providing transparency.

Running with a dog does not always provide faster times. On one memorable occasion, a Rother Valley parkrunner and her dog were sprinting the last fifty metres and heading for a PB. But all thoughts of a fastest time evaporated when the dog suddenly put the brakes on and tottered to the side of the path for a wee! And sometimes dogs stop to poop, or for a quick drink part way round the course.

For some runners, there appeared to be a simple solution to the 'PB with dog' and 'PB without dog' problem: register twice, for example as 'John Smith' when running without the dog and 'Rover Smith' when running attached to your four-footed friend Rover, and keep the two identities for the unassisted and assisted runs respectively. While this might seem a sensible solution, it produces further problems. For one thing, it puts false numbers into the data on the number of runners registered and the number of times they run. These data are more important than they might appear since parkrun uses this information to show the effectiveness of parkrun in getting people out and running, the age groups involved and so forth, which are important to attract sponsorship and support from other organisations. While the absolute numbers of people with such 'double identities' might be small, nevertheless this is a source of data error which the parkrun HQ team are keen to avoid.

Much more problematic from the point of view of the volunteer teams, and what can really confuse the results, is a runner insisting on taking a finish token for him or herself plus one for the dog! Since the timers only press the timer button for humans crossing the line, not for dogs, a runner taking two tokens instantly puts all the results out of sync and it can be a real pain sorting it out.

Some dogs enjoy their parkrun so much that they positively sulk if their owner brings them to the park and then takes up a non-running volunteering role, or goes running without them. Nicki Bowen runs with her dog Tally, a Springer Spaniel; he's one of two regular canine participants at Eastleigh parkrun. Nicki started running with Tally when he was about ten months old, when Nicki, who had been injured, was just looking for a nice steady parkrun. Tally was welcomed from the first week and he really enjoys it. Now he gets quite upset if Nicki gets into her running gear and leaves him in the house on a Saturday morning.

For some dogs the five kilometres is a bit too far; it's not unknown for small dogs to be picked up and carried for a while during the run. At Barrow parkrun, Donna Speirs recalls she was marshalling one day and one runner's tired black Labrador was holding him back rather, so she offered to take it for him. A while later, the dog started pestering to be allowed to hold its own lead and, without thinking, she let him. This meant, of course, that *she* was no longer holding the end of the lead – and just as she realised this, the rested dog took off again after the runners. 'And I didn't even know the dog's name, then, so I couldn't try to call him back!'

Bouncing buggies

Rather like running with dogs, people parkrunning with a buggy wasn't planned; it just happened, with someone turning up one day and asking if they could do it. Of course the answer was yes, and this enables people to run when otherwise they might be unable to participate due to not having someone to look after the baby.

> *It sat in my garage for six or eight weeks. Every time I took the washing out of the dryer or went to grab a cold beer it was there – waiting. A generous gift from a cousin after the birth of my second daughter. A running buggy. Dark red. Designed for exactly the kind of thing I love doing – running. But the streets of Bradford didn't feel like quite the right place. Or maybe I thought, 'dads don't run with prams.' I know, I thought, I'll take it to parkrun – shoot a load of photos for my cousin – and pretend I used it. So I just about manage to feed, clothe and organise a seven-month-old baby on a warm, dry Saturday morning in August and make it to my local parkrun. I feel a bit odd, but it's suddenly a bit easier as I catch sight of another buggy in the distance. Then I'm at the start line and people are smiling and waving into the pram. Then my daughter's laughing. Then everyone's shouting 'teeny tiny hill' like everyone always does, and then we're off. Then I realise this is ace. I won't lie, it's partly helped because – unbelievably – I can still run fast enough to actually pass other runners. But it's also hearing my daughter shouting out as we pass runners and the joy of being out together. We've done fifteen now and I love it. I get time on my own, Mum gets a lie-in and the only downside I can see is that she always crosses the finish line first!*
>
> Tom Paget, Bradford parkrun

Bounding dogs and bouncing buggies

Unlike dog-assisted and some wheelchair athletes, runners with buggies are usually slower than when they run without the buggy, and no course records have been set running with a buggy. Despite this, some of the people pushing their young children around are really quite speedy. However, there is absolutely no intention to start a separate category in which to mark runs with buggies: if such a category was developed, there's a risk that the competitive instincts of some runners might get the better of them, and the results could be dangerous both for the toddlers in the buggies and for other parkrunners.

Andrew Gould runs with a buggy containing his son George, when the course is not too wet and muddy. It makes the run really hard work for Andrew, given that the Eastleigh course is all on grass except where it's on mud, includes a little hill which has to be tackled three times, and contains lots of corners. 'You can't use your arms to help you, it's all in your legs and on that third time up the hill...' George finds it rather more relaxing and often falls asleep during the run. If he is awake he really enjoys it, cheering and shouting 'catch them!'

In August 2013 my husband and I adopted a one-year-old boy and took it in turns to run and to marshal, with the small boy in his buggy looking cute and clapping the runners. Shortly after purchasing a running buggy on eBay I ran pushing him. And running that course with a buggy is no stroll in the park! I am always the last buggy runner to finish but never mind! I hope I'm showing my son a good example and he will join the Roundhay parkrun family one day.
Kieren Balkwill, Roundhay parkrun

Running with a buggy is definitely harder work than running without one. 'It's about three, three and a half minutes slower with the buggy than without, especially with that hill,' said Steve Cooley at Banstead Woods. 'Bushy parkrun is easier, and Brighton &

Hove parkrun – the tarmac course is quite easy; this is harder. But it's good being able to run with the buggy and it's good training as well – it's much easier after when you run without the buggy. And Josh [in the buggy] enjoys it as well.' At Leamington parkrun they often have four or five buggies; regular volunteer Simon Teale is always impressed with the runners who manage to push these up the hill and over all the roots.

> *parkrun is an integral part of our family life. I started parkrunning at Cannon Hill parkrun in 2011 and my wife soon became interested and joined me most parkrundays. Following the birth of our daughter, we bought a running buggy so that we could continue to parkrun as a family. Sometimes I parkrun on my own and aim for a PB, sometimes I push the buggy, and sometimes all three of us parkrun together. We really appreciate the fact that parkrun allows parkrunners to push their children in their buggies as it means we can do something fun, active and healthy as a family.*
> *Nathan Warren, Cannon Hill parkrun*

Martin Yelling doesn't just run with a buggy – he runs with a double buggy, containing twin sons Sonny and Beau. 'I started running with a buggy when Ruby, who is now four, was about five or six months old. Now I run with the boys in a BOB Duelly, which is quite sizeable. The first couple of times we just went around at the back, enjoying the boys' first experience of parkrun – I remember saying to Liz at the end, "the boys have just done their first parkrun!" Now sometimes we're at the back, and Liz and I might swap who is pushing the buggy. Other times I decide to hammer round and I've found that it's best if I can get a fast start at the front, that way both I and the people around me get a clearer run. I've done 17:22 with both the boys and I have a secret ambition to see if I can sneak under seventeen minutes with the double buggy.'

Martin acknowledges that Poole parkrun, which he describes on the *Marathon Talk* podcast as 'the fastest parkrun course', is close to ideal for running with a buggy, being pretty much flat and on paved paths, without difficult curves or other obstacles: 'not like running Forest of Dean with a buggy.' Martin also recognises that it's a real privilege to be able to run the parkrun with the twins in their buggy when he wants to: 'One of the great things about parkrun is that it has broken down the barriers of what's acceptable in a running event.'

Another runner with a double buggy is Corey Unwin running the hilly Larne parkrun course and bringing his time down under 21 minutes – quite an achievement on that course which is challenging enough that the record is 17:29 – and always with a smile.

When my wife and I found out we were expecting our first child I decided it was time to make changes and to take up running again (after a fifteen year hiatus since my childhood!) My aim was to do something that would eventually make my daughter proud and getting fit seemed like a good place to start. A friend let us know about Valentines parkrun so we turned up not really sure what to expect; I was amazed by how many people were there and how friendly everyone was and from there I was hooked. Whenever training has got stale or hard and I've found it hard to hit the streets, parkrun has always been there as my rock to keep me going. This year I'm competing in my first triathlons... I've had the pleasure of pushing our daughter Freya in her running buggy most weeks since she was four months old and thoroughly enjoy the different perspective running with a buggy gives. Freya usually laughs at the first lap and is fast asleep on the second lap! My wife has also now completed 22 parkruns, reducing her time by ten minutes! parkrun improves our fitness and gives us a great family start to the weekend. Thank you parkrun.

David Bell, Valentines parkrun

Another parent tackling hills with a buggy – and a double one at that – is Scott Northey who mostly runs at Blackbutt, arguably the most challenging course in Australia. He pushes his two young sons, who are three and four. At first he just had a standard pram and the front wheels wobbled rather, so he got a three-wheeled running version which works much better. The uphills are tough, particularly when he's leaning forwards, trying not to slip and with his sons trying to talk with him, but he admits that he can actually cover the final one and a half kilometres downhill section a few seconds faster with the pram and sons than without.

In September 2013 I gave birth to my third son, Flynn, and I knew the time had come to have a go at a parkrun. Huddersfield has an excellent course for buggies, so when Flynn was ten days old, with my doctor's permission we did our first parkrun together, slowly, in 49 minutes. I am still not a runner but I love getting my family up and organised every Saturday morning, my PB has improved to 33:22 and I recently had two weeks off due to injury and had a brilliant time barcode scanning. I run with my ordinary buggy (I dream of a proper running buggy) and Flynn loves it although he does keep getting heavier which makes it more difficult. My biggest parkrun fail was during the Christmas Day run which my husband and I ran with all the boys in buggies (my eldest two together with my husband) and me and Flynn together. I found it so incredibly hard and I was really disappointed with myself. It wasn't till the following parkrun that I realised that I had run the entire 5K with the buggy's brake on! No wonder it was bloody hard!

Sarah-Jane Pattison, Huddersfield parkrun

Dog-and-buggy run

And occasionally a runner comes to parkrun with both a dog and a buggy. For example, at Leamington parkrun Ben Smith regularly attends with both, and commonly overtakes quite a few people. Obviously a very well-behaved dog is essential if you are going to do this, together with a hefty dose of common sense and extra care for the legs of other parkrunners.

Bounding dogs and bouncing buggies

And try not to copy the parkrunner at Bournemouth who tethered his greyhound to the buggy while he tied his shoelace – only to have the dog go racing off pulling the buggy behind him, while the toddler inside squealed in delight!

18

Location, location, location

The park itself is lovely; it's just beautiful in spring with the trees coming into blossom – it really lifts your heart.

Amanda Woodham, Brighton & Hove parkrun

parkruns are held in an amazing variety of locations, from city centres to beaches and large nature reserves, and from reclaimed land to World Heritage Sites. Some runs are held entirely on wide tarmac or concrete paths, others on grass, sand, gravel or bark-covered trail, and many on mixed surfaces. Formats vary from single-lap courses to two-, three-, four- and even a five-lap course, as well as out-and-back courses and more complex layouts. And they are all traffic-free.

Each parkrun website's course page includes a map and a description explaining the format such as the number of laps. What the maps don't show is how flat or undulating the course is. In general, courses fall into one of two categories: they are either praised by their regulars as being 'flat and fast' or proudly described as being 'undulating' or 'challenging'. A few events bluntly state that their course is hilly.

There is no 'best' parkrun – they all have unique features, whether the terrain, the views, the café or certain event traditions. Some are easier to navigate than others. On the day of the Colwick trial event, with about fifteen runners, the Run Director described the course, sent the runners off – and was somewhat astonished when they reappeared from five or six different directions. Obviously the course or the course markings needed to be rethought. And Forest of Dean parkrun is widely recognised as being very picturesque, but more than one visitor has suggested that it is best enjoyed while accompanied by a native guide.

To describe all the parkruns worldwide would take a complete book in itself. This chapter illustrates the variety of parkruns and some of their unique features.

UK

It is impossible to include here any reasonable proportion of the UK's nearly 300 parkruns; the following are, therefore, a mere taster.

The Bushy parkrun course is a flat single lap, with the start and finish sections on grass and a central two to three kilometre section on gravel paths. It can be quite magical on misty autumn mornings with red deer likely to pop out at any moment, particularly down the starting avenue.

Hull parkrun also has a flat course, two and a bit laps on tarmac paths around a large, irregularly shaped boating lake and an animal centre in East Park, producing some fast times. It has permanent start, finish and kilometre markers, making it ideal for people wanting to time themselves on a freedom run.

Some other flat UK courses
Cardiff: an out-and-back course along the River Taff.
Poole: two laps around a boating lake followed by a final short lap around a cricket pitch and cycle oval.
Bromley: two and a third laps around the park.
York: about one and a half laps of the tarmac service road around York racecourse.
Newcastle: crossing the Town Moor on a tarmac path as well as skirting the perimeter of the Military Vehicle Museum.
Newport: two anti-clockwise laps with a few twists and turns through the beautiful grounds of Tredegar House, on gravel tracks, bark-lined paths, grass and compact earth.
St Albans: 800 metres along a path, three times round the lake then returning down the path.
Beeston: gravel and tarmac single lap around the recreation fields plus a little switch-back.
Mansfield: three laps on concrete and gravel paths.
Riverside, Chester-le-Street: nearly three flat laps, mainly on tarmac paths but including a grass section, with half of each loop alongside the River Wear, home to numerous ducks and swans.
Dulwich: three flat loops on smooth tarmac paths; particularly suitable for wheelchairs.

Sea views are provided by a number of coastal courses. Edinburgh, out and back along Cramond/Silverknowes Promenade, borders the Firth of Forth, so it can be rather breezy. Aberdeen parkrun starts near Donmouth local nature reserve and takes you up and down the Beach Esplanade beside Aberdeen Bay. Greenock runs along the Greenock Esplanade, Whitley Bay provides 'bracing seaside conditions', Hartlepool runs along the promenade; and Southsea is another esplanade run.

Location, location, location

Banstead Woods is nearly two laps, starting a little way up the hill, so that runners only have to run the full length of the incline on the second lap. The forest paths have enough give in them to make striding out on the long downhill section very pleasant. The woods are particularly beautiful in spring when bluebells carpet the ground. Barrow parkrun in the English Lake District is two and a half laps and definitely undulating (hilly!), while Keswick parkrun, also in the Lakes, is an out-and-back along the Keswick Railway Path: trail, sometimes muddy, but 'quite flat for Keswick' (!) and with lovely views of the River Greta the whole way. St Andrews parkrun in Craigtoun Country Park is a gentle mixed-terrain course of gravel and tarmac paths through woods, with a small section on grass.

The original Eastleigh parkrun course was at Lakeside and held beside the lake. The first Event Director, Brett Briton, coached triathletes. parkrunner Henry Hopkins said, 'I'll never forget arriving to find about ten hardy souls who had already done their 2.4 mile swim and were just going to do a quick parkrun before cycling fifty miles home!' The designated winter course got too muddy with the pounding of many feet and the event had to move again, this time to Netley Abbey. Then the parkrun split, the original Eastleigh parkrun moving to its new home (an all-grass three-lap course up and down the disused fairways of Fleming Park's old golf course) while an offshoot stayed at Royal Victoria Country Park as the new Netley Abbey parkrun (a fairly flat three-lap route mostly on tarmac and gravel paths).

Conkers parkrun in the East Midlands is a scenic and undulating trail out-and-back with a loop around a wood at the far end; part of the loop runs alongside Ashby Canal. Graves parkrun is a pleasant two-lap course, mostly on tarmac paths, taking runners past a small boating lake and fish ponds as well as past Highland cattle at the far end and through the animal farm at the end of each lap. Ashton Court, on tarmac road and gravel path, is out with about 100 metres of ascent, two parts quite steep, then back again; views over Bristol and the surrounding countryside make the climb worthwhile – and at least it's downhill on the way back! Heaton Park parkrun in north Manchester is complex and definitely undulating, on paths, passing a stately home at the highest point and a lake at the lowest point. Ipswich combines gravel paths on the first half of each lap with a cross-country section, downhill then gently climbing, for the second half.

Ingenuity has sometimes been needed to fit a parkrun into the limited available space. Highbury Fields parkrun in London is a backwards-D shape with *five laps*, on concrete paths but with the finishing section on grass. Aberystwyth parkrun in Wales uses an out-and-back lap on the wide central path through Plascrug Park, then three anticlockwise laps up one side path (separated from the main path by grass and a row of trees on either side), across and down the other, before a last dash back up the central path.

Tilgate parkrun near Crawley, West Sussex starts with a gentle grassy slope down to reach and circumnavigate the lake, which is home to ducks, herons and swans with, in season, fluffy grey cygnets. It then heads out through the mature woodlands of the park and over some hills before returning for a second lap of the lake. Kingsbury Water parkrun in the West Midlands is also through woodland; it starts with 800 metres on tarmac road, moving onto gravel paths as it passes Willows pool and takes a circuit around Bodymoor Heath Water, Causeway Pool and the Model Boat Pool before finishing back down the road. Worcester parkrun is also mainly in woodland, starting and finishing around playing fields, with two circuits of the Nunnery Wood woodland paths in between.

Lloyd parkrun, Croydon was described by a visitor as 'a proper cross-country course'. The two laps, all on grass (and mud in winter) each incorporate a sharp, speed-stealing turn into the main hill. Wimpole Estate parkrun is a single lap which starts and finishes on estate roads but with most of the course cross-country on trail and paths across undulating parkland. Killerton is also undulating; on a mixture of grassy tracks and stony trails, it is a single lap course taking you into the countryside, with lovely views across the fields. Medina, I.O.W. parkrun on the Isle of Wight is about 3K on grass, 2K on paths, slightly undulating, with views of the River Medina and of Newport. Gunnersbury is a figure of eight, quite twisting, on grass, tarmac and uneven paths, and past pretty ponds and follies; it starts downhill on grass – and finishes up that hill. Hampstead Heath parkrun is definitely undulating, on woodland paths and concrete, the two laps passing through ancient woodland and past ponds. Brighton & Hove parkrun also has its hills, although Amanda Woodham says that the tarmac surface of the paths is quite springy.

Margate parkrun on the east coast of Kent can be a challenge to pace properly, not because of any hills – the mixed tarmac and grass course is flat, along the coastline at Palm Bay and using part of the Viking Coastal Trail – but because of the wind coming off the sea. Durham parkrun crosses three bridges (one providing the only incline on the course!) and offers beautiful views of the River Wear (often with university rowing crews), Durham Cathedral and the eleventh-century Durham Castle. At Telford, a short starting section is followed by a long lap and a short lap of Randlay Pool, and you run past animatronic dinosaurs. Parke parkrun uses trail paths, tarmac path and gravel cycle path, with a very stony section near the start and end; it has notably steep hills in the wooded section.

Portrush parkrun in Northern Ireland is run along East Strand Beach from the promenade to the end and back again. Matt Shields said, 'The course is never the same two weeks in a row:

the tide can be in and you're running on soft sand, or the tide can be well out and you can have flat, hard sand. The difference [in running time] would be five or ten minutes. There are some weeks when you turn up and think: "You know what? Let's just chill out and enjoy it!" because there's no chance of running a PB. There are days when there's rough seas and the breakers are coming up beside you... it's hard to have a bad day. It's also near the Giant's Causeway, and it attracts lots of English parkrun tourists.' If you arrive early, you sometimes get to watch racehorses galloping along the beach.

Larne parkrun in Carnfunnock Country Park, twenty miles north of Belfast, overlooks the sea. With footing including tarmac, gravel and trail paths, and a number of twists and turns, it is described on its website as 'an undulating picturesque course'. It's proudly known locally as hilly, challenging and tough, ideal for building strength and stamina, but also absolutely beautiful, on a good day providing views clear across to Scotland. Citypark parkrun, Craigavon, is a single lap on tarmac paths around two lakes; Queen's parkrun, South Belfast, is two fast laps on gravel paths; while Derry City is an out-and-back alongside, and crossing over, the River Foyle, on paved and bitmac paths.

Denmark

Three of the Danish courses are in the Copenhagen area: Amager Fælled is a fast, flat, two loop course on paths mainly covered with gravel or sandy soil; Amager Strandpark, in Amager Beach Park, is a single lap, very flat on paved roads with beautiful sea views throughout, while Fælledparken, also a single-lap course, is in Copenhagen Park at the heart of Copenhagen, on gravel paths. Of the others, Brabrand parkrun takes place on varied terrain with hills and scenic countryside, with views across Aarhus. The rest are forest courses: Esbjerg in Vognsbøl park is a single-lap course on gravel and soil forest trails; Vejen is a single-lap course, mainly on forest trail, in a beautiful natural area; and Nibe is a two-lap forest course, hillier than the others, with varying substrates including asphalt, gravel, grass and ordinary forest floor.

Australia

There are already more than ninety parkruns in Australia, with at least one in every region of the mainland and on Tasmania. With fewer large city parks than in the UK but plenty of cycle paths which can be repurposed as parkrun paths on a Saturday morning, many are out-and-back courses, often beside rivers, lakes or seashores.

Kirra, in Queensland, is probably the fastest course in Australia at present: dead flat, out and back along a beach promenade. Wynnum parkrun is also a flat coastal course, fast despite its two turnaround points. Cleveland parkrun is another coastal out-and-back Queensland event, partly on concrete paths and partly on wooden boardwalk, with just a 'playful' incline in the middle and lovely views. Kingscliff, also an out-and-back coastal run, is one of the most beautiful, on a boardwalk along a beach, with golden sand and surf waves rushing in; some runners leave the boardwalk for the return leg, running on the sand for fun instead.

Sonia O'Sullivan is particularly fond of Albert parkrun in Melbourne, where the course along the lake gives backdrops of the whole skyline of the city, and you get the swans on the lake and in winter the freezing fog just lifting off the water.

Pioneer parkrun in Western Australia is partly on an elevated boardwalk leading up to a treetop walkway! Claisebrook Cove parkrun in Western Australia takes a route out and back along the Swan River, then runs around the man-made cove which gives the run its name, and finishes up a short, sharp, twenty metre hill known locally as Heartbreak Hill. Notable features include the black swans, cormorants and even dolphins swimming up the river in twos or threes.

Albury-Wodonga parkrun crosses the border between the Australian states of Victoria and New South Wales. Starting at Hovell Tree Park, Aldbury, the out-and-back course follows the Murray River Trail, initially on the western shore before crossing the Murray River (the state boundary) and continuing north on the eastern shore to the turnaround point.

Shellharbour parkrun at Killalea Reserve, New South Wales, is a beautiful, undulating one-lap cross-country course, mainly on grass, but including 300 metres on sand along a popular surf beach before heading inland past a lagoon and round the reserve, with the final section along a gravel track. Fingle Bay is another picture-postcard run with blue water, tropical white sand and a couple of hundred yards of the course being on the sand.

Rockingham parkrun in Western Australia is an out-and-back, mostly flat, shoreside route in a long, beautiful park. It's mainly on concrete with about 800 metres of grass around the perimeter of the Naval Memorial Park, which is home to a ship's cannon, a submarine's fin, and various monuments; the onshore breeze can be challenging in winter. Sandon Point parkrun in New South Wales is possibly the most scenic, with its meeting point on cliffs overlooking the ocean, while Penrith Lakes parkrun is a flat course, looping around the lake that was built for the rowing regattas at the Sydney Olympics. Launceston parkrun, Tasmania, starts and finishes with about one kilometre along a compacted gravel flood levee before heading down a ramp and around the Heritage Forest, also mostly on gravel, with pleasant tree-lined areas. A couple of barricades to stop motorcycles mean that the run incorporates a right-then-left shimmy feature.

Currently, the most challenging routes in Australia are Blackbutt and Bunyaville parkruns. Bunyaville, in Queensland, is a beautiful run, starting on a grass field, continuing on a gravel track followed by an uphill stretch on a one-person-wide track created for the parkrun. It then continues on fire trails, down to the creek and up again. The return leg is tougher than the out, with a long uphill section. A variety of birds may be seen or heard, including cockatoos, mynahs, quail, kookaburras and others. Blackbutt, through a national park in the Newcastle area, New South Wales, is mainly on tarmac trails, but includes an uphill start and multiple hills in the middle, giving about 130 metres of ascent during the run. You get to run past an enclosure of kangaroos and emus as a bonus.

St Peters parkrun, Sydney, also has an infamous hill – but one well worth climbing for the sweeping views of the Sydney skyline at the top – and Augustine Heights has two hills on each of its two laps.

The first three events in South Australia were all scenic out-and-back courses: Torrens, along the Torrens River; Mount Barker, on paths through established wetlands; and Mount Gambier, circling three quarters of the Blue Lake. The Australian Capital Territory around Canberra also has three parkruns. Gunghalin, north of Canberra, is a rarity in Australia, using a circuit course of just over one lap around Yerrabie Pond. Ginninderra, a little way south, is a lollipop-shaped course, taking in a circuit of the Lake Ginninderra Peninsula between the 1.2 kilometre start and finish sections. Tuggeranong, south of Canberra, is a more typical out-and-back course using tarmac and gravel paths skirting around Lake Tuggeranong.

South Africa

There are more than thirty parkruns in South Africa. Delta (the first event) and Roodepoort parkruns in Johannesburg are approximately 1,700 metres above sea level, making these the highest altitude parkruns in South Africa – or indeed anywhere, at present. Willem Loison, who ran 75 times at Bushy parkrun in London before moving back to South Africa, really noticed the difference when he started running at Roodepoort parkrun: 'The first one I felt I was going to die!' Not only was there the altitude difference but the two-lap course is a lot hillier. Delta's single-lap course is also far from flat; one of its hills has earned the nickname 'Polly Shorts' after a famous section of the Comrades ultramarathon route.

Greenpoint parkrun is worth running for its ever-changing views: 'initially you see Signal Hill, then you run towards the stadium, then along the road and if you look up you can see Devil's Peak; on the way back you're heading towards the sea then you go around the corner and see the Lion's Head then Signal Hill again,' said Suraj Valand, who designed the course. The beautiful Woodlands parkrun features a mixture of surfaces including tarmac, grass, brick paths, a wooden bridge and stepping stones; there are some short but steep hills. Part of the course is in an animal reserve, so no dogs are allowed and you need to watch out for ducks (sometimes right on the route), guineafowl, peafowl, dassies (rock hyrax) and even springboks. Summerfields parkrun is another beautiful run, along the bank of the Sabie river by Kruger National Park.

North Beach parkrun in Durban uses a wide, flat out-and-back course along the beach front, with great coastline views on one side. Nahoon Point parkrun in East London goes across the beach (whales may be seen offshore) and into thick indigenous forest. Big Bay parkrun in Cape Town is an out-and-back course with runners starting on a grass embankment then running out along the concrete beach promenade and back again. Once a month, when the tide is right in, part of the course has to divert inland slightly.

Voortrekker Monument parkrun in Pretoria is all on tarred roads and has a long steep hill up to Fort Schanskop – providing magnificent views of Pretoria, although I'm not sure how many of the parkrunners appreciate it by that time. Naval Hill also provides great views, over Bloemfontein, but the course starts and finishes well up the hill by a massive statue of Nelson Mandela and is actually quite flat. The hill is also home to Franklin Nature Reserve and there's a chance to see some of the local wildlife including ostrich, zebra and giraffe.

Poland

parkrun Poland's first thirteen events provide a wide variety of courses including city parks, wooded areas and seaside locations. Those looking for a PB can head to the flat, fast courses of Gdańsk, Gdynia and Kraków. Gdańsk and Gdynia are both on the coast of the Baltic Sea and are therefore quite windy courses; Gdynia, an out-and-back course right along the seafront, is particularly scenic, while Gdańsk parkrun is a two-lap course in pleasant wooded parkland; Kraków offers its natural beauty as well as stunning views of the old town. Runners who prefer cross-country type courses should definitely visit Żary in western Poland, Leszno (between Poznań and Wrocław) and Konstancin-Jeziorna south of Warszawa; all three offer beautiful but more challenging runs. Leszno is a single-lap anticlockwise course on dirt road, bike path, sandy road and asphalt. Żary parkrun takes you on a figure-of-eight course, with one loop much larger than the other, through the Green Forest on compacted earth paths as well as gravel roads and some tarmacked road, while Konstancin-Jeziorna is a two-lap course, on gravel, packed earth and sand paths through the forest.

Those who love city parks are advised to attend Łódź, Poznań, Szczecinek, Cieszyn or the two Warszawa events, Warszawa-Praga and Warszawa-Żoliborz; these are all located in quiet parks in the city centres. Łódź provides an opportunity to visit the old Ponia-towski Park with its big trees and wide paths. Szczecinek parkrun, situated by Lake Trzesiecko, is a long thin loop of a course taking you along the lake shore, beside the river and past the headquarters of the Regional State Forest situated in a former castle before returning to finish just thirty metres from the start. Warszawa-Praga is completely flat, run on gently curving, wide tarmac paths lined with mature trees (home to red squirrels) and with a long finish straight down the centre of the park after two and a half laps of the periphery. Warszawa-Żoliborz's two-lap course uses narrower tarmac paths in more open parkland, with one stretch of gravel and one of sand past the children's playground; there's a little hill before the final 300 metres.

Two of the most unusual of all parkrun courses worldwide are Poznań and Cieszyn. Poznań parkrun takes place in Park Cytad-ela (Citadel Park) which, although the biggest park in Poznań, is still not huge. Nevertheless the course has sufficient twists and turns that the whole 5K is fitted into a single lap. Generally, parkrun teams are encouraged to keep their courses simple, making written descriptions easy and minimising the need for signs and marshals, but this course was specifically designed to encourage people to look around and appreciate their natural and cultural surroundings, and to lead them past some of the amazing features within the park. On their way around the course, runners pass not only trees and shrubs, roses and annual bedding plants but also tanks, aircraft and memorials. Cieszyn goes one better than Albury-Wodonga: rather than crossing a state border within a country, it has the honour of being the only parkrun course which takes place in two countries. Starting and finishing in Poland, the course crosses over the River Olše and into the Czech Republic, with nearly half of the route being within that country, before returning into Poland. Fortunately, you are not asked to show your passport at the border!

New Zealand

The first five events to be set up in New Zealand were all in the North Island. Cornwall parkrun, in the sanctuary of Cornwall Park right in the middle of bustling Auckland, provides the feeling of being transported into the English countryside. It's also a working farm with sheep and cows grazing in paddocks and chickens and pheasants foraging. The out-and-back course is undulating with one relatively long hill. Just south of Auckland is Barry Curtis parkrun, a mainly flat two-lap course in a lovely, large open park with wetlands and boardwalks, beautiful bush landscaping and interesting artwork, as well as a great children's playground right near the start. Just over an hour's drive south from Auckland is Hamilton Lake parkrun, around the lake shore in a very pretty location with an abundance of wonderful birdlife and native bush plantings making this setting a very special place; it's a flat, easy course, if somewhat exposed to the weather as you run around the lake.

Lower Hutt parkrun at the southern end of North Island, not far from Wellington, was the first parkrun in New Zealand; it's run along the bank of the Hutt River. This is a scenic flat, fast, out-and-back course on a calm day but locals pride themselves on having the strongest headwind or tailwind when the Wellington wind is blowing! The nearby Porirua parkrun is also out-and-back, although more undulating. The Event Director, Astrid van Meeuwen-Dijkgraaf, really liked the potential for faster and slower runners to encourage one another as they pass during the run, which she saw at Lower Hutt and wanted to duplicate. It takes place in Bothamley Park; tucked away in a protected gulley, the course runs along the Kenepuru Stream lined with pines and native bush.

The birdsong is lovely and the surroundings are very peaceful; the outward leg climbs slowly, so the return is an easier downhill.

Dunedin parkrun in the South Island is fairly far south; it changes its start time in winter to 9 o'clock because of the dark mornings. It's situated in beautiful botanical gardens, looping around exquisite manicured, formal gardens then crossing over the river to go up rather steeply through some wilder bush areas; the view at the top is worth it – and is followed by a welcome downhill section. The second South Island parkrun to start was Hagley, in Christchurch. It runs on flat, hard paths except for the start and finish on grass. Millwater in the North Island is out and back along a smooth but undulating path alongside the Orewa River Estuary.

Ireland

Malahide parkrun, in the grounds of Malahide Castle, was the first Republic of Ireland event. After a short lap around a golf course, the longer lap takes runners further out into the grounds and through some wooded sections. This fairly flat event has arguably the best tea house of the Irish parkruns and is the pride of north Dublin. Marlay parkrun, held in the popular Marlay Park, is the pride of south Dublin. A long lap around the golf course and outer perimeter of the park is sandwiched between laps of the concert field – run anti-clockwise initially and clockwise to finish. Griffeen parkrun in west Dublin is a flat two-lap course around the perimeter of Griffeen Valley Park in Lucan, crossing the river twice on each lap and including some wooded areas, while St Annes in eastern Dublin is in a picture postcard park, once part of the Guinness estate and now owned by Dublin council. Run mainly on gravel and tarmac paths, runners finish on a 600-metre straight down the main wide tree-lined avenue.

Location, location, location

Sonia O'Sullivan loves Castle Demesne in Macroom, where you enter the grounds through the castle gates and, 'it's a lovely setting, a little forest park, and you go have to go under an archway – the only problem with it is that you have to go up this hill twice; it's definitely not a PB course.' The arch is quite a draw with parkrun tourists, who always want to be photographed standing next to it.

Clonakilty, near the south coast, is in the grounds of the local agricultural show, and involves four anticlockwise laps of the flat, fast course. Westport is an out-and-back course on a disused railway track which has been tarred over as a cycle and running track. Participants run gently downhill to the Westport Quay, then gradually uphill on the way back. Castlebar, a little way northeast, is a two-lap course around Lough Lannagh; the second lap is lengthened with a loop around the playground and outdoor gym. This course provides views of Croagh Patrick, the holy mountain.

Naas, southwest of Dublin, uses the racecourse ambulance track to give a two-and-a-half-lap course. It looks easy and fairly flat, but it's a long haul up the back straight, and exposed to the winds. Ardgillan parkrun, tough but beautiful, lies on the east coast of Ireland, overlooking the Irish Sea. It starts and finishes at Ardgillan Castle, with a figure-of-eight course on stony paths and tracks through both open and wooded sections of the castle grounds. There are some pleasant long downhill sections but the final kilometre is back up the hill.

Knocknacarra parkrun, Galway, is also set in a lovely park and run on gravel and tarmac paths. The course is full of twists and turns so you might get lost – but won't be bored! As a bonus, there's great west of Ireland hospitality in the community centre afterwards. Oldbridge parkrun, a single, but somewhat complex lap, starts and finishes at the Battle of the Boyne Visitor Centre, Oldbridge estate, Drogheda, while Tymon parkrun is a two-lap, mostly flat course on tarmac paths, with some undulation, and Waterstown parkrun in Palmerston is another two-lap course on tarmac. The single-loop course of Bere Island, in contrast, starts with a hill for the first 400 metres then rewards runners with views of the Atlantic and Lonehort Viking harbour.

USA

Livonia parkrun, Michigan is mainly flat and mostly on grass, with some sections on asphalt and cement paths; it goes around a sports fields and beside lovely wooded areas. It can get rather snowy in the winter. Durham, North Carolina, an out-and-back course, is also fairly flat. The paved path along the Third Fork Creek Trail includes boardwalks and bridges over the creek. There are plenty of trees and lots of wildlife. Clermont Waterfront, Florida, is definitely flat, on asphalt paths alongside Lake Minneola.

Russia

Of the first seven parkrun Russia courses, five are around Moscow. The most central, Gorky Park, is an out-and-back along the embankment of the Moscow River, as is Kolomenskoe parkrun a bit further south. Severnoe Tushino parkrun, with a bit of undulation, is on tracks partly along the waterfront of the Khimki Reservoir, where the marine museum with a real submarine is located, and partly further into the park. Meshchersky parkrun provides clean air and silence; it's fairly flat, on granite-chip paths, running among giant pines and birches. Izmailovo parkrun is another forest run along a track to a large pond and back, and undulating. Yelagin Island parkrun in St Petersburg follows a path around the circumference of the island. Stavropol parkrun in southern Russia, between the Black and Caspian seas, is an out-and-back course. It uses the central avenues of the park, starts and finishes near the zoo and runners pass the café – which is an actual aeroplane!

Singapore

East Coast parkrun in Singapore is an out-and-back following the coastline of East Coast Park, with coastal views throughout.

Extreme parkrun locations
Northernmost*: Yelagin Island parkrun, St Petersburg, Russia (59°56'N)
Southernmost: Dunedin parkrun, South Island, New Zealand (45°52'S)
Closest to Equator: East Coast Park parkrun, Singapore (1°17'N)
Highest Altitude: Delta and Roodepoort parkruns, South Africa (1,700m)
*Record previously held by Elliðaárdalur parkrun, Iceland (64°08'N)
[Data to October 2014]

19

Partnership and sponsorship

For me that's what parkrun is all about – inspiring people to get into running as well as helping them to explore these special places available to them.

Rob Joules, Sports Partnership Manager, National Trust

parkruns do not happen in a vacuum. Each event needs a physical location where the run can be held. Additionally, one of the pillars on which parkrun is based is that it is completely free to the participant; for this to continue it is necessary for parkrun to secure funding to cover all the costs, from course markers to computer servers. Partnership and sponsorship have been, and continue to be, vital to parkrun.

Partnership and sponsorship

Local governments and park owners

In the UK, most parkruns are held in municipal parks and permission has to be granted by the local council. Councils vary in their initial reactions to the idea of having a parkrun, some practically rolling out the red carpet while others are uncertain. However, once parkrun is explained, most local authorities recognise that it provides a valuable service in encouraging healthy exercise. In some cases, very strong relationships have been developed.

Paul Sinton-Hewitt admits that getting permission to hold the first run at Bushy Park never entered his head – after all, he was simply timing a 5K run for some friends. It was only after the next couple of events had been started up – with all the necessary permissions in place – that the manager of Bushy Park called Paul and asked to see him. 'I was embarrassed,' Paul recalls, 'expecting to get told off, and when he came out into the reception area and over to speak to me I started to apologise – but he grinned and said that of course he'd been aware of what had been happening in his park, several hundred runners (and assorted dogs) being somewhat hard to miss, but wasn't it about time we put this on some sort of official footing?'

There's little doubt that it was probably easier to get acceptance and permission at that time, with BPTT and the Wimbledon Common and Banstead Woods events established and becoming more appreciated, than it would have been in advance.

While proper permission was secured for the start of WCTT, it was at the third event that a special relationship started with the various authorities. Banstead Woods is a designated Site of Special Scientific Interest (SSSI) and from the start it was essential for this event to be accepted by the council and by English Nature (now Natural England). Chris Phelan, the Event Director, has always emphasised to everyone involved with the parkrun that it is important to respect and care for the woods – keep to paths, pick up litter and so on. Additionally, parkrun has provided some valuable assistance to the council, making it a real partnership with benefits in both directions.

In 2008, the local council chose forty fixed points, and every month parkrunner Tricia Cue takes photographs of each of these, providing a visual record of any changes. These are passed to the council, which now has a fantastic archive which otherwise would probably never have been developed.

Starting in 2009, Banstead Woods parkrunners have contributed many volunteer-hours to help with control of a highly invasive plant, Himalayan balsam. This plant damages habitat needed by local rare species such as woodcock and it sends its seeds far and wide, so it's important to pull it up before it seeds each year. On the plus side, it has shallow roots and is easily identified, so volunteers don't need much training to remove it. Six times each summer, Chris asks at the pre-run briefing for people to stay for a while after the run; about thirty or forty people stay and pull balsam for half an hour or so before repairing to the pub for tea or coffee. By 2012, the council asked Chris if they could start treating a different area of the woods: the weed was no longer a problem in the areas they had been managing. 'Being able to tell this to the runners was great,' said Chris. 'They were really proud of what they had done.'

Developing such a good relationship with the council and Natural England has led to benefits for the parkrun. The runner limit has been increased and the council prioritises clearing paths used by parkrun if these are blocked by fallen trees after a storm.

Glasgow parkrunners have similarly started helping Pollok Park to control Himalayan balsam. They held three uprooting sessions in 2012 and another three in 2013, although as Richard Leyton noted, 'On the days we have pre-planned to do this, it has always absolutely poured down. We're hoping for better weather on the scheduled dates this year!'

Another parkrun with a great relationship with their local council is Porirua parkrun in New Zealand. Astrid van Meeuwen-Dijkgraaf and George van Meeuwen started up Porirua parkrun because they wanted a parkrun closer to where they lived, rather than having to get up early to drive over to Lower Hutt. In this aspect their plans backfired: 'We now get up even earlier, to get ready for the parkrun,' Astrid said.

Initially they had problems finding an appropriate location: they wanted an out-and-back course, on paths wide enough to cope with eighty or one hundred runners, with a café nearby and no roads to cross. 'I was at a meeting, happened to mention this to one of the people from the council and they suggested Bottomley Park,' said Astrid. The council had a large project to redevelop the 'unloved' park, so, 'When we said we could get maybe sixty to one hundred people using the park every Saturday morning, they thought we were great.' The council has provided signs, including a board explaining about the parkrun and permanent kilometre marks so that people can easily use the course for freedom runs. They have provided a picnic table near the finish, advertised the parkrun on a billboard beside the major state highway for the whole of April 2014, and featured parkrun repeatedly in their newsletter. During November 2013, the anti-graffiti department provided vouchers for a free cup of coffee for anyone who ran a PB, 'because they liked the fact that parkrun was giving young people something to do instead of tagging buildings.'

Rockingham parkrun, the second event to start up in Western Australia, also had a good relationship with their council from the beginning. One of their regular participants, Ashley Pittard, is the Community Infrastructure Planning Manager for the City of Rockingham. At his suggestion, the council put in special aluminium composite signs for the parkrun, applied directly to the concrete path, showing the start/finish line and giving the website address and the 8 o'clock start time, as well as kilometre distance markers. These were unveiled by the mayor at the anniversary run and much admired. Claudia Wells, the Event Director, says she has noticed when she runs how useful it is to have the distance markers and know exactly how far she has to go: 'It's really made a difference to my mindset when I'm running.' She also greatly appreciates that if the signs ever need to be removed they can be recycled.

Some councils have been very proactive. Brueton parkrun was set up by Solihull Council in July 2010 and organised by them for the first five weeks then handed over to the parkrunners. At Brueton's first anniversary celebrations, to thank the council not only for setting up the parkrun but also for their continuing help and support, the Brueton team and parkrunners presented Brueton Park with a tree, with Councillor Mrs Diana Holl-Allen accepting the gift.

Serious misunderstandings with local authorities have thankfully been rare. In September 2011, Cardiff parkrun was temporarily suspended by the Parks Department after a few complaints from other users of the Taff Trail. However, following a review of the parkrun's risk assessment (which had apparently been mislaid by the council) and an overwhelming outpouring of local support for the event, the decision was reversed within 24 hours.

The National Trust is a UK conservation charity, 'protecting historic places and green spaces, and opening them up for ever, for everyone.' It looks after historic buildings and gardens, but also forests, farmland, moorland, coasts and islands, including several nature reserves and even whole villages. Running in natural spaces is one of the activities which the National Trust encourages. This has led to the National Trust becoming an important partner of parkrun, making a number of its places available as parkrun event locations.

By June 2014, the National Trust was hosting fifteen parkrun events. Newport parkrun, in the grounds of Tredegar House, started in March 2011, but this was before the National Trust starting looking after it. The first new partnership was Killerton parkrun, Exeter, which started in April 2011. The property team at Killerton expressed their interest in providing a venue to the local community, who were looking at starting a parkrun. Rob Joules, the National Trust's Sports Partnership Manager, saw that the partnership worked, let parkrun know that the National Trust would be happy to host other parkruns, and let the property teams know that this was a good idea. 'From there it happened very organically, from the bottom up.'

Killerton was followed by Plym Valley, Sheringham and Wimpole Estate parkruns in 2012. South Shields in The Leas, Clumber Park, Osterley, Yeovil Montacute and Blickling parkruns began in 2013, with Lanhydrock, Gibside, Lyme Park, Fountains Abbey and Parke parkruns starting during the first four months of 2014.

In a parkrun UK newsletter in November 2013, Rob Joules commented on how closely their principles and parkrun's principles were aligned. He noted that the National Trust is all about looking after special places for people to enjoy and that their motto is 'for ever, for everyone' – which dovetails very well with parkrun's all ages, all abilities inclusivity and strong community involvement.

Often, Rob said, people ask tentatively whether they are allowed to run in National Trust properties (the answer is: 'of course you can – you just walk a bit faster'), and parkrun is a great way to encourage and enable people to run around the Trust's green spaces. For Rob, parkrun is ideal because it's a community event organised and delivered by volunteers. The National Trust can assist quite easily, by helping ensure there's a suitable route and having the café open at the right time on winter Saturday mornings, for example.

Several parkruns are university-led. This theme started early, with Leeds parkrun, and continued with Sunderland and with South Manchester parkrun at Platt Fields Park.

In South Africa, partners providing venues have included local authorities, private landowners and Reserve owners. Modderfontein Reserve is owned by the Endangered Wildlife Trust and they allow parkrunners to enter the reserve free of charge every Saturday morning. The Reserve Manager, Luke Strugnell, and his team even helped with car parking when the May 2014 special event brought more than 1,800 parkrunners to the reserve. The pay-off for the reserve has been greatly increased awareness that the reserve exists and is a good place for an outing.

Partnerships also play a role in parkrun volunteering. Naturally, there are the partnerships between individual events and local running clubs. Additionally, volunteers may be directed towards their local parkrun by local or national volunteering organisations, such as Join In in the UK.

Join In aims to build on the volunteering spirit demonstrated by the 'Games Makers' of the London 2012 Olympics and Paralympics. David Moorcroft, the former 5,000 metres world record holder and still UK 3,000 metres record holder, is Join In's Director of Sport and has been promoting parkrun volunteering for several years. For Dave, parkrun is fantastic because of its combination of promoting healthy activity and building community. He said, 'I love the simplicity of parkrun, the fact that it's free, that it's an achievable distance, that it's brought people from all walks of life together. It's more than just a running event, it's a community built around the running.' Join In was launched by Dave, together with the Brownlee Brothers, at Leeds parkrun the

Partnership and sponsorship

Saturday after the Olympics finished in August 2012. Dave notes that 'parkrun reflects a lot of what Join In is about, which is to get more people to be physically active and involved in sport and physical activity, both through volunteering *and* taking part, not one or the other.' He wants to increase the celebration of volunteering within parkrun.

Globally, there are also relationships with local organisations, from businesses donating equipment to their local parkrun, such as the hardware store which provided a tent for Bunyaville parkrun, to parkrun events which adopt a local charity and help them with fundraising.

Sponsors and supporters

parkrun could not have expanded as it has (more than 500 events and still growing) without its sponsors. Many of these sponsorships have developed because of individuals associated with the various organisations, who have seen first hand what parkrun does and wanted to support it.

Hugh Brasher, son of the late Chris Brasher (Olympic athlete and co-founder of the London Marathon) is a long-term parkrun supporter. He first ran Bushy Park Time Trial in July 2006, finishing in under eighteen minutes. Hugh thinks that parkrun is an amazing concept: 'it's free at 9 o'clock on a Saturday, accessible, totally inclusive; it gets people together in a completely supportive way.' Over the years, he has shown his support in many ways, including helping Paul to get initial introductions to Nike, and later a re-introduction to adidas, plus helping in parkrun's dealings with other running organisations. As Managing Director of the Sweatshop running stores, he has for many years provided the amazing monthly Sweatshop prize to each UK parkrun. Hugh is now Race Director for the London Marathon, but he still supports parkrun, sitting on the parkrun Board, and the Sweatshop prizes continue to delight parkrunners. Hugh would like to see more support of parkrun from councils and central government, and greater recognition of the role parkrun plays in motivating people to run and to exercise regularly.

Nike's Simon Charlesworth was introduced to parkrunning by Hugh Brasher, who took him and his colleague Alex Pellew to Bushy event number 185 in 2008. Simon was impressed from the start with how much community spirit was galvanised around parkrun, not just at Bushy Park but also at the other events as they developed. He found this particularly impressive in London, where in general people who do not already know each other just don't talk to each other. He was also amazed at the fact that Paul Sinton-Hewitt and the team managed to keep the events free. 'I always used to walk away scratching my head at how Paul managed, did such amazing things,' he said. Simon really embraced parkrun, wanted to support the organisation and to recognise the volunteers supporting parkrun by their efforts. He was the driving force behind distribution of jackets, and later tops and baseball caps, for volunteers – many of which are still worn with considerable pride today.

In 2009, Nike donated 200 technical T-shirts celebrating the fifth anniversary of Bushy parkrun; these sold like hot cakes, with many people sadly being disappointed as they were too late in trying to order one. The proceeds went towards buying laptops for more events as they started up.

Simon helped to develop parkrun's branding, bringing in graphic designers from the company Popcorn, who produced the parkrun logo and the basic parkrun website design, with its trees, rolling hills and wildlife – influenced by Simon's memories of autumnal parkruns. Simon also pushed parkrun to introduce the 50-club, 250-club and, for junior runners, 10-club T-shirts. At the time he suggested these, the black 100-club jackets seemed like an impossible dream to many beginning parkrunners. The new clubs made it easier for people to reach a point where their persistence in running was visibly rewarded, which provided a greater incentive to make parkrun a regular habit.

While constantly amazed at what the parkrun team achieved with limited resources, Simon also challenged them to do more, building into the sponsorship additional rewards if parkrun managed to set up more events than originally expected in a given year. The partnership lasted until 2011.

From 2009 to the end of 2013, Lucozade Sport was a major sponsor. Lisa Pinder had experienced parkrun and recognised that this was something quite special – the people, the atmosphere. She thought that parkrun, although small at the time, could make an ideal partner, and she fell in love with Paul's vision of a parkrun in every town. Her visionary attitude, recognising the potential of parkrun, helped parkrun to expand into more locations across the UK.

Over their years of sponsorship, Lucozade provided, in addition to sponsorship money, the feather flags used for years to mark the starting area (very useful to assist visiting parkrunners in finding the parkrun when visiting an event for the first time), marshals' bibs and finish funnel tape. They also took bottles of sports drinks to parkrun events all around the UK; provided a 20% discount on Lucozade products bought online directly from Lucozade; and offered entries for lucky parkrunners to a variety of races over the years, including the Royal Parks Foundation Half Marathon and – via their Chase the Place competition – even the London Marathon, together with running kit, training advice and other support. Towards the end of 2013, Lucozade Sport changed hands and this era of sponsorship came to an end.

Back in 2007, adidas provided the first ever outside funding for parkrun (then still the Time Trials), which helped Paul Sinton-

Hewitt and the team to develop the early events outside Bushy Park. In 2011, adidas once more became a sponsor in the UK and then became sponsors in several other countries.

London Marathon started to support parkrun in 2009. Dave Bedford, who was the London Marathon's Race Director at that time, brought parkrun to the attention of Nick Bitel, the Chief Executive. Dave emphasised that parkrun was a very worthwhile initiative and Nick decided to support it.

He said, 'The London Marathon believes that it has a role to play in getting more people to take part in sport and exercise. Whilst the Charity [The London Marathon Charitable Trust] only funds capital projects, London Marathon does look at revenue projects that it believes complement its core values.' For Nick Bitel, the most important aspects of parkrun are: 'The fact that it is free and takes place at the same time always helps remove barriers to participation. We also like the way in which it uses data to help understand its customers.' Also starting in 2009, parkrunners became important volunteers at the London Marathon, helping at the starting area.

Additional supporters of parkrun in the UK have included the Mayor of London, providing funds to set up another twenty parkruns within London; the mobile communications company Three, providing mobile internet dongles to UK events; and the messaging specialist company aql, enabling UK parkrun results to be sent to participants by text.

parkrun Denmark receives funding from a region of DGI, an organisation which presently covers more than 6,000 local associations and clubs in Denmark and part of northern Germany. DGI is 'a strong advocate for a healthy, challenging and community-based sports environment' and wants to help individuals to achieve 'both personal and shared victories'.

Partnership and sponsorship

parkrun Australia has had three main sponsors: adidas, Stockland and Suncorp Bank. adidas was their first sponsor and Tim Oberg is very grateful to them. 'They took a real punt because they backed us right from the start, even before we had any events running, just based on the history of parkrun in the UK.' For Suncorp Bank, parkrun is a natural grassroots running programme to invest in alongside their sponsorship of a variety of running events such as the Gold Coast Airport Marathon and the Sydney Running Festival.

Unique to parkrun Australia is Stockland, a large property development company which specialises in constructing complete new communities in developing corridors, as well as large shopping centres. Stockland sponsors parkruns starting in these new developments, to help create and promote the spirit of the new community; development of a parkrun alongside a new shopping centre has also featured.

In South Africa, the first sponsor was Blue Label Telecoms. Gary Harlow, a board member at Blue Label and now parkrun South Africa board chairman, persuaded his board, including Brett and Mark Levy, the founders and CEOs, to back parkrun South Africa with their enterprise development money when the beginning organisation had just 22 registered parkrunners. adidas is also a sponsor, and Bruce Fordyce is really pleased to have Discovery Vitality ('the wellness programme which rewards you for getting healthier') as their third main sponsor, important not just for financial support but also in marketing. In addition to their parkrun points, people earn Vitality points for completing a parkrun – 500 a time, which is a lot more than for a gym session, for example, which only earns 150 points. Vitality likes parkrun, because parkrun records people finishing, not starting, so there's no doubt that you really have completed the 5K of exercise.

parkrun: much more than just a run in the park

In New Zealand, the main sponsor is New Zealand Home Loans. Allan Hartley, a business owner of New Zealand Home Loans in Lower Hutt, ran at the first Lower Hutt parkrun and pretty much as soon as he crossed the finish line he approached Richard McChesney, the Event Director. Allan remembers, 'I recognised that this was a great concept and I wanted to be involved at a sponsorship level.' He met Paul Sinton-Hewitt and facilitated a meeting with Mark Collins, the CEO of New Zealand Home Loans.

For Mark, 'This sponsorship was an opportunity to promote something I am passionate about, which is getting people into healthy community activity without having to be an athlete. The biggest health threat in New Zealand is obesity and the related poor health outcomes that come with that. I see parkrun as a wonderful way to give access to people to adopt a healthier lifestyle in an achievable way.' He's felt the magic of parkrun for himself: 'It's also a brilliant way to spend time with family and friends and having run the Hamilton parkrun many times I love the feeling of getting out with my wife and our children and watching them progress and achieve their potential.' The different offices around the country are encouraged to get involved with support for each local parkrun. In 2014, much to the delight of local parkrunners, the company agreed to sponsor the parkrun 50-club and 100-club T-shirts and a number of New Zealanders are now proudly wearing these.

parkrun Poland finalised a contract with their first sponsor, adidas, in 2013. In 2014, they gained a new sponsor, the cosmetics company Ziaja Ltd. Ziaja became active in promoting physical activity through sponsoring of a number of sport events across Poland, including running, in 2013. After initial contacts with parkrun in Gdynia, they decided that parkrun would be a good partner for them nationally.

Partnership and sponsorship

In Ireland, parkrun is being supported by both the Irish Sports Council and the Irish Health Service, HSE. John Treacy, Olympic marathon silver medallist and twice World Cross-Country Champion, is now Chief Executive of the Irish Sports Council, which aims to encourage as many people as possible to go out and exercise. He finds the simple format, informality and accessibility of parkrun is encouraging people to graduate from walking to running, and provides a stepping stone assisting at least some people to move on to longer races. He also sees the fact that parkrun is timed as being an important element; as he said, 'We all like to see our progress.' parkrun, he thinks, is important because it provides venues where people can go and jog at their own pace, and not feel intimidated, and can jog with friends. The informality and the family atmosphere are important. 'And people start their weekend with a 5K run, and they might knock a second or two off their best time, and they feel good about the start of the weekend.'

When John attended the first anniversary of Marley parkrun and helped to hand out the prizes, he arrived early and there were few people there – then he got to witness the parkrun phenomenon whereby suddenly at 8.50 you're surrounded by people. He sees the role of the Irish Sports Council as facilitating the development of parkrun by acting as enablers, helping to open doors so that parkrun Ireland can meet with and partner with other organisations such as park managements.

In Australia also, support has come from a retired international athlete – Olympian Ron Clarke AO MBE. When Tim Oberg was just starting up parkrun Australia he approached Ron, who was at that time Mayor of the Gold Coast, and explained the parkrun concept. Ron said: 'As I had long been an advocate of the benefits of consistent running/walking for everybody in a community, when Tim explained the various elements of parkrun, I became very enthusiastic.' Ron particularly likes the combination of the fact that the runs are free and that each person's results are stored, so that each participant can look at their own records and compare themselves to the general standards for their gender and age group. 'That the runs are organised by ordinary community folk voluntarily, and the courses similarly managed, adds that community spirit that so epitomises each and every venue.' Having been involved in getting the 55 kilometre Harbour Walk constructed, he also thought it would be good to see some regular, organised use of this for walking and running.

On a global level, in September 2014, parkrun launched a new partnership with the online retailer Wiggle to sell a small range of parkrun-branded goods. Proceeds from sales to parkrunners in each country will be used to support and expand parkrun within that country.

20

Tales of the unexpected

The pathways were frozen and you couldn't really run,
people were sliding everywhere and you had to walk,
but it was really fantastic!

Willem Loison, remembering a snowy Bushy parkrun

For the most part, parkrun events happen smoothly, week after
week, and run reports on the individual event pages concentrate
on particularly outstanding performances, noteworthy running
milestones, marriage proposals, birthdays and other happy events.
However sometimes something remarkable, beautiful or even ter-
rifying happens.

In Poland, for instance, all runners at Gdańsk remember New
Year's Eve 2012, when it was suggested that all the events in Po-

land should run their courses in the reverse direction to usual. However, somewhere along the way the message reaching Gdańsk parkrunners became garbled and the runners were asked to run the course running backwards – which about fifty of them did!

At Sunrise-on-Sea, visitors from the nearby Nahoon Point parkrun participated in a 'swimming parkrun' requiring navigation of two flooded gullies: 'Many didn't navigate too well and ended up in water to their waist – the photos were hysterical, but it was the most popular week of the year so far,' said Tracy Mackay.

Travel woes and timing

Occasionally, unfortunate coincidence of timing threatens to disrupt an otherwise smoothly organised event. At Graves parkrun's inaugural event, while the runners were out on the course, a large van drove up to one corner of the course. Several workmen in hi-vis jackets got out, set out some stakes and, while the volunteers watched in astonishment, set about inflating a large inflatable slide. For the runners it was somewhat surreal, coming round the corner and thinking, 'that wasn't there on the first lap!' Thankfully they were able to run around the newly fenced off area and finish the run with only a couple of seconds delay.

Kingston parkrun also had fun and games for their inaugural event. The 'dress rehearsal' had gone off perfectly, but on the day of the first 'real' run there was a regatta on the river and people were carrying their boats down to the water – right across the course. A rapid rethink ended up with the course starting three-quarters of a mile further along the river. Paul Sinton-Hewitt thinks that the revised course is actually better than the original, but it did cause some confusion on that first day, with runners turning up at the 'start' only to find that they needed to jog a kilometre or so to the new location.

Tales of the unexpected

Barrow parkrun had been up and running for a couple of years when one Saturday morning a large hedge-cutting vehicle arrived, drove down the path and – despite the evident event in progress, with lots of runners approaching down the path – workmen started to put out cones to keep people away and off the path. Rapid diplomacy persuaded them to wait fifteen minutes and not block off the path until the run was over.

parkrun tourists occasionally encounter some difficult conditions just getting to their destinations. Chris Cowell remembers failing to reach Cardiff parkrun because of ice falling off the Severn Bridge closing the motorway, and a winter's morning when he and Linda stayed overnight near Warrington, carefully ventured to Pennington Flash parkrun and found it cancelled due to ice. The backup plan was Wythenshawe, so they dashed there and found it too was cancelled due to ice and they had to drive 200 miles back home with no parkrun to show for it. Visiting Walsall Arboretum parkrun in June, they knew there would be no such problems. Instead they arrived to find that it had been cancelled due to flooding! The flood waters had actually subsided by the Saturday morning, so they and about twenty others ran the course as a freedom run.

Nneka Okonta's trip to Northern Ireland also didn't go quite as planned. 'I'd worked it all out; the events in Northern Ireland start at 9.30 and I'd found a flight which landed at 8.55 just 700 metres away from Victoria parkrun, Belfast – perfect.' However, she realised on the Friday night that Victoria parkrun started at 9 o'clock. Luckily the plane landed early and she hurried to the park – where she found no parkrun, but five other people standing around looking puzzled – the venue, she discovered later, had been temporarily changed while park paths were repaired. With assistance from one of the other parkrunners and her mother-in-law – who had a car – she managed to reach Ormeau parkrun just in time. Nneka said, 'I am indebted to Joanne Little, who was just brilliant – she not only got me there, but also waited while I had a shower in the nearby leisure centre afterwards and then dropped me off in central Belfast where I could spend some time being a tourist and get a bus back to the airport.'

Visiting friends in Cardiff for the weekend, we decided to fly into Bristol on Saturday morning. I found out that the plane was due at 8.15 am and the nearest parkrun was Ashton Court, just 8 miles and fifteen minutes drive from the airport. Our friends agreed to pick us up. We made it into Bristol on time, and it was a fine sunny day, but our friends were not there... a text message told us they slept through their alarm. 8.20, 8.30, 8.40 no sign of them... at 8.45 we caught a glimpse of their car. Reaching Ashton Court just before 9 o'clock we shot out of the car and towards the start line. We got there just as the safety briefing was finishing and managed to start with everyone else. It's a tough course going up that hill and then down! On the way down I was tired but the heavy breathing of a dog kept me on my toes! One of my slowest parkruns, but a great adventure and thoroughly enjoyed!

Nadhim Bayatti, Lyme Park parkrun

Come rain, ice, flood or snow

Christmas Day 2012 I woke to rain lashing at the windows and drove towards Lloyd Park with water cascading off my windscreen. Water was flowing off the side roads in wide streams and the gutters were struggling to contain the torrents. Lloyd Park itself was sodden. Nevertheless, the volunteers arrived and at 9 o'clock 32 brave souls set off running through the lakes and streams where previously there had been football pitches and grassy paths.

For the Flynn family, running at Banstead Woods parkrun, the Christmas Day downpour was even more exciting. 'First,' said Phyllis Flynn, 'we heard the sound of running water inside the house and discovered water was pouring into the utility room, so we had to set the buckets out to catch it. By then it was too late to run to the woods as we had intended, so we got into the car for the short drive. Part way there the road was closed due to flooding – so we abandoned the car and ran for the woods. We came running down the course towards the start, waving at the marshals not to let them start without us! What a day!'

Tilgate parkrun's management team were pleased to be allowed to store some of their equipment in the boathouse in winter. However, with the prolonged heavy rainfall in winter 2013-14, the water level in the lake rose several feet. One of the team waded in thigh-deep and opened the boathouse door to see if any of the equipment could be salvaged – and they all watched as the plastic crates holding the volunteer hi-vis vests and other equipment came floating out...

In Australia, back when there were just four courses in the Perth area, one particular Saturday they all had to be cancelled due to severe storm warnings. However, the only time that Wynnum parkrun, Queensland, has been officially closed due to weather was when the Run Director of the day got up to address the assembled runners... only to see, over their heads, a large waterspout in the bay. As there was no way of knowing whether this was going to stay out to sea or come into land, he took the only safe option and cancelled. parkrunners being parkrunners, of course, about half of them decided to freedom run the course anyway.

At Nahoon Point, Eastern Cape, South Africa, Bob Norris admits that they don't really get cold weather and even the rain is comfortably warm. However, the finish is on a sand dune and whether the wind is from the east or the west it can blow sand into runners' faces and really make things difficult for volunteers carrying out timer duties.

One of the tasks of Event Directors is to assess the state of the course in inclement weather conditions and if necessary to either modify the course or, on occasion, cancel the event. At Lloyd parkrun, two winters in succession I have found myself jogging around the course in the snow, wearing a head torch, at 9 o'clock on a Friday evening, deciding whether it would be safe to send the runners around the next morning. Both times I decided that the run could go ahead, with additional precautions.

Bramhall parkrun has also had occasional problems with snow. As Rob Downs explained, 'two laps, a few hundred runners and the fresh snow can turn into something more resembling a bob-sleigh run.'

At Wimbledon Common, when the course is covered in snow, the usual flour markings have to be replaced by temporary spray paint. 'The first time this happened,' said Ian Higgins, 'I used red marker paint, making neat red dots and arrows, beautifully visible against the snow. At least until the runners had been around; after the trampling of a few hundred feet it looked like there had been a Wimbledon Common Massacre! Never again; I switched to blue paint after that.'

A number of courses which are held on tarmac have alterna-tive off-road courses to use when the usual paths are icy. Pollok parkrun's winter course is three laps of a distorted hourglass shape around football and hockey pitches. Many runners have said that they enjoy the different challenge provided by this course – al-though some dislike the associated wet feet!

Tilgate's management team have been known to shovel snow and put down grit on the path round their lake to create a safe course in winter. Meanwhile, in Poland, Russia and Michigan, parkrunners keep on going through the winters despite some seri-ously cold temperatures and snowy conditions, just bundling up in more layers, hats and scarves, and wearing ice spikes as needed.

Health scares

There are very few accidents and injuries at parkruns. At Lloyd, the worst I can remember is a runner slipping on ice while walking across the car park one winter morning and cutting his hand. One sticking plaster later and he went off and was first to finish, so obviously no real harm done. However, every parkrun develops a risk assessment at the planning stage of the event and reviews it regularly, including considerations for medical emergencies.

Over the past ten years there have been a handful of serious medical incidents at parkruns. When you realise that by the end of May 2014 more than 600,000 parkrunners had been participating at parkruns for an aggregate time in excess of 277 years, this should not be surprising.

In 2011, a runner collapsed halfway round the course at Banstead Woods. When the initial report came in Sue Esslemont, the Run Director, took the first aid kit over. At first they thought he might be having a heart attack. He was getting cold and wasn't very coherent. This was when prior planning was important. Recognising the limited vehicular access at the woods, the parkrun had previously made contact with the local air ambulance and provided them with a map of the course. When the parkrun team reported a runner in serious difficulties in the middle of the course, the helicopter was sent out and landed in a field as close as possible, while a four-wheel-drive ambulance came into the woods from the adjacent farmer's land and took him to the helicopter. He was airlifted to hospital and successfully treated for a stroke.

This incident encouraged Event Directors everywhere to check our risk assessments and consider how we would be able to respond to such an emergency. When you request an ambulance, you are always (at least in the UK) asked for the postcode. But who knows the postcode of their park? I certainly didn't. Now that is included with other information on cards given out to all our marshals.

In May 2013, a runner collapsed with a heart attack just before the start of Huddersfield parkrun and was successfully treated by medically qualified parkrunners. Sadly, when mountain biking journalist Steve Worland collapsed with a heart attack during Ashton Court parkrun in April 2014, he could not be resuscitated, despite the attentions of fellow parkrunners who were medically qualified. In May 2014, Nikki Herbison collapsed due to a brain haemorrhage at Rushcliffe parkrun while raising money for St Mary's Community Park Project and was looked after by doctors running behind her, but died the following day. The following week, parkrunners at Rushcliffe paid tribute to her with a minute of applause to celebrate her life.

Close encounters of the parkrun kind

While people running with dogs can occasionally cause problems, there are also other dogs being walked in the park which are, with or without their owners, capable of causing chaos. Those on extending leads have the best chance of tripping up runners or tying up their legs, while dogs jumping up at runners are always a possibility. It is important for all parkrunners to remember at these times that we *share* the parks, and to remain courteous to the owner of the canine – however frustrating the encounter may be. The run report for the ninth running of Wormwood Scrubs parkrun commented that there were some great times, 'despite runners having to hurdle a rather large dog that decided to lie down across the narrowest part of the course...'

Part of the Bramhall parkrun course passes alongside a lake and it's not uncommon for there to be ducks and Canada geese sitting on the path. Usually they move once they realise runners are coming – but sometimes they don't. 'There was one time,' says

Rob Downs, the Event Director, 'when there was a complaint that a runner had kicked a goose. Now, he claims that he hurdled it, and I don't know which version is true, but since then, as well as the general announcements to all the runners, I give an extra talk to those at the front and remind them no kicking of the ducks or geese: that would be a fowl offence!'

Similarly at Barrow parkrun the geese occasionally decide to congregate on the paths near the start – not just one or two but dozens – needing to be gently shooed away. And at Bedford parkrun every summer a female swan stands on the path hissing and trying to bite the ankles of the runners going past. The runners are used to this, and just keep running. The swan does have an excuse – she's protecting her cygnets, cute balls of fluffy down.

Occasionally, rather more exciting close encounters occur.

In summer 2014, towards the end of the run, one of the Bushy juniors volunteers looked up, pointed and yelled 'swan!' As Nicki Clark, the Run Director, said, 'That was accurate, but "duck!" might have been more useful.' Trevor, the funnel manager, threw himself flat on the ground to avoid collision with the low-flying swan, which landed by the funnel and looked incredibly confused, obviously thinking, 'this wasn't here this morning!'

A larger bird nearly made Karien Potgeiter late for the inaugural Naval Hill parkrun, Bloemfontein. Arriving at the last minute, she discovered an ostrich in the car park and decided she had better walk gently until she was some distance away, rather than run for the start and risk being chased. She later learned that this particular bird is very tame: 'Unfortunately one doesn't know that when you first see her!'

At Wimpole Hall in Cambridgeshire, cows are loose in the park and have to be managed during the run as they can get rather assertive near the finish line! There are loose cattle *and* sheep at Yeovil Montacute parkrun; the sheep tend to stand by the side of the course then, as the runners draw level, run out in front of them, making everything more interesting.

Pollok Park, Glasgow, has is a fold (herd) of prize-winning Highland cows with long shaggy coats and curving horns. Normally, they are inside a fence, but one Saturday morning the whole lot escaped and went charging down the finish straight before turning round and running round the course in the reverse direction, rather surprising the runners, before heading out of the park. Luckily, the Event Director Richard Leyton had maintained a good relationship with the park managers so had a telephone number handy and was able to inform them quickly, so the cattle were all recaptured before any got hurt. On the other side of the world, in New Zealand, there was a very similar event at Cornwall Park with cows getting loose and walking across the turnaround spot.

At Summerfield, just outside Kruger National Park, the nocturnal hippos are back in the river by the time the run is held but the organisers do have to check that there are no springbok on the course.

Checking for deer on the course and if necessary waiting for them to clear is standard for quite a number of parkruns. During one Bushy parkrun a red deer stag calmly walked into the finish funnel and stood there. With the runners expected back any minute, volunteers carefully pulled out a couple of the poles and laid the tape down on the floor, after which the stag strolled out and across the park. Similarly, one Bushy juniors parkrun had a delayed start while waiting for a couple of battling stags to finish their contest and move away from the run route. At Richmond parkrun, deer occasionally dart across in front of the runners; Livonia parkrun, Michigan, has also had a near-miss between a parkrunner and a deer, while on another occasion a couple of white-tailed deer calmly stood around near the start while the pack of runners dashed past them. And at Riddlesdown parkrun the smaller local roe deer are usually seen only before the run starts, but one morning in summer 2013 one bolted across the path of the lead runner, Alan O'Connor, resulting in a brief collision and bruised legs. He still finished first, exclaiming, 'I got run over by a deer!'

Darwin parkrun in Australia has an entry in their risk assessment saying, 'If a crocodile is on the course, delay the event until clear or change the course,' and several Australian events warn of the possibility of venomous snakes. At Kawana parkrun, a deadly eastern brown snake was seen on a tree by the parkrun course a couple of days before the run: 'there were lots of PBs that week from people running particularly fast through that area,' said Mel Erbacher, their Event Director.

When Lian and Noel de Charmoy, the New Zealand Country Managers, ran at Delta parkrun in South Africa with their daughter Kelly on Christmas Eve 2011, Kelly had only run a few hundred metres when she stopped and limped back to the start with twin puncture wounds in one ankle – a possible bite from a rinkhals (spitting cobra) – necessitating a quick trip to the local hospital. It was not until 2014 that they returned to Delta parkrun, where, after the run, Kelly was congratulated on the longest time ever to finish a parkrun!

At St Francis, Eastern Cape, a lynx was photographed knocking over a course marker soon after it had been set up. The same action a few weeks earlier had led to some runners taking a wrong turning, but at the time the identity of the culprit had not been known.

And several years ago at Bushy Park it was parkrunners to the rescue: sitting outside the Pheasantry Café, Danny Norman noticed that there was a bunch of crows in the trees overhead, there was a piece of fishing line dangling down from the tree – and, he realised, the line was attached to a crow's foot. Danny grabbed hold of the line and carefully pulled the protesting bird down; Chris Wright's wife, Mary Hickson, held it; someone found a pair of scissors, and they snipped the line off and let the poor bird go!

Natural wonders

With a number of parkruns in various countries being held in nature reserves, runners sometimes have the chance to see some fantastic wildlife.

The very first event at Ebotse parkrun on the East Rand in South Africa took runners past flocks of guinea fowl, and they were outpaced by springbok. In January 2013, a crowned lapwing laid her eggs right in the middle of the parkrun route, with the poor bird having to endure more than one hundred runners running around both sides of her nest once on the way out and again on the way back. For the next several runs the area around the nest was cordoned off and the brave bird stayed on the eggs throughout the runs. Early in February the nest was empty but a lapwing with three chicks was seen nearby. A week later, a newborn springbok was seen not far off the course, lying absolutely still, head and ears down, waiting for its mother to return to it.

parkrun tourist Chris Cowell had a memorable parkrunning experience at Medina, Isle of Wight, when he saw a red squirrel – perhaps not so unusual for parkrunners on the courses in Poland, but unfortunately very rare now in England, where the American grey squirrels have almost completed their takeover.

Runners at Rockingham parkrun in Western Australia frequently see dolphins in the bay area near the start/finish. A pod of dolphins has also showed up by Wynnum parkrun in Queensland, and one runner even saw a dugong. Half an hour south at Cleveland parkrun they have koalas and wallabies in the park as well as dolphins and whales off the coast. Volunteers setting out the course there were lucky enough to see a female koala with a well-grown young on her back. And at Kawana parkrun, brush turkeys are common and, again, there is a chance of seeing whales or dolphins.

And several of the beachside parkruns in South Africa, including Nahoon Point and PE (Port Elizabeth) Hobie Beach, sometimes get southern right whales frolicking just offshore. Bruce Fordyce said he couldn't quite believe it when he was at Nahoon Point for the inaugural event and joked about the organisers getting people to dress up in whale suits for the occasion – very special!

21

So you want to start your own parkrun

Do it; it's a lot easier than you think and a lot more enjoyable too.
Mark Connelly, Event Director, Darwin parkrun

You've got that promotion you always wanted, but it means moving to a new city. In addition to all the usual inconveniences of moving house, your new location lacks one major requirement: a parkrun. As you settle in and find your feet in your new community, you continue to feel that hole in the week where parkrun ought to be. Finally, you decide there's only one thing for it: starting your own parkrun. Then you wonder what on earth you're letting yourself in for.

The good news is that – particularly if you're in a country where parkrun is already established – this should be possible. After all, one of parkrun's goals is for there to be a parkrun wherever anyone would like one, with a preference not for a few, large events but a large number of small events, each involving the local community and providing a supportive environment where people can engage in physical activity. If parkrun has not yet reached your country, then it might still be possible, but more steps are needed, including someone who is willing and able to do everything needed to set up parkrun in your country, from forming a company to securing sponsorship.

Moving from deciding to start up a parkrun to the first official run at your new event will take time – probably three to six months – commitment and determination. Also, your life will never be the same again. However, you'll have lots of help and make many new friends along the route of your amazing journey.

I had a number of heart attacks in early 2010. Walking became boring so I downloaded a Couch to 5K app for my phone – I haven't looked back. When I heard that a Corby parkrun was to begin in April 2013 it was music to my ears! Come July when there was still no parkrun I called and spoke to Jackie at Northamptonshire Sport; a lovely lady with the ability to charm... the next thing I knew I'd agreed to be the Event Director! I have met so many inspirational people through parkrun and continue to do so. It truly is a community event for the community by the community, bringing runners and non-runners together. I love that our elite runners remain to cheer on the slower athletes, we all love to see the younger runners giving it their all and we just love the looks on the faces of runners who know they've run a new PB as they cross the line. The phone call that I made in July 2013 ranks alongside a small number of best conversations I have ever had.

Andrew Bennett, Event Director, Corby parkrun

Building a team

As the initiator, you will need to act as a champion for your potential parkrun, extolling its virtues to your local community: to individuals, running clubs, your local authority and the owner or manager of the park where you intend to hold your event. However determined you are, you can't manage a parkrun on your own, so you'll need to develop a core team of volunteers committed to making their new parkrun thrive.

While parkruns have been started based on one person's passion to make the event happen, it is really important to have like-minded individuals around you. People who are, like you, enthusiastic about getting your local parkrun going; people you can bounce ideas off, discuss problems with.

The number of volunteers needed to manage each parkrun varies depending on how many marshals are needed around the course and how many runners there are. A parkrun with an easy to follow course and a relatively small number of runners might really only need three volunteers to manage the run, covering the timer, finish tokens and barcode scanning. However, as numbers grow a back-up timer and a second person scanning barcodes become useful, as well as perhaps a funnel manager and a finish token assistant.

Sometimes, committed non-running volunteers will appear and be very happy to be involved every week. 'They're like gold dust,' says Matt Shields, 'every team, starting up, I tell them they will find people like that emerging from the community – and when they do, jump on them and keep them!'

Funding

You'll also need to raise some funds locally. parkrun is totally free to the runners but there are considerable costs involved in starting up and maintaining each parkrun. Currently, in the UK, for each new parkrun, the local community is asked to raise a start-up fee of £3,000, matching a similar amount from parkrun's major sponsors. After that, parkrun commits to support the event indefinitely.

What is this money needed for? While the details vary a little from country to country, start-up costs may include a laptop computer for managing the volunteers, processing the results, communicating with HQ and so forth, and a computer bag to keep it safe; a set of barcoded finish tokens (plus blank tokens and replacement barcode stickers for the ones that go astray); timing devices and a barcode scanner to capture the finish data; a parkrun feather flag; equipment for marking up the course and setting up a finish funnel; hi-vis vests for the marshals; clipboards and various other bits and pieces. Then there are costs involved in parkrun HQ setting up the new event's website.

There are also the ongoing infrastructure support costs, such as computing costs, the input of the hard-working parkrun HQ staff and public liability insurance. The start-up funds, in addition to parkrun's sponsorship monies, are absolutely necessary to enable parkrun to continue providing free events for tens of thousands of runners every week.

I name this parkrun...

Obviously your parkrun will need a name. Sometimes this is simply the name of the town or the name of the park. If it's named after a park then the 'Park' part usually gets left off, as it's rather implied in the 'parkrun' part of the name, and for those held in a country park, 'Country' is also omitted. Exceptions are made for clarity: Black Park Country Park ended up as Black Park parkrun, because Black Country parkrun would have wrongly suggested the Midlands, while Black parkrun just sounded wrong! Sometimes the geographical location is added as a modifier for clarity: Albert parkrun, Middlesbrough versus Albert parkrun, Melbourne, for example. Very occasionally a nickname is used, such as Ally Pally parkrun in Alexandra Palace Park in London and Newy parkrun in Newcastle, Australia, but only if this is widely known.

Local council and landowner agreement

You will need to get agreement from the local council, or other landowner, to hold the parkrun on their land. This could be a challenge when parkrun is new to a country or to a region. Once there are a few parkruns in the local area the councils are more likely to know what parkrun is and does and it becomes easier to make contacts. Additionally, you can provide case studies from other nearby parkrun events to show how much parkrun has benefited the local park and local community as well as how expected problems have failed to materialise.

There are occasional difficulties with local authorities which, for whatever reason, do not appreciate parkrun and do not want one in their area. Thankfully most councils are really happy to welcome an event which gets people of all ages up, moving and using their local park, with minimal or zero ongoing costs for the council. Rarely, it can take months, even a year or more to persuade a council to cooperate, but more commonly it's fairly easy once you've identified the right contact. Sometimes the local council gets really engaged, which is hugely beneficial.

It is also worth considering involving other landowners. In the UK, the National Trust has welcomed parkrun events onto a number of its sites; in South Africa the Endangered Wildlife Trust has opened Modderfontein Reserve to parkrun, while Summerfields parkrun is held on the privately owned Summerfields Estate.

Developing the course

Every parkrun is five kilometres long (two kilometres for juniors events), but the layouts of the courses differ widely – whatever accommodates the required distance in the space available. It is helpful to consider one, two or even three possible routes at an early stage and measure them approximately using one of the online distance measuring tools. The better organised you are at this stage, the more likely it is that the local authorities and park managers will take you seriously. Before the inaugural run, the course should be measured properly by an official course measurer from a local running club, or using a measuring wheel.

All sorts of surfaces can be used, but prepared paths of one sort or another are preferable when available to reduce damage to the park grounds, particularly in wet weather. If the course will be on grass, then ideally a relatively wide route should be available to reduce wear. Additionally, simple courses are suggested, easy to describe (for example, 'keep going around the perimeter path just inside the park fence, heading clockwise') and not needing large numbers of marker arrows or marshals to prevent parkrunners from getting lost. For lapped courses, experience has shown that interference between faster and slower parkrunners is minimised if there are no more than three laps, although four- and five-lap courses are in operation. Out-and-back courses also work well.

Essential elements for safety are: not following or crossing any open public roads (Roma parkrun in Queensland cunningly sends runners around a cul-de-sac to avoid this); not including cross-country style obstacles and not running down steps (although running *up* steps is permissible if necessary). Some events which use tarmac paths find that they need to designate an alternative route for use when the path becomes icy, while other events have developed alternative courses to cope with unexpected flooding.

parkrun: much more than just a run in the park

Richard McChesney, who set up Lower Hutt parkrun after getting hooked on parkrun in the UK and then moving to New Zealand, highly recommends that if you have not got years of local knowledge, you should take advice from people who do know the area very well, and take the time to look at the course over several months, in different conditions. This can avoid problems such as he had at Lower Hutt, where the course had just been approved when heavy rain and resultant riverside flooding showed that it would be unsuitable and he had to rethink the location.

James Saunders, who has been involved in three parkruns and a junior parkrun as Event Director, agrees that you must consider the suitability of the course at all times of the year. He also strongly recommends thinking about the fact that not everyone will see easily what to you seems to be the obvious route, so more signage might be needed than you originally expected. You should also consider who the users are going to be and how the course will look to them – including beginners and children, who may find overwhelming a hill which would be just a mild slope for an experienced cross-country or trail runner. On the other hand, Nat Glenn happily bills Larne parkrun as a beautiful but challenging event, encouraging even beginners to try it.

It would be boring if all parkruns were held on simple flat paved paths with no inclines and no tight corners. Nevertheless, it's good to consider whether your proposed course is usable for partially sighted runners, wheelchair users or runners with buggies: or whether it could be made more friendly to these groups with a little modification.

Occasionally, developing the course can prove very challenging. Finding a route for Greenpoint parkrun in Cape Town which was acceptable to all the parties concerned, including the local council, the park manager, the local police and the next-door stadium, didn't cross any roads, and started and finished outside the park, involved many re-drawings and recalculations of the distance.

Learning from other people's mistakes

Richard McChesney has found it's good to both run at and volunteer at several different parkruns and note what works, aspects you would like to copy, or anything you think you might prefer to do differently. Astrid van Meeuwen-Dijkgraaf and her husband George started up Porirua parkrun after running at Lower Hutt and Astrid notes that she happily stole all the good ideas from that event! At both locations, scanning of the finish tokens takes place at the end of the finish funnel, 'and we don't let them out until they've been scanned,' said Astrid; she thinks this is why they haven't had any finish tokens go missing (yet).

Paul Graham's advice, having started up the pioneering Bushy juniors event, is, 'build up slowly, be prepared, have a team in place. That's the thing to do. Patience is the key.'

Risk assessment

A mandatory part of setting up a parkrun is the development of the risk assessment. There's a form to fill in for this, which at first sight can seem daunting, but is mainly a matter of common sense: for example, the risk of extreme weather such as thunderstorms or blizzards may be low in your location, but the chance of disruption if one occurs is high. These forms make you actually *think* about potential hazards, which is the first step towards avoiding them if possible and being prepared to handle them if they arise.

Additionally, the fact that each event has an official risk assessment can be key in persuading local authorities that you are part of a serious, knowledgeable organisation and this could help you to get the necessary permissions.

junior parkruns

For the junior parkrun events there are extra requirements, including additional child safeguarding policies to be followed.

As with the 5K events, a trial run is important. At Southampton juniors, for example, the trial identified a need for taller cones pointing the way to the finish line, emergency action cards for marshals to wear on lanyards and extra stakes for the funnel and signs.

New countries

If there is no parkrun yet in your country, then the situation is more challenging, although it has (obviously) been done.

Starting up parkrun in a new country is also a considerable challenge for parkrun. Based on past experience Paul Sinton-Hewitt has developed a set of conditions which need to be met for such an expansion:

- A strongly enthusiastic person to be parkrun's local ambassador and drive forward the development of parkrun.
- Support in-country by appropriate sponsors.
- Likely development at more locations.
- A certain degree of political stability.

Anyone who wants to initiate parkrun in a new country will need to contact Paul, demonstrate their enthusiasm and start a dialogue to see whether their proposal could work.

Support from parkrun

One of the great things about starting up a parkrun is that you get support from parkrun HQ and, more and more often now, from a local parkrun Ambassador. Ambassadors are people who have been involved with their local parkrun and have decided that they wanted to do more to help; commonly, they assist in parkrun activation. Previously, someone from headquarters would have helped with everything from talking to your local council to getting your course measured. Now, you are likely to be helped by someone from a parkrun close by – or at least in your region – who has probably previously been through everything you are presently wrestling with and come out the other side with a functioning parkrun.

Having a more experienced mentor such as a parkrun Ambassador is great, whether you are navigating the bureaucracy of your local council or getting to grips with the volunteer management system on the computer. In addition to the useful practical support, it gives you a chance to get to know other parkrun enthusiasts and to make friends.

Once you have your core team, park chosen, permissions in place, funding secured, course chosen and measured, post-run café or coffee shop chosen and website pages sorted, you are ready for your first event. A test run is important – for example, by inviting clubmates from your running club, or family and friends. This is when you can discover and solve any unexpected issues, such as people finding an alternative route where you had thought the course was unmistakable, before the official inaugural run. And then the date of the inaugural run comes, and you set up the course and wait for runners to appear…

'Don't be discouraged if you don't get very many people at first,' Anita Afonso said. 'It's better that way, gives you time to iron out any problems. And don't worry about the number of participants. There don't need to be lots of people to make your parkrun successful. It will grow organically, and we're fine with small events.' Small events, Anita points out, are less likely to run into problems with swamping the park's car park or damaging the grass or the paths, and it is easier for everyone to fit into the local café for post-run coffee and chatting while the results are being processed and the finish tokens sorted.

A key example of 'small is beautiful' is Summerfields parkrun, just outside Kruger National Park in South Africa. This has the lowest average number of parkrunners of any parkrun (9.8), with a high of 38 runners and lows, on a few occasions, of one.

Advice to the would-be Event Director

I asked several Event Directors what they would advise for people setting up a parkrun and they all agreed they would say 'go for it!' There are many benefits, particularly watching people crossing the finish line with a smile on their faces – and the only down side is losing that Saturday morning lie-in!

James Saunders said, 'Try to develop a team early, people who are passionate. Try not to take on too much responsibility yourself and then burn out. Delegate, assume that people can and will take on the responsibility.' He added, 'I can't imagine life without doing these things and being so involved. I can't imagine what I did beforehand.'

Claudia Wells at Rockingham parkrun in Western Australia says to remember that it really doesn't matter if you make mistakes occasionally – if a runner is annoyed because something has gone wrong and they won't get a proper time, you can always offer them the chance to come back next week and run it for free! Besides, 'Every Saturday you'll have a great time with friends.'

And a final word of advice from Anita Afonso for anyone thinking of setting up a parkrun: 'Keep it simple.' Remember, the core of parkrun is a free, timed, 5K run with friends. That's all.

22

The future: beyond 1,000,000 parkrunners

I could list so many people whose lives it's changed – just from a thirty minute, forty minute, fifty minute run on a Saturday morning – who would have thought it?

Danny Norman, parkrun UK Social Media and Communications Manager

In 2004, Bushy Park Time Trial started with thirteen runners and five volunteers. Since then a lot has changed, including the ways runners are identified and timed, how the results are distributed and how the events are funded. The greatest change is the sheer number of events, parkrunners and volunteers. However, the pillars of parkrun remain constant: the free, weekly 5K run, inclusive and open to all, which builds on and extends local communities.

Tenth anniversary

When I interviewed the thirteen parkrun pioneers in late 2013 and early 2014, every one of them wanted to return to Bushy Park for the tenth anniversary run. On 4 October 2014, all of them were there, as were those first volunteers.

The atmosphere in Bushy Park that morning was fantastic. By 8.15 there were already hundreds of runners gathering, many in 50-, 100- and 250-club tops, others wearing tenth anniversary T-shirts or running club vests. Runners had come from all over the UK and from all over the world, from Russia to Australia. First-time parkrunners were there and dedicated tourists such as John and Joanna Cassells.

At about 8.40 the masses drifted from the car park area and congregated near the start, forming a colourful, buzzing crowd. After the annual prizes had been presented to Bushy parkrunners and volunteers, the pioneers lined up to great applause and were given unique gold parkrun athlete IDs and 'parkrun original 13' medals. Finally, the huge group of excited runners was persuaded to retreat to the start line and the run began.

As ten years previously, Paul Sinton-Hewitt started the run. This time however there were 1,705 runners and it took about fifty seconds for all the runners – some with buggies and some with a dog – to cross the start line. At its peak, the finish line crew were dealing with more than one hundred runners a minute, and for a while the double funnel had to become a triple funnel. It was amazing, and a huge credit to the forty-eight Bushy parkrun volunteers who made it all run smoothly. One of the volunteers scanning in the finishers' barcodes was none other than Paul Sinton-Hewitt.

The future: beyond 1,000,000 parkrunners

The first runner entered the finish chute in 15:59, while the first of the parkrun pioneers to finish was Matthew Morgan, in 17:23. His time, over ninety seconds faster than ten years earlier, gave him 23rd place. Rachel Rowan's 19:25, also some ninety seconds faster than in the first run, brought her in as second woman. Steve Rowland's run finally brought him into the 50-club, ten years after his first appearance here; James Russell was running his 292nd parkrun, while Tanya Wolken started parkrunning again just this year and has now reached five runs. The final parkrunner reached the finish funnel in 56:57.

Around the globe, 77,694 runners and 5,993 volunteers took part in 477 parkruns in ten countries for International parkrun Day. Including junior parkruns held the following day, there were 503 events on the tenth anniversary weekend, and more than 80,000 runners.

Growth and recognition

The growth of parkrun over the last several years has been nearly exponential. During 2014, parkrun passed some fantastic milestones, including 500 locations, 750,000 individual people having run at least one parkrun, 1,000,000 registered parkrunners, and 6,500,000 individual runs. It's amazing.

Alongside the increase in number of events and number of parkrunners there has been an increase – initially very gradual, now faster – in the recognition of parkrun amongst runners of all standards, and by external organisations. In the early years, events were included in the race listings in some UK running magazines. Now, with more than 300 events countrywide each week, they would completely swamp those listings. The widespread presence of parkrun is acknowledged in marathon training plans which suggest incorporating parkruns and is demonstrated in the repeated references to parkrun in online discussions in websites from *Runner's World* to *Run Mummy Run*. In the early years, parkrun results were listed in some local UK newspapers. More recently, parkrun has featured in articles in local, regional and national newspapers, on the radio and even on television in various parkrun countries, not to mention a growing number of YouTube videos. On the morning of the tenth anniversary, parkrun even featured on the BBC News.

For several years, the value of parkruns has been recognised locally with parkrun Event Directors being nominated for and winning local awards for volunteering. In 2009, when there were still just eleven parkruns in the UK, Paul Sinton-Hewitt was named as one of the 'Heroes of Running' by *Runner's World*.

Fast-forward five years and in the 2014 Queen's Birthday Honours list, 'Peter Paul Sinton-Hewitt, founder of parkrun' was awarded a CBE 'for services to Grassroots Sports Participation'. This is, without question, an appropriate recognition of Paul's efforts over the last ten years in guiding parkrun from that first run to the amazing global organisation that it is today. The CBE was presented to him by the Duke of Cambridge, Prince William, on 2 October 2014 – the exact tenth anniversary of that first run – and he wore it at the tenth anniversary celebrations.

Recognition of and partnership with parkrun is also increasing within the athletics community. Shortly before the tenth anniversary, Tom Williams met with representatives from England Athletics, jogscotland, Athletics Northern Ireland and Welsh Athletics. They discussed collaboration to increase running at all levels from grassroots to elite performance, including for example how talented parkrunners could be encouraged to step up into club athletics. And just days after the anniversary, Paul Sinton-Hewitt announced that parkrun had joined forces with the International Association of Athletics Federations (IAAF) to become a partner of Athletics for a Better World.

The future

I asked many people, from parkrun HQ staff and Country Managers through Event Directors to a variety of parkrunners what they would like to see for the future of parkrun.

John Treacy, head of the Irish Sports Council, would like to see a parkrun in every town in Ireland.

Tourist Chris Cowell wants 'more of the same with smaller attendances at the larger venues.' He added, 'But don't change the formula.'

Bruce Fordyce and Bob Norris are both certain that parkrun South Africa is going to be the biggest running movement that South Africa has ever seen. They want parkrun to continue exactly like it is now in every way – the friendliness, the relaxed atmosphere, the inclusivity, the family participation, people smiling at each other. But they want more events, including more rural events and more events in less affluent communities, bringing parkrun to more people. Bob also thinks that there is a great future in parkrun tourism, drawing people to places that would not otherwise be obvious tourist locations. Certainly a growing number of parkrunners are looking at possible holiday destinations with parkruns in mind.

Jakub Fedorowicz wants 50,000 registered parkrunners and thirty events in Poland in the next two years.

Ron Clarke, parkrun Australia's Patron, said, 'I see parkrun's future as extending this concept worldwide and throughout every country including all the regional areas. The formula is simple, and very successful, and needs no further tinkering.' He added that all that was needed was to maintain parkrun's present standards and ethics, and avoiding excessive influence from commercialism.

The National Trust would like to continue to work closely together with parkrun, see the relationship deepen and grow, and support communities as they start up more parkrun events. Rob Joules would also like to see more parkrun junior events on Trust properties if there is interest, as it's a great way of encouraging children and their families to get outdoors and closer to nature.

Liz Yelling also would particularly like to see more junior parkruns, ideally one associated with every single parkrun event. 'That would be brilliant because that's the real grassroots of our running.' She also thinks that the main parkrun events can have a major impact in helping to tackle obesity and improve fitness: 'parkrun has mobilised a lot of people into the running community, people who otherwise maybe wouldn't have done that. I've seen my friends who have gone to parkrun and gone on to run marathons, who have had no background in running before.'

I could go on, but in summary, practically everyone I have spoken to while researching this book wants parkrun to continue doing what it is doing now – providing free, 5K runs at a set time and place every Saturday morning. And they want to see more of them, in more locations and more varied communities.

This presents a variety of challenges to parkrun. Many people would like to see parkrun targeting disadvantaged communities, both urban and rural, and bringing to them the many benefits of parkrun: exercise and fitness, a positive outlet for children's energy, an event in which the whole family can participate, enjoy, cooperate and (if they wish) compete with each other, an opportunity to grow communities and improve community cohesion.

However, parkrun, with its volunteer model, works best where a community really *wants* to have its own parkrun. Paul has said, 'It does not matter whether that community is small or large. We are just as happy to have a parkrun with only a handful or a few dozen people as one with hundreds, but the community has to want that parkrun, has to adopt, manage, run and volunteer at their parkrun, or it won't work. It's not something which can be imposed.'

The vision

Paul's vision for the future of parkrun remains, like parkrun itself, very simple in concept: 'I want parkrun to be available to all communities. My vision is that there will be a parkrun in every town and city that wants one.' Paul wants to make it possible for every parkrun country to run a professional organisation, with core employees who can drive the growth of parkrun, assess the courses properly and enable every community which wants a parkrun event to have one. He recognises that this will need ways for each country organisation to make enough money to fund those core personnel; he's optimistic this will fall into place.

Paul also wants parkrun to take a lead in changing the minds of people in government regarding people taking part in regular run/walk/jog activities.

And, importantly, one of his main ambitions for parkrun is to influence and change how running is perceived by children. He said, 'I would like young people to associate participation in running with *joy*, and for running to relinquish the shackles that bind it with punishment. Running will forever be hard – however, that does not mean that we cannot enjoy the experience.'

It's an exciting time. More parkruns and more junior parkruns are starting up all the time. More people, children and adults, are discovering the joys of parkrun. Several new parkrun countries will soon join the family.

Here's to the future of parkrun!

Training plans

12 weeks to 5K

When starting out on your training, running non-stop for fifteen minutes may seem like an impossible task. However, you'll soon build up to it with a little patience and a run/walk strategy. Walking is not cheating and by taking regular short walking breaks you'll soon be running further than you believed possible whilst also reducing your risk of injury.

So pick a ratio that is suitable for your ability; you may start with 30 seconds of running to 1 minute of walking, then in week 2 try 1 minute of running to 1 minute of walking, then progress to 2 minutes:1 minute, then 3 minutes:1 minute and so on.

However if you can already run for 5 minutes start there, 5 minutes running to 1 minute walking, you could then progress by reducing your walk break. So 5 minutes run: 30 seconds walk might be your option for week 2.

Whatever ratio you choose, stick to a timed walk break – don't let it get longer or be an endless rest and each week make sure you are running a little more and/or walking a little less.

Good luck, and remember that hard work and consistency and following a gradually building programme will ensure you develop your running in a safe and enjoyable way.

Karen Weir, Event Director Richmond parkrun
www.runwithkaren.com

Training plans

Week	Mon	Tues	Wed	Thurs	Fri	Sat	Sun
1	Rest	15 mins run/walk	Rest	15 mins run/walk	Rest	45-60 mins walk	20 mins run/walk
2	Rest	15 mins run/walk	Rest	15 mins run/walk	Rest	45-60 mins walk	20 mins run/walk
3	Rest	15 mins run/walk	Rest	20 mins run/walk	Rest	45-60 mins walk	25 mins run/walk
4	Rest	15 mins run/walk	Rest	15 mins run/walk	Rest	45-60 mins walk	20 mins run/walk
5	Rest	20 mins run/walk	Rest	20 mins run/walk	Rest	45-60 mins walk	25 mins run/walk
6	Rest	20 mins run/walk	Rest	20 mins run/walk	Rest	45-60 mins walk	25 mins run/walk
7	Rest	20 mins run/walk	Rest	25 mins run/walk	Rest	45-60 mins walk	30 mins run/walk
8	Rest	15 mins run/walk	Rest	20 mins run/walk	Rest	45-60 mins walk	25 mins run/walk
9	Rest	25 mins run/walk	Rest	25 mins run/walk	Rest	45-60 mins walk	30 mins run/walk
10	Rest	30 mins run/walk	Rest	30 mins run/walk	Rest	45-60 mins walk	35 mins run/walk
11	Rest	30 mins run/walk	Rest	30 mins run/walk	Rest	45-60 mins walk	40 mins run/walk
12	Rest	20 mins run/walk	Rest	20 mins run/walk	Rest	5km run!	Rest

12 weeks to improve your 5K

In this plan, note that:

Monday, Wednesday and Friday are rest days.

Tuesday sessions should always start with one mile easy running to warm up and finish with one mile easy running to cool down.

Thursday sessions should always finish with five minutes of easy running after the 80% effort segment.

The effort percentage is a guide and can be related to a rate of perceived exertion. For example: 60% effort is a comfortable conversational pace, 70% is a steady pace requiring focus and low levels of discomfort, 80% is controlled discomfort and approximates to your 10K pace, 90% is hard and you are unable to converse, 100% is maximal effort, something that you can maintain for seconds only.

Karen Weir, Event Director Richmond parkrun
www.runwithkaren.com

Training plans

Week	Tues	Thurs	Sat	Sun
1	5 x 2 mins @ 95% effort [2 mins recovery]	5 mins 60% effort 5 mins 70% effort 5 mins 80% effort	parkrun (easy)	30 mins easy run
2	6 x 2 mins @ 95% effort [2 mins recovery]	6 mins 60% effort 6 mins 70% effort 6 mins 80% effort	parkrun (80% effort)	35 mins easy run
3	7 x 2 mins @ 95% effort [2 mins recovery]	8 mins 60% effort 8 mins 70% effort 8 mins 80% effort	parkrun (race)	45 mins easy run
4	5 x 2 mins @ 95% effort [90 secs recovery]	5 mins 60% effort 5 mins 70% effort 5 mins 80% effort	parkrun (80% effort)	30 mins easy run
5	5 x 3 mins @ 95% effort [2 mins recovery]	8 mins 60% effort 8 mins 70% effort 8 mins 80% effort	parkrun (race)	45 mins easy run
6	6 x 3 mins @ 95% effort [2 mins recovery]	9 mins 60% effort 9 mins 70% effort 9 mins 80% effort	parkrun (80% effort)	50 mins easy run
7	7 x 3 mins @ 90% effort [2 mins recovery]	10 mins 60% effort 10 mins 70% effort 10 mins 80% effort	parkrun (easy)	55 mins easy run
8	5 x 3 mins @ 95% effort [90 secs recovery]	7 mins 60% effort 7 mins 70% effort 7 mins 80% effort	parkrun (80% effort)	40 mins easy run
9	6 x 3 mins @ 90% effort [1 min recovery]	10 mins 60% effort 10 mins 70% effort 10 mins 80% effort	parkrun (race)	50 mins easy run
10	5 x 4 mins @ 90% effort [2mins recovery]	10 mins 60% effort 10 mins 70% effort 10 mins 80% effort	parkrun (80% effort)	55 mins easy run
11	6 x 4 mins @ 90% effort [2 mins recovery]	10 mins 60% effort 10 mins 70% effort 10 mins 80% effort	parkrun (easy)	60 mins easy run
12	10 x 2 mins @ 95% effort [1 min recovery]	8 mins 60% effort 8 mins 70% effort 8 mins 80% effort	parkrun (target PB!)	45 mins easy run

Acknowledgements

This book could not have been written without input and assistance from a large number of people.

I want to thank:
- Paul Sinton-Hewitt for believing in me when I brought him my book proposal, and giving me the support of parkrun which enabled me to do the research.
- Shelagh Yospur for editing and Aidan Dixon and Eva Jacobs for proofreading and general comments before the manuscript went to the publisher.

Acknowledgements

- Everyone in UKTT, parkrun UK, junior parkrun and the Country Managers – Chris Wright, Danny Norman, Tom Williams, Joanne Sinton-Hewitt, Richard Leyton, Alan Dempster, Anita Afonso, Jane Niven, Helen Hood, Paul Graham, Chrissie Wellington, Bruce and Gill Fordyce, Rick and Lori Brauer, Matt Shields, Lian and Noel de Charmoy, Tim Oberg, Jakub Fedorowicz, Jonathan Sydenham, Maxim Egorov and Semen Serikov – for sharing with me their parkrun journeys and what goes on behind the scenes, and for correcting my mistakes. Any remaining errors are my own fault.
- All the parkrunners, parkrun volunteers and parkrun supporters who have given me their time and input.
- Everyone who kindly talked to me before and after parkruns, and everyone who sent in their parkrun stories. I only regret that I couldn't include everything that everyone shared with me, or this book would have included another 50,000 words.
- All the photographers who have allowed me to use their photographs.
- Rachel, Richard and Emily Tanner, James Moore, Foong Cheek, Kevin Caley and anonymous beta readers, for your comments on various drafts of the book.
- Aidan Dixon, my husband, for general support and coping with me obsessing about parkrun while researching and writing this book.
- Scott Reeves and his team at Chequered Flag Publishing, for publishing this book.

Also from Chequered Flag Publishing:

ONLY GOLD MATTERS
CECIL GRIFFITHS
THE EXILED OLYMPIC CHAMPION

by John Hanna

He was one of Wales' greatest athletes. But he could have been even greater.

Cecil Griffiths won an Olympic gold medal in 1920. Then his running career was shattered, banned by the athletics authorities for receiving prize money in wartime charity races as a junior. Although this working-class Welshman broke into the world dominated by graduates from Oxford and Cambridge, he was denied his chance to line up with the 1924 Olympians who would later find fame in Chariots of Fire.

In this very personal biography by the husband of Cecil Griffiths' granddaughter, John Hanna traces the life of Griffiths and his unequal struggle against the athletics establishment that singled him out.

INNOVATIVE AND EXCITING SPORTS BOOKS

Chequered Flag
PUBLISHING

www.chequeredflagpublishing.co.uk